A BEGGAR IN PARADISE

LIVING WITH THE INCA INDIANS

CHRIS CONROY

MENTOR PRESS

First Published in 1997 by

MENTOR Press
43 Furze Road,
Sandyford Industrial Estate,
Dublin 18,
Republic of Ireland.

Tel: (353)-1- 295 2112 / 3   Fax: (353)-1- 295 2114

Paperback: ISBN 0 947548 92 0
Hardback: ISBN 0 947548 87 4

First Print (PB) 1997
Second Print (PB) 1998

A catalogue record for this book is available from the British Library

Cover Design: Design Image

Cover Photograph courtesy of SlideFile
All other photographs courtesy of Chris Conroy

Edited by: Claire Haugh
             John McCormack

Design and Layout: Kathryn McKinney
                     Tony Hetherington

Printed in Ireland by ColourBooks Ltd.

3 5 7 9 10 8 6 4 2

CONTENTS

Preface

Peru is a country of many contrasts and contradictions. In spite of its great beauty and hidden riches, it is one of the poorest countries in Latin America. The distinction between the rich and the poor is immediately evident to those arriving by plane in Lima. As they make their way to the luxurious hotels in Miraflores and San Isidro, the magnificent houses of the wealthy are in sharp contrast to the shanty towns which surround the city. But in spite of the huge influx of these poor Indians, the city has retained much of its imperial inheritance. The wealthy Peruvian families who live there still like to think of Lima as the 'City of the Kings'.

Arriving from the north along the Pan-American highway, visitors are greeted by a vast coastal desert which stretches all the way from Ecuador to Chile. Inland in the distance rise the tall peaks of the Andes. Here and there along the way rivers meander to the sea, forming oases of lush vegetation on the way. The more adventurous travellers enter from the north-east by way of the great Amazon river. Many Indian tribes still live in this vast jungle basin, parts of which contain some of the last unexplored areas of the world. Entering from Bolivia involves crossing the snow-capped Andes. At first sight the Inca Indians inhabiting this region appear rugged and austere, somewhat like the climate – they have adapted well to their barren surroundings.

I must explain that the Indians do not use the term 'Indian' to describe themselves. This was the name given by Christopher Columbus to the native inhabitants when he landed on the Caribbean island of Hispaniola in 1492 – he thought he had reached the East Indies. This misnomer is still used to describe the indigenous peoples of North, Central and South America. In Peru today the word 'Indian' is a derogatory term. The Indians prefer to call themselves 'campesinos'. These are peasants who gain their living from land that is held in common by the rural community. I use the term 'Indian' throughout the book in the best possible sense to refer to the descendants of the indigenous people who lived in Peru before the coming of the Spanish. Much of their culture and lifestyle is fast disappearing and many are now living like beggars in paradise.

Chris Conroy

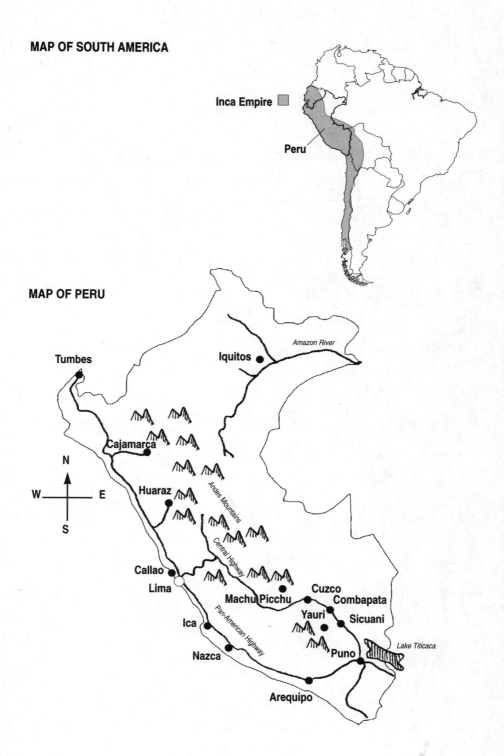

MAP OF SOUTH AMERICA

Inca Empire

Peru

MAP OF PERU

Tumbes

Iquitos

Amazon River

Cajamarca

Andes Mountains

Huaraz

N

W   E

S

Central Highway

Callao

Lima

Machu Picchu

Cuzco

Combapata

Yauri

Sicuani

Ica

Pan-American Highway

Nazca

Puno

Lake Titicaca

Arequipo

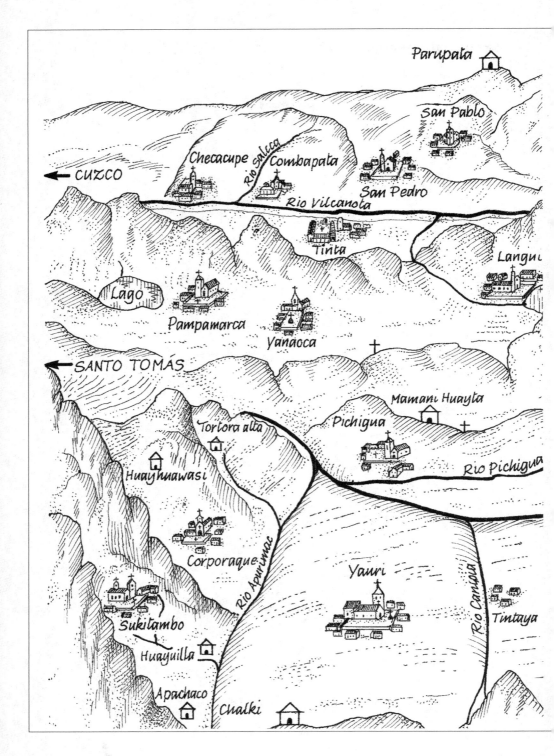

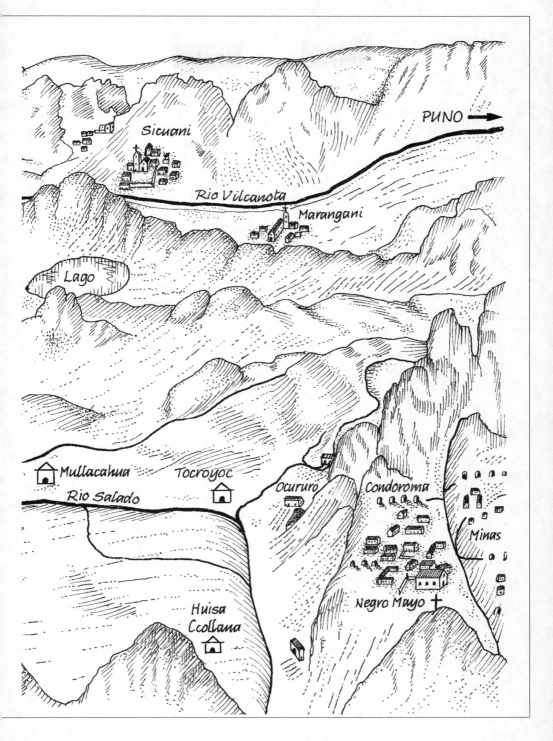

1
Journey from Lima

At last I was on my way to my final destination in the mountains. The sky was grey and overcast and the air was hot and humid. I was happy to be leaving the oppressive heat of Lima for the cooler atmosphere of the Andes. Jorge Chavas Airport, named after a famous Peruvian aviation pioneer, was mobbed with people and another coachload of tourists had just arrived from one of Lima's downtown hotels.

"Everyone wants to go to Cuzco," remarked Pedro, my taxi driver, as I paid him the fare. He had talked non-stop on the way to the airport, delighted no doubt that a foreigner could understand Spanish.

"Good luck, Padre," he shouted as I struggled with my cases. "Be sure to get a seat by the left-side window. You'll get a great view of the mountains." His battered Volkswagen backfired as he pulled away.

The airport was utter chaos. It was not even organised chaos. No one seemed to queue or wait patiently in line. They just crowded around the ticket desk and shouted for attention. This is South America. This is Peru. Normally life here is laid-back and easy-going. '*Mañana*' is their favourite expression. 'Tomorrow is another day.' But when it comes to catching a plane at six o'clock in the morning it's everyone for himself.

I wondered where the Cuzco desk was . . .? Just follow the tourists. They were the ones with the blonde hair, blue eyes and white faces. Their young Peruvian guide was looking after all the necessary checking in. Most of them carried only hand luggage. I had three heavy cases which I thought were surely overweight. To my surprise the check-in clerk never even bothered to put them on the scales.

My flight was with *Aero Peru*, the national airline. The waiting lounge was an open smoky space with an inadequate number of plastic chairs. Six o'clock arrived and nothing happened. We must be back to '*Mañana*' again. An overweight American lady turned to her husband and exclaimed in a loud voice,

"George, I thought you said the plane leaves at six."

"It's supposed to leave at six. That's what it says on the programme," he replied, taking a piece of paper from his inside pocket.

"They haven't announced that it's been delayed. Maybe we are in the wrong place!" she persisted.

"Nancy, you worry about everything. Just relax and be patient."

"How can I relax at this hour of the morning. We should still be in bed. Why did we get here so early if the plane doesn't leave at six?" she wondered. "Where is the goddamn guide? She's never around when you need her."

Just then an *Aero Peru* hostess arrived to tell us that the weather in Cuzco was overcast and our plane would be delayed until the clouds had cleared.

"George, what did she say?"

As George didn't understand a word of Spanish, he hadn't a clue what she had said. It didn't look good. A German tourist intervened.

"Perhaps one hour, we go. This is Peru. Never on time."

By now the lounge was full of smoke and I could hardly breathe. A young Peruvian boy arrived with the morning papers.

"*Expresso . . . Republica . . . Caretas,*" he shouted.

There were no takers. I just wanted to go to the toilet.

Just then the door opened and another hostess appeared. At last we are on our way. I moved quickly to the front of the line. Once on the plane I was lucky to secure a window seat on the left-hand side.

The flight from Lima to Cuzco takes about an hour and most of the passengers are tourists, except for the odd Peruvian businessman who is most likely involved in the tourist trade anyway. Pedro was right. The view was breathtaking as the morning sunshine broke through the clouds. Range after range of snow-capped mountains appeared below and little streams meandered through the deep valleys. I saw a lake in the distance. The mountain slopes were barren with no sign of vegetation. It was impossible to imagine how anyone could cross these hills on horseback. I thought of Pizarro and his small army of horsemen who in the sixteenth century had to negotiate these mountains, clothed in armour, swords in their scabbards, ready for battle. My thoughts were interrupted when a middle-aged lady leaned across me to get a better view.

"*C'est magnifique!*" she exclaimed. Speaking English with a very pronounced French accent, she asked me if I would mind if she took a photograph. Funny how French people always seem to presume that you speak English.

When she had taken numerous photographs, which I doubted would ever come out, she asked;

"Have you been to Cuzco before?"

"No," I replied, "this is my first time."

"For me this is a journey of a lifetime," she said. "My husband always promised me that he would bring me to Machu Picchu for our silver wedding anniversary. By the way this is my husband, Jean." He was sitting next to her but didn't seem to speak English.

"*Enchanté*," I said.

"We will stay a week in Cuzco," she continued. "We hope to visit all the ruins. I'm a little worried about the altitude. They say it is hard to breathe at 12,000 feet. I have often climbed in the Pyrenees near our home, but never at 12,000 feet."

Just then the hostess arrived with soft drinks. Fresh orange juice, Coca Cola and Inca Cola. Inca Cola, a variation of Coca Cola, is yellow in colour and produced in Peru. She also had *mate de coca*, a kind of tea made from the coca leaf. The coca was the sacred plant of the Incas. We are more familiar with the coca leaf as the basis for the drug cocaine. The *mate de coca* reduces the effects of altitude sickness. It is also green and to me it tasted terrible. The French lady asked for a second cup.

"*Trés bon*," she said, as if she was tasting a glass of Bordeaux.

"Are you staying long in Cuzco?" she enquired.

I knew that this question would come up sooner or later. This is where a casual conversation can turn into an interview. I could have just said I was on holiday and left it at that but you always get caught out in the end, so I decided to explain.

"I will be in Cuzco for a few days, but I'm not really a tourist. I'm on my way to a place called Yauri, way out in the mountains beyond Cuzco. I am going to live among the Indians."

"Oh, how wonderful!" she exclaimed. "Are you an anthropologist?"

"No, I'm an Irish Carmelite priest and I'm going to work on the missions, among the native Indians."

"I guessed you were Irish," she said, "from your accent. It is much easier to understand than the English accent and I did think you might be a priest. There is something about priests that gives you away, even though you are not wearing your robes."

I wasn't trying to hide anything but I hadn't worn a Roman collar for years.

"I think you priests who go on the missions do wonderful work," she continued. "Did your superiors send you, or did you decide to go yourself?"

"I volunteered," I replied, trying not to sound too heroic.

"You have great courage," she said, "at your age!"

"I am forty-eight," I said. "I don't feel too old."

"I am fifty-two," she replied. "I don't think I would be able to do it. But I'm afraid I'm not a very good Catholic. I haven't been to church for a long time. But I do believe in God and I always pray. I was nervous before this flight, but I feel much safer now that I have a priest beside me. You can give me absolution if anything happens."

Just then, the 'Fasten your seatbelt' sign came on. We were almost there. Time had gone by quickly in conversation. Cuzco is situated in a high Andean valley south-east of Lima. Through a break in the clouds I got my first glimpse of this dramatic red-roofed city surrounded by high mountains. I couldn't see how we could possibly land. There was no sign of an airport. We seemed to have passed by Cuzco when suddenly the plane banked to the left. The lower wing seemed to almost touch the top of the mountain. We levelled out between two peaks and as we approached the city a narrow runway appeared in the distance. As the plane touched down the French lady suddenly grabbed my arm.

"Oh, *mon Père*, I thought I would need absolution then." Out of the corner of my eye I could see her husband looking at me.

Suddenly a gush of cold air swept through the plane as the door was opened. I put on my warm jacket. The plane had come to a halt a long way from the terminal building. I could feel myself taking deep breaths as I walked along and by the time I reached the luggage collection area I was exhausted. Although thousands of visitors pass through here each year, there was little in the way of modern conveniences. There was no automatic conveyor belt for the luggage. Instead it arrived from the plane on an open trolley and cases were handed out individually to the passengers. A young boy dressed in rags offered to carry my cases. I was glad of the help because there was no way I could have managed them alone. It was almost impossible to get out through the airport exit door. There seemed to be hundreds of people waiting outside, all shouting at the arriving passengers, "Mister, hotel, taxi . . .?"

I felt a tug on my coat and turned around to find a little child begging with her hand out. She didn't have to say anything. The look on her face was enough. Eventually I chose a taxi, an old battered Volkswagen beetle that had seen better days. But then there wasn't much to choose from. None of the taxis was less than ten years old. Anyway I wasn't too particular. I just wanted to get to the Hotel Ollanta on the Avenida del Sol. As there are no meters in the taxis, one has to haggle over the price before the journey. Many a tourist has learned to his cost not to leave it to the end.

"Hotel Ollanta, *sí Señor*, fifteen dollars."

The price is always quoted in dollars for tourists and it's usually double the normal. He was hoping that I didn't speak Spanish.

"I don't have dollars," I said, "only soles. How much is it in soles?" I offered him the equivalent of five dollars and he was happy to accept. He loaded the luggage into the car, putting the smaller case under the bonnet and the other two on the back seat.

I have learned from experience never to judge a place by the journey from the airport. Yet first impressions can be very important. Cuzco looked so beautiful from the air with its red-tiled roofs. Here on the ground we were passing through a shanty town. Mud huts with tiny windows. Dirty streets. People everywhere. Children on their way to school. The sky was overcast as the hot morning sunshine that we had flown through had not yet penetrated the clouds.

"Do you go to Machu Picchu tomorrow?" asked the taxi driver.

"No, not tomorrow," I replied, "perhaps another time." But I didn't really want to pursue the conversation. By now we had reached Avenida del Sol, a wide double-lane thoroughfare leading to the centre of the city.

"That's the Palace of Justice," said the driver, "or Palace of Injustice, as we like to call it." He said this in such a sarcastic way that I got the impression that he was speaking from personal experience.

He pulled up outside the Hotel Ollanta on the opposite side of the road. As there was no porter I asked him if he could bring my cases into the hotel. I was too weak to carry them. He very kindly obliged. I paid the fare and added a tip.

"*Muchas gracias, Señor*," he said, and with that he rushed back to the airport to look for another tourist.

The hotel was small but clean and comfortable. By now altitude sickness was really setting in and I was getting weaker by the minute. At the desk I asked if they had a "*simple*" which in Spanish means a single room. It always seems to me that you are asking for a simple room, but then all the rooms are simple anyway. I was on the fourth floor. There was a small lift that could hold about two people and I hoped it would take the cases as well. As the lift began to move I felt a lightness in my head. Lifts are not to be recommended for people with altitude sickness. I just wanted to lie down on the bed. I had been warned in Lima that the only thing for altitude sickness is to remain still. The problem is that there is only about half as much oxygen in the air as there is at sea level. The body has to readjust. It does this by increasing the number of red corpuscles in the blood. It's during this process that one feels terrible. It begins with dizziness and a slight headache but gradually gets worse.

I tipped the boy who had shown me to my room and I stretched out on the bed. In spite of the cold I was beginning to perspire. As I lay there motionless I couldn't help thinking that here I was at the centre of the Inca Empire and I could have been anywhere in the world . . . in bed. I was eager to get out and see the sights. I wanted to explore, but now my teeth began to hurt, the nerve endings were pounding. Funny how the altitude affects your teeth.

I began to feel hungry but I didn't want to eat. I rang down for some *mate de coca*. I could put up with the taste if it would ease the pain. Altitude sickness has all the symptoms of sea sickness together with a few more sensations. My forehead felt as if it was shrinking and my eyes seemed to be receding into the back of my head. It's the most nauseating and debilitating sickness I have ever experienced. And I was to suffer from it every time I came back to the mountains. Now I know why mountain climbers need oxygen masks to reach the summit of Everest.

I lay awake all night, but by the next morning I was feeling much better. It takes a couple of days to get really acclimatised. I heard every clock in Cuzco strike on the hour. At four o'clock the first bells sounded for Mass. I felt a little dizzy as I stood up. My room faced on to the street and as I pulled back the curtain it was already bright. I could see the Palace of Justice. The Spanish loved to call their seat of justice a palace.

14

It is a massive building with giant steps leading up to the entrance. This was to give the impression that the law was towering above the people. I could just imagine how a poor Indian felt when walking up those steps.

'The law is dispensed from a palace so it must be just'. But the taxi driver wasn't convinced.

I set out to explore Cuzco, one of the most beautiful cities in the world. When the Spanish soldiers led by Pizarro first entered the city, they too were impressed. One of them wrote back to King Charles;

> This city is the greatest and finest ever seen in this country or anywhere in the Indies. We can assure Your Majesty that it is so beautiful and has such fine buildings that it would be remarkable even in Spain.

Plaza de Armas, Cuzco

I made my way to the Plaza de Armas which was just around the corner from the hotel. Every city and town in South America has a Plaza de Armas. This was where the soldiers would have gathered the arms for battle. There are few squares that can compare with the Plaza de Armas in Cuzco however. This was the *Wakaypata* (Holy place) for the Incas, and the area where all their great festivities took place. It is a great square with a beautiful park and fountain in the centre. The two most important buildings overlooking the Plaza are the cathedral and the Jesuit church (*Iglesia de la Compañía*) both of which were built on the

15

stone foundations of former Inca palaces. This is the same all over Cuzco. Walls were built of huge stones placed one on top of the other without the use of cement. They fit so perfectly together that not even a razor blade can be pushed between them.

As I looked across at the cathedral I felt a sense of pride that it was a Carmelite bishop, Bernard Serrada, who completed its construction in the eighteenth century. He was Bishop of Cuzco from 1725 to 1735 and was also responsible for dividing the diocese into deaneries, one of which is the present Prelature of Sicuani where I would be working. Mass was just beginning as I reached the cathedral. Most of the seats were occupied, many of them by Indians. I gave thanks to God for my safe journey so far. The inside of the cathedral is awe-inspiring. Apart from the main altar there is a beautiful cedar altar behind the choir, covered with gold leaf and baroque ornaments. In the centre of this altar is a painting of Our Lady of the Nativity, a masterpiece of the Cuzco School of Painting. Everywhere vast amounts of gold and silver ornaments can be seen – all part of the El Dorado that Pizarro had set out to find. No modern church could ever be so ornate. The cathedral was built in a different time, in a different style and with a different mentality. I wondered what the young people back home would say to this. They were always complaining about the wealth of the Vatican. As I left there was an old Indian woman sitting by the door, begging.

The next couple of days were spent walking around Cuzco. I visited museums, churches and ruins. Yes, there are many ruins, silent reminders of a glorious past. There are many other reminders too that are not so silent. Indians in multicoloured clothes were selling their wares everywhere – alpaca sweaters, rugs, ponchos and *chullos* (knitted hats that are tied under the chin). Children with unwashed faces were selling Chiclets and pop ices. I sat for hours in the Plaza just watching the world go by. Young and old gathered around me to sell me things. They look at you as if you have dollar signs in your eyes, and persist, "Mister, alpaca very cheap."

They never take "No" for an answer. They seem to think that if they persist for long enough you will be shamed into buying something you don't really want. Then they suddenly spot another tourist and run after them. Maruja was a young Indian girl who came to sell her wares in the Plaza every day. She sold little home-made Indian dolls and handwoven bracelets and belts. She was very friendly and liked to talk. I asked her where she lived.

"I don't live in Cuzco, I live in Pisac, a little town about an hour away in the Sacred Valley of the Incas."

"How many are in your family?" I asked.

"I have one brother and two sisters. My Papa works in the *chacra* (field). My Mama is not well. I come to Cuzco every day to earn some money for my family," she explained.

"What age are you?"

"I was fifteen on my last birthday."

"Don't you go to school?"

"I went to school up to last year. Then my mother got sick and I couldn't go anymore."

"Where do you buy the dolls?"

"I don't buy them, I make them. Look at their smiling faces. I painted them."

Just then two tourists carrying rucksacks passed by.

"Quick," I said, "they might buy a doll!"

"They never buy anything. They have no money. They stay at the hostel and always look for the cheapest things."

The mornings in Cuzco at this time of year are cold and miserable. The sky is overcast and a damp mist descends from the mountains. This can quickly change to a sudden downpour which can last for a couple of hours. It is April and the rainy season will soon be at an end. No wonder the Incas had such a devotion to *Inti*, the Sun god. The sun transforms everything. Even the gloomy faces of the people brighten up, although they don't exactly put on a happy smile. Indians always seem to have a solemn expression on their faces, but they appear to be in better humour once the sun is out.

I took an early taxi to catch the train to Sicuani, which is situated southeast of Cuzco and further down the valley. The train station wasn't far, just at the other end of Avenida del Sol but there was no way I could carry my three heavy cases. The *micros* (small chubby buses) are always full, with people hanging on from the outside. Actually, a Peruvian bus is never 'full'. When it stops, it is up to you to get in or hang on.

There was a great throng waiting outside the station when I arrived, Indians of all shapes and sizes. Whole families were huddled together – the women with their long coloured skirts, babies on their backs and little bowler hats perched on top of their heads. These hats give them a very comical appearance as they always appear to be a few sizes too small. Why they wear them no one really knows. Perhaps it's just for style. The men and the other children are busy with the animals – sheep, pigs, goats, ducks and hens. There are sacks of all kinds of vegetables. Many of the women have great *bultos* (bundles) on their backs. No Indian ever travels without a *bulto* on their back. Often it contains a baby but it could just as well be a sack of potatoes.

The train was due to leave at eight o'clock but it was now half past seven and the gates were not yet open.

"Mister, will I mind your cases?" asked a little boy with matted hair and a dirty face. He had dark chocolate-drop eyes and was the very picture of innocence. But I was thinking of *Oliver Twist*. I had been warned that Cuzco was the most notorious city in the world for pickpockets and robberies. I had no choice as I would need help to carry the cases onto the train. Besides I couldn't imagine this boy running off with my cases.

"What's your name?" I asked.

"Alfonso," he replied timidly.

"Alfonso, do you have a friend who could help me with my cases?"

"I could carry them," he replied, attempting to lift one of my cases.

"You could carry the small one," I suggested.

He ran off and returned with his pal, César. The gates opened and everyone surged forward. I was carried anxiously along with the mob, sweat streaming down my face. Alfonso and César struggled with the cases.

"A single to Sicuani," I shouted.

The man in the kiosk took a quick glance at the two boys, but said nothing.

We pushed our way onto the train in front of a sheep and a woman with a huge *bulto* on her back and a oil lamp in her hand. Alfonso got me a seat by the window. I thanked the boys and gave them some soles, the equivalent of a dollar each. They grabbed the money tightly in their little hands as they left the train. Today they would have something to eat. They waited on the platform until the train began to move.

18

"*Gracias, Señor,*" they shouted, as the train pulled out of the station. I looked at my watch. It was half past eight in the morning.

The train was crowded with people and animals, and just like the *micros* some passengers were clinging onto the outside, others were riding on the roof. I recalled scenes from the Wild West frontier or the West Clare Railway. I was the only gringo on the train and the object of much curiosity. A little baby, peeping out from behind her mother's back, just stared at me. He wore a multicoloured *chullo* tied around his chin. Everyone was babbling in Quechua, the Inca language. I didn't understand a word they were saying and I wondered why I had spent the last few months trying to learn Spanish.

There were no doors on the carriage and some of the windows were missing. The train followed the valley, south alongside the River Vilcanota, passing through fields of wheat and maize. There was little in the way of any other vegetation apart from the odd eucalyptus tree. In the fields people were working with primitive tools. A woman was leading a pair of oxen while a man guided a wooden plough behind. On the train people pushed their way through the carriage selling all kinds of food – roast potatoes, maize and little pieces of roast meat on sticks.

"*Papas, maiz, anticuchos, tamales,*" they shouted, as they passed along.

The beautiful smell of roast meat filled the train, but it all looked terrible. Youngsters carried huge crates of bottles on their shoulders, shouting "Inca Cola, Pepsi, Coca Cola."

The train stopped at intervals along the way. Immediately local people rushed to the windows with their wares, home-made jumpers, ponchos and more food. Children were shouting "Chiclets" and various other things. Little piglets roamed around the track unhindered. I looked to see where we were and to my surprise there was no name on the station, nor did the stationmaster call out the name. Actually there didn't seem to be anyone in charge of anything. We were in the middle of nowhere. Soon the train was on its way again.

I began to feel very anxious and uneasy. How would I know when we had reached Sicuani? The train goes on to Puno near the Bolivian border and then on to Arequipa, two days away. Suppose I got off at the wrong station and found myself sitting on the platform in some isolated place with three heavy cases and not being able to speak the language. I didn't want to think about it.

Just then the ticket collector pushed his way through the crowd, checking the tickets. Lots of people didn't seem to have any. I knew then why they were riding on the roof. All kinds of arguments ensued.

"Who owns that pig?"

"Is that your child?"

"Where did you get on?"

Of course everyone said they had just got on at the last station. They haggled over the price of the ticket. The ticket collector ended up accepting about half of what the ticket cost. One old woman didn't have any money at all, so he took her little bowler hat.

"Are we far from Sicuani?" I asked as he checked my ticket.

"Oh it's a long way off, we haven't reached Checacupe yet. Sicuani is the stop after San Pablo," he explained, and with that he moved on.

Now I was more anxious than ever and there was another problem. I noticed at every stop that the people getting on the train would not let the people get off first. How was I going to get off the train in Sicuani?

Another station, another stop, and I am wondering where we are when suddenly I see the tall figure of Bishop Albano Quinn standing on the platform. This is it. This is Sicuani.

"Tiny?" I shouted through the open window, "I'm over here."

We call the bishop "Tiny" because of his height. He is six feet four inches. A tall good-looking man with white hair, wearing a Roman collar, he turned when he heard his name. So did everyone else when they heard the two gringos speaking English.

"Get out quick," he urged, as he hurried towards me.

"I can't, I'm blocked in. There are people everywhere."

"Through the window," he said, "cases first."

I pushed out my cases and then climbed out myself. A rather undignified arrival but I was relieved to be off the train. Tiny welcomed me with open arms, happy to have another Carmelite in the Prelature of Sicuani. This was once part of the Diocese of Cuzco but was separated in 1959 when the first Carmelite bishop was appointed. Tiny succeeded him in 1971. (A prelature is what an area is called while it is in the process of becoming a diocese. It has to show that it is capable of being self-sufficient.) There were about fifteen priests working in the prelature altogether, and only five of these were native Peruvians, the rest were volunteers from various countries.

Sicuani is a sleepy town. Although there is plenty of movement, little is happening. As we left the station, Tiny told me a little bit more about the place.

"It is a fairly large town of about 35,000 inhabitants. The majority of the people are Indian, but there is also a large number of mixed race called *mestizos*. These *mestizos* run most of the businesses in the town. They are also the teachers and the policemen. The Indians sell mainly on the side of the street and in the market place. Most Indians are part of a vast underground economy and they don't pay taxes. Unfortunately most young people are unemployed."

Crossing the bridge over the River Vilcanota, I noticed a peculiar mode of transport, a type of rickshaw with a square pannier in front over the wheels. Perched on top was an Indian woman with a bowler hat together with all her belongings. She looked so elegant as she was pushed along by a young boy peddling behind for all he was worth.

"That's the local taxi," remarked Tiny, "great for going down hills, but not so good for going up; everyone has to get out and walk."

"And that is the convent and school built by the Chicago Sisters of Mercy. Unfortunately they have long since left. The Indians never really accepted the gringo Sisters' methods which were modelled on the methods used in the United States. The Sisters also found it very difficult to get volunteers to come to Peru. The school has now been taken over by the government. It has deteriorated a lot but at least it's still being used."

With that, hundreds of young girls in grey uniforms and white shirts streamed out of the gates on their midday break. The paved road ended finally and we moved slowly in our little Volkswagen along a dirt track full of water-filled potholes. Tiny dodged around them, skilfully moving from side to side. Two policemen armed with pistols and submachine guns stood at a large wooden door. I imagined they were noting the arrival of a strange gringo in town.

"That's the jail," remarked Tiny. "There are over a hundred Indians locked up in there with little hope of ever getting justice. Some are there for years, lingering in appalling conditions. From time to time there is a breakout, or when they have money they just bribe the guards."

The bishop's residence, known as 'Tintaya', is surrounded by a high wall, capped with red-brick tiles. Built on recovered swampy ground, a stream flows by on one side. It is also a meeting place for all the priests of the prelature. As we entered the double iron gates two Alsatian dogs came running towards us.

I spent the next week in bed suffering from a mixture of altitude sickness and a heavy dose of flu. I had a lightness in my head and a sick stomach. Food was out of the question. I felt hungry but I couldn't eat. A nurse from a nearby district just happened to be visiting. Her name was Olga and she was from Liechtenstein. She had volunteered to work with the Indians for two years. Although she had no medicine she was able check me over and assure me that all would be well.

☆   ☆   ☆

Early one afternoon we set out south-west on the final stage of my journey to Yauri. There wasn't a cloud to be seen in the clear blue sky. Apart from my wide-rimmed sombrero, there was no escape from the burning heat of the sun.

"Best fill up with gasoline," said Des Kelleher, as he pulled the Dodge truck in to a dilapidated looking gas station with two old-fashioned pumps. They had handles on the side for those occasions when the power went off, as it frequently did. Des was a fellow Irish Carmelite. He had arrived in Yauri a month or so before me and had driven down to Sicuani to collect me.

"This is the last gas station until we reach Yauri and more often than not it has a sign which says, '*No hay gasolina*' (Out of gas). The gas has to come from Lima and there is usually some hold-up so it's always wise to have an extra can in the back of the truck."

We passed a row of tall eucalyptus trees which stood like sentries on the side of the dirt track. After the rainy season the mud had turned to dust and as we sped along we blew up a huge dust storm behind us. There was an old wooden bridge on stilts across the river, with a plank missing in the centre. The bridge creaked and swayed as we passed gently over it. A sharp turn to the right and we began to climb. The truck bounced up and down on the uneven surface. The heat was stifling. I opened the window and a cloud of dust filled the cabin.

"Shut the window," shouted Des, "or we'll be smothered in dust."

It was a choice between sweating and choking to death. On and on we climbed, twisting and turning as the dirt track seemed to get narrower and narrower. The side of the mountain was tiered with terraces ascending to the summit like steps of stairs. Des explained that these were built in the time of the Incas. This was where the Indians grew their maize and potatoes. The soil had to be carried on their backs from the fertile valley below. The terraces were built so that the soil wouldn't be washed down again when the rains came. I could only imagine how many thousands of Indians it must have taken to build such an extraordinary construction. These terraces are still used for cultivation today.

As we passed a forlorn bush on the side of the road Des remarked, "Take a good look at that bush. It's the last one you'll see for a long time. Nothing much grows above this point."

Higher and higher we climbed, the old truck moaning and groaning under the strain. At times we negotiated hairpin bends with scarcely an inch to spare. It was a bone-shaking and terrifying trip. We came to a fork in the road. No signposts.

"Both roads lead to Yauri," explained Des, "but we have to go to the right. It's a little longer but less hazardous. There was a landslide on the other road a short time ago and a lot of lorries got stuck. Some of them are still there."

As we reached the top of the mountain we had a wonderful view of the lake at Langui. On the side of the lake was the little village with its church surrounded by mud huts. Langui resembled a typical village in the Swiss Alps. Yet there was something barren and unwelcoming about it. I was soon to discover that it was a troubled place in spite of its tranquil setting.

Llamas and alpacas were grazing on the side of the road. They are called the 'sheep' of the Andes. There didn't appear to be much for them to eat except for a kind of spiky straw grass called *ichu*. They raised their long necks as we approached, unaccustomed to being disturbed on their lonely mountain. They stared at us in surprise, cocking their baby faces in the air. As they did so, I could see the coloured threads hanging from their pierced ears. This was the only way of distinguishing ownership I suppose. Each herd has a leader who leads them out in the morning and home at evening time. In the distance a little boy was sitting on a rock. He is the shepherd who stays out here all day minding his precious animals.

Des recalled how an English doctor who visited once couldn't stand the sight of llamas.

"Stupid animals," he used to say. He was an alcoholic and may have

Llamas on the 'road' to Yauri

been suffering from impaired vision. I thought they were really beautiful animals and I hoped one day to keep a baby llama.

We passed through a little village called Descanso, which means 'resting place'. It was probably an ancient staging post for the llama trains that plied their trade between Bolivia and Peru. We didn't delay as we wanted to reach Yauri before nightfall. I could hardly believe I was reaching the end of my long journey. I began to feel excited at the prospect of finally seeing this place that I had heard so much about.

"There's the tower of the church," said Des, pointing to a little speck between two hills. We were almost there.

My first sight of Yauri was unforgettable. We came upon it suddenly as we rounded a sharp bend. There it was in the distance perched on a little plateau in the middle of a vast plain. This region is called the *Altiplano* or High plain, and is a six-hundred-mile long plateau. The setting sun was casting its last rays over the sleepy town. Another day had ended. Small herds of llamas and sheep were returning lazily to their corrals. They appeared like dragons as their breath turned to steam in the cold evening air. There were little huckster shops on each side of the street. They were dimly lit, some by candle, others by kerosene lamp. A few Indian men in ponchos and women with long skirts hurried along in the dim light. There is very little twilight in the mountains.

It was already dark as we entered the Plaza in front of the church. On

My first sight of Yauri

the far side of the road some young policemen were standing idly in front of the police station. Armed with pistols and machine guns they eyed us menacingly as we approached but they said nothing. The priests' house was to the right of the church. We entered through a little door set in the centre of a great Spanish door. The little door led into a cobblestoned patio off which were various rooms. Des lit a candle and showed me into a room near the entrance to the patio.

"This is your room," he said proudly, as if he was showing me into the Hilton Hotel.

The room was empty except for a bed in one corner, but that was all I needed at that moment. I began to shiver in the cold night air. I was covered in dust and my mouth was parched with the thirst. I took a swig of water from a plastic bottle, unpacked some things from my cases, blew out the candle and went to bed. I was exhausted but I couldn't sleep. I thought of all that had happened since I left Ireland. I thought of my mother at home in Wicklow. Perhaps she couldn't sleep tonight either. Why in the name of God had I come to this dreadful place . . . ?

2

The Big Decision

I had been ordained a priest in 1959 as a member of the Carmelite Order. This Order is spread throughout the world and has many missions in Africa and South America. After my ordination I had ambitions to work in the foreign missions among the poor in Zimbabwe. However, I was considered to be a good preacher and so I was appointed to the home mission instead. I was sent to the Carmelite community in Whitefriar Street in Dublin where I spent many years giving parish missions and retreats around Ireland and England. Next I spent seven years as chaplain to hotels in Birmingham, England. I then decided to do further study in youth work in Brussels, Belgium where I founded a young Christian community.

Later I moved back to Ireland where I gave retreats for young people at the Carmelite Conference Centre (Gort Muire), Dundrum, at the foot of the Dublin mountains. One evening as one such retreat was ending, a group of students and I sat on the floor of my room talking. As one girl looked around my room at the pictures and music records, she asked me a simple question.

"Do you have a vow of poverty?"

I was a little taken aback, but I had no difficulty answering her question.

"Yes, as a Carmelite, I have three vows: Poverty, Chastity and Obedience," I replied. She still looked puzzled as she continued to gaze on the pile of records in the corner of the room.

"Poverty doesn't mean not having things," I added. "It means not becoming attached to things; not being preoccupied with them."

She still wasn't satisfied. For her, poverty meant not having things; not having enough to eat, not being able to pay the rent, not being able to buy nice clothes. That's real poverty. I did not seem to lack for anything.

That night I began to think. I was perfectly happy with everything that I had done as a priest. But my life was going by very quickly and I had never really lived with poor people. I was almost fifty years old now and I wanted to spend part of my life with the very poor. This was the real message of the Gospel. I became more and more taken with the idea and I couldn't get it out of my mind.

Shortly afterwards I happened to meet Des Kelleher who was home on holidays from Peru. We had been students together. After becoming a priest Des had gone to Peru and for the past fifteen years he had lived and worked with the Inca Indians in the Andes. He spoke their language and visited them in their communities which were scattered over a wide area. I was fascinated by the fact that he was living at fifteen thousand feet above sea level! He had recently been appointed to a new area which covered a whole province about the size of Belgium. He was going to be working on his own as there were very few priests in this mountainous region of Peru. Then he said something which really touched me very deeply.

"These Indians must be the poorest people in the world. They have a constant struggle just to exist in the barren Andes. They have no hospitals, no doctors and no nurses. They are a forgotten people. Half their children die before they reach two years of age. They have a very strong faith and trust in God. They are crying out for help and they are the most beautiful people in the world."

I was hooked. I just had to go. But there were many things that I hadn't thought about. I was booked to give retreats for the next two years. I was very happy where I was. Why should I change? I would have to leave my family and friends. I would have to learn not just one, but two new languages; Spanish and Quechua.

My father had died the year before and my mother who was over eighty was living on her own in Wicklow. She needed me now more than ever. How could I possibly leave her? It would break her heart. I told Des how I felt. He was silent for a moment, then he just quoted from the gospel.

"And Jesus said to them: 'I tell you most solemnly, there is no one who has left his house, wife, brothers, parents or children for the sake of the Kingdom of God, who will not be repaid many times in this present time and in the world to come, eternal life.' "

The next day I went to see the Provincial and volunteered to go to Peru.

"Are you sure you know what you are doing?" he asked with surprise.

"I was never as sure of anything in my life," I said, "I have been thinking about it for some time."

"It will mean the end of the youth retreats," he said, "there is no one to take your place."

"I will write and cancel all those who have booked," I said. The Provincial smiled.

"If we have to decide between retreats and the missions, the missions will win every time," he said. "You know I volunteered to go to Peru myself a number of years ago, but never got the chance."

Now I had to break the news to my mother. I will never forget the journey home to Wicklow. Telling her that I was leaving was going to be one of the most difficult things I ever had to do. It would be the last thing in the world that she would expect to hear. But I knew my mother had great faith. I had seen how she reacted when my oldest brother Eddie was killed in a motorbike accident at the age of only twenty-six. She was heartbroken and yet she accepted it all as the will of God. Many years later my other brother Davy died from cancer. And now she was a widow after almost sixty years of marriage. God had given her some heavy crosses to carry and I wondered how much more could she take.

She loved to see me coming home and looked forward to Mass in the house when she could no longer go out to church. We were having a cup of tea and a chat when I decided there was no right time or easy way to tell her.

"Mam, I am going on the missions to South America to work with the poor Indians in the mountains of Peru."

There was silence for a moment which seemed like an eternity. Then she said;

"I'm sure you'll find those people very strange. When are you going?"

"Oh, not for while yet. I'll be here for Christmas."

"That's great," she said, "we'll have a good Christmas anyway."

After that we didn't talk about Peru anymore, mainly because she hadn't an idea where it was. I wasn't too sure myself so I looked it up on the map. I discovered that it was a vast country with three distinct regions; the arid coastal plain, the mountains and the jungle. It was just below Ecuador and above Chile and Bolivia. I knew nothing about the country or its people. I remembered reading a wonderful book on the life of St Rose of Lima. The place I was going to work was called Yauri but when I looked for it on the map I couldn't find it. The nearest place I found was Sicuani.

Once I had made up my mind to go I felt a great peace of mind. I knew I had made the right decision. Of course the question that everyone asked was "Why?" That was one question that I couldn't easily answer. Some of the biggest questions in life are not easy to answer. Everyone was very enthusiastic and offered me every encouragement. No one said I shouldn't go.

I hate saying 'Goodbye' and I was dreading the final farewells. I remembered what Alicia, an English girl who lived near home, said at the end of the summer holidays long ago. She was about eight years old at the time and we used to go everywhere together, hunting in the woods, swimming at Brittas Bay and picking flowers in the garden. The day before I was due to go back to Terenure College she said to me;

"Christy, I won't be around tomorrow when you are leaving. You see I get these awful butterflies in my stomach and I don't like them. So I will hide in the woods until you are gone."

I knew exactly how she felt.

As the plane to New York left Shannon I was happy to be on my way at last. Although I still had some butterflies I wasn't feeling very sad or lonely. The anticipation of such moments can be much worse than the reality. Just as I was about to doze off, a young American teenager beside me began to talk.

"Are you going to the States on holiday?" the teenager asked.

"No, I'm just passing through. I'm going to work in South America," I replied.

"I'd love to go to South America. What kind of work do you do?" he enquired.

"Well, actually I'm a priest. I'm going on the missions to Peru," I explained.

"What kind of priest are you? Are you a member of a religious order?"

"Yes," I replied, "I'm a Carmelite."

"Really! I'm a Carmelite student with the New York Province. My name's Mike Feeney. I have just been visiting my grandfather in

Donegal. Do you know Charlie Graham?" he quickly asked.

"Yes, I do. He is a Wicklow man, like myself. Actually he's picking me up at the airport."

"What an extraordinary coincidence!" he exclaimed.

From then on there wasn't a dull moment until we landed at John F Kennedy Airport in New York. I was amused by one of his questions.

"What do you call that street in Dublin with the river running down the middle of it?"

I wasn't quite sure what he was talking about. Then it dawned on me.

"Oh, you mean the quays on either side of the River Liffey!"

☆　　☆　　☆

I had never been to the United States before. As the customs officer looked at my passport he remarked;

"What are you smuggling today, Father?"

Everyone looked around to see what I had in my cases.

Charlie Graham was waiting for me in the Arrivals. With him was Alf Isaacson, another Carmelite, and Mike Feeney's mother. We all set off for downtown New York.

The Carmelites have a monastery on 28th Street. The New York Province was founded from Ireland and has remained 'more Irish than the Irish themselves'. Twenty-eighth Street is one of those New York streets that has no name, just a number and not a lot of character. It is opposite Bellevue hospital. On arrival I got a great welcome from the Carmelite community and Charlie showed me to my room.

"Some very important people have stayed in this room," he said, as he opened the door.

"This was Lar Flanagan's room and it was here that De Valera (revolutionary leader and later prime minister and president of Ireland) stayed after he escaped from Lincoln Jail, England in 1919. Lar was chaplain to Bellevue hospital at the time and one morning he returned from night duty to discover De Valera asleep in his bed. They were great friends, you know, having been to school together in Blackrock College, Dublin."

Charlie offered to show me around New York. Although well into his seventies he was very quick on his feet. His new pacemaker had given him a fresh lease of life. I found it hard to keep up with him especially when he decided to catch a bus that was about to take off. He had an embarrassing habit of entering the exit door so he didn't have to pay. The driver would shout,

"That's okay, Father. You don't have to pay," and as we were leaving, "Have a nice day, Fathers."

Walking up Fifth Avenue we visited St Patrick's Cathedral, dwarfed by the surrounding skyscrapers. We watched the skaters on the open-air ice rink and strolled around Macy's, the most famous department store in the world. If you can't buy it at Macy's it just can't be bought! Travelling on the subway I was surprised to see that every inch of it had been scrawled with graffiti. None of the graffiti made any sense. It was as if some monkeys were let loose with crayons. Charlie said that a famous psychiatrist explained this phenomenon by saying;

"It is the youth of today freely expressing themselves."

God help the youth of today if that is all they have to say!

I climbed the Empire State Building which at 1,250 feet high was once the tallest building in the world. Charlie didn't have a head for heights so he waited in a nearby coffee shop. From the top of the building there is a magnificent view of the city and on a clear day you can see for almost eighty miles. It was very windy at the top. Apparently a few weeks earlier a woman had tried to commit suicide by jumping off the top, only to be blown onto a lower storey before she hit the ground. She survived with a few broken bones.

I found New York a rather strange place. People on the street would suddenly start shouting, or singing or dancing, for no apparent reason. It is probably the greatest open-air lunatic asylum in the world, without the bars.

The two great cultures of South America before the arrival of the Spaniards were the Aztecs of Mexico and the Incas of Peru. Whenever I speak about the Incas, people often confuse them with the Aztecs. Although there are some similarities between the two, there is no evidence to suggest that they were influenced by one another. My flight from New York to Lima was via Mexico City so I decided to stop off for a few days and learn a little about the Aztecs.

Arriving in Mexico was quite a culture shock. The city was covered by a dense cloud of smog when I arrived. It was summertime in Mexico and the air was warm and sultry after the bitter cold of New York. On my way to the city centre I thought I was caught in the rush hour until the taxi driver exclaimed;

"*Carramba!* It would be quicker to walk. Mejico is getting worse all the time."

It was funny to hear him pronouncing Mexico without the 'x'.

"There are over twelve million people in Mejico City and every one of them must have decided to come out today," he complained.

He dropped me off eventually at a small dingy hotel where I was lucky to get a room. The wallpaper was once a bright yellow with a floral pattern, but it had faded badly and was peeling off at the edges. The carpet was frayed with a bald patch in one corner of the room. There was no sink and no running water, just a table with a basin and a large jug of water. The toilet was at the end of the corridor. It had an overhead cistern and chain. When the chain was pulled the sound of gushing water reverberated throughout the hotel. (There is a lot to be said for the toilets in Buckingham Palace which are said to have a delayed action, so that the Queen is well out of earshot before a sound is heard!) The bed was comfortable or maybe I was too exhausted to notice. Within minutes I had fallen asleep to the roar of the traffic and the sounding of horns.

I woke with a headache and a sick stomach, the first effects of altitude sickness. Mexico City is 7,350 feet above sea level. The city was originally built by the Aztecs on an island on top of a volcano, surrounded by water and mountains. Over time the water drained away and the city expanded, but many of the older buildings are now sinking into the spongy soil. The cathedral has recently been saved from sinking out of sight.

The Mexicans are a very friendly people and are always ready to help. The only problem is that sometimes they give you directions even though they don't know the way themselves. They are too polite to say they don't know. Dressed in brightly coloured clothes they always seem to be smiling. In spite of the large crowds no one is in a hurry and everyone seems happy and easy-going. I walked to the Museum of Anthropology in Chapultepec Park on the outskirts of the city. Walking is always much more interesting than taking a taxi and, as I had discovered, it is quicker too.

Everywhere children were begging on the streets. Mexico has a very high birth rate and there is an intensive government campaign for birth control, but no one seemed to be taking any notice. It was raining heavily from early morning which was unusual for this time of year. But as they say at home it was 'warm rain' and I certainly wasn't going to let it spoil my visit.

Outside the museum there is a large monolith to the rain god, Thaloc. He was having a field day today! The Museum of Anthropology is a museum for those who don't really like museums. It presents marvellous graphic representations of man's evolution, following race, flora and fauna. It also shows the ancient civilisations and cultures of Mexico. Although the Aztecs are the best known, there were many other tribes that preceded them. Many traces of these early tribes can still be seen all over Mexico, notably in the City of Teothuacan or City of the Gods, about thirty miles northwest of Mexico City. I decided to pay it a visit so I shared a taxi with some other tourists.

Along the way we stopped beside a huge cactus plant and our driver demonstrated the many uses that the Indians made of this desert plant. There was no part of it that wasn't used. They could even survive in the desert by sucking the sap from the stem.

Teothuacan was a thriving city about one thousand years ago, when most European cities were little more than villages. There still remains two great pyramids dedicated to the Sun and the Moon. It was on top of these pyramids that human sacrifices were offered to the Gods. In between the two pyramids is the Queue of the Dead where the sacrificial victims made their final journey to the summit. I climbed the hundreds of steps to the top of the Pyramid of the Sun. The view from the summit was breathtaking, although I'm sure it didn't look so good to the poor unfortunates who would have stood here waiting to be sacrificed.

The city of Teothuacan declined and disappeared in about the seventh century AD and no one knows why. After this many different tribes appeared, among them were the Mexicas or the Aztecs as they are better known. They held sway until they were conquered by the Spaniard, Cortez, in 1521. Like all Spanish conquests it was carried out for God and for the Crown and within a single generation Franciscan missionaries had converted the Aztecs to christianity. The Indians were accustomed to adapting imposed religions to their needs. However, there was one important factor that helped with their conversion and that was the miracle of Our Lady of Guadalupe.

A simple Indian, Juan Diego, soon after being baptised, saw visions of the Virgin Mary. The bishop refused to believe him until Juan Diego showed him a miraculous image imprinted on his cloak. Science has never been able to explain the origins of the image of the dark-skinned Madonna now venerated as the Patron Saint of Mexico and South America.

Early on Sunday morning I made my way to the basilica of Our Lady of Guadalupe, just outside Mexico city. I found myself caught up in a crowd of thousands of people from all over South America. Women with lace mantles on their heads, their hands held high, clasping their rosaries and praying aloud. Little groups of people were waving flags and banners to the accompaniment of music. There were stalls everywhere selling anything from a sandwich to a holy picture. One little boy was selling birds so tame that they flew around and returned to rest on his shoulder. In this way he never had to replenish his flock. Many Indians were dressed in traditional costume and one group was jumping around doing what looked like a war dance.

As I approached the shrine, old men and women crawled along on their hands and knees, their knees bleeding from the rough pavement as they made the last few yards of their pilgrimage. This was my first experience of Latin American religion. The basilica is an immense ultra-modern structure made from concrete and marble in the shape of a volcano. It holds over twenty thousand people and contains just one image above the altar, the dark-skinned Virgin Mary imprinted on a sixteenth-century cloth. Masses were being offered continuously. A moving escalator carried the pilgrims behind the altar where they could have a closer look at the Madonna. As I moved underneath I said a silent prayer to Our Lady.

The next morning I sent a telegram to the Carmelites in Lima. It read simply, 'Arrive Tuesday 8.00 am Flight A.P. 621 Chris.'

The sky over Lima was covered with a dense blanket of thick clouds. From above, it looked like a great eiderdown had been laid out over the city. Underneath, it was dull and sultry. As we broke through the clouds

I got my first bird's-eye view of Peru; a long narrow desert coastline, grey, arid and uninviting. There was no sign of vegetation as the desert stretched for miles to the foothills of the Andes. Out in the bay there were hundreds of little fishing boats bobbing up and down like ducks. We flew low over some flimsy shacks and appeared to be landing in the desert; the runway sliding underneath us at the very last moment. To the left I noticed the green camouflage of military aircraft and helicopters, a grim reminder that Peru is governed by army generals. Once in the terminal building I passed quickly through immigration as I had a permanent visa from the Peruvian Embassy in London. The customs officer took a cursory glance at my cases and asked;

"Do you have a medal or a holy picture for me?"

I had to admit to him that I did not. That was the last thing I thought of bringing to Peru. Afterwards I was told that they always ask priests for medals. It hasn't got anything to do with religion. They just like to keep them as lucky charms. From then on I never travelled without a plentiful supply.

There were two Carmelites there to meet me, Albano 'Tiny' Quinn, who had come down from Sicuani, and Mike La Fay, the parish priest of the Carmelite parish in Miraflores. They welcomed me literally with open arms. Shaking hands is considered very formal in South America. Outside the airport it was the early morning rush hour, but there was no rush. *Micros* trundled along with great puffs of smoke belching from the rear and people hanging on for dear life.

The streets in this part of Lima were unpaved and pot-holed. People sat around little kiosks eating sandwiches and drinking coffee. An enterprising mechanic had dug a hole by the side of the road and was fixing the exhaust pipe on an old battered Volkswagen. No car appeared to be less than ten years old. The streets were dirty and untidy. A scraggy dog was rummaging through the rubbish piled high by the river. Mike took the coast road from the airport to show me Miraflores from sea level. Even at this early hour there were crowds on the beach and in the water. Chocolate brown youngsters with long black hair were riding the surf like torpedoes. Inland, the cliffs rose sharply with tall multi-storey houses sitting precariously on the top. As we approached Miraflores it soon became apparent that we were entering a much more affluent area. Even the streets were cleaner. Large flat-roofed white houses of Spanish style stood surrounded by high walls or iron railings. The windows were caged in with iron bars. This was obviously 'bandit country'.

"This is not the real Peru," remarked Tiny, as he noticed my surprise at the luxurious surroundings.

The Carmelite monastery is typical of this part of Lima. The priests' house is situated beside the church and the primary school. The whole complex takes in the entire block. A little further away is a huge secondary school which is considered one of the best in South America. It is co-educational and caters for the better off, including children of government ministers and army generals.

The Carmelites have achieved a lot in a relatively short time in Peru. It all began in 1949 with the arrival of two Carmelites from the Chicago Province with no missionary experience. They were given a derelict area here on the outskirts of the city. There was no church, no school and very few houses. Just ten years later, in 1959, the first Carmelite bishop was appointed to Sicuani. You could hardly imagine two more diverse missions. The affluent middle-class residents of the suburban district of Miraflores contrasted sharply with the impoverished forgotten Indians of the Andes. I was happy to be going to the latter. In the meantime I would have to go to a language school to learn Spanish.

Tiny returned to Sicuani and for the next three months I stayed in Lima and went back to school. Each morning I would take a *micro* on the thirty-minute ride to Barranco where César and his wife, Esperanza, ran a language school. It was beside the central house of the St James' Society, a missionary foundation of secular priests started by Cardinal Cushing. As there were always new recruits, César and Esperanza were assured of a thriving business. The teaching was on a one-to-one basis and you progressed at your own pace. The school wasn't just for priests but had a constant sprinkling of business people and embassy staff. The new Norwegian ambassador was there at the time and when I was lucky I got a lift in the ambassador's car.

César didn't confine himself to teaching boring Spanish verbs, however, but talked freely about the state of the country.

"There go the generals for their morning coffee," he remarked one day as six helicopters flew past. He didn't think much of the forthcoming elections.

"The junior generals will find it hard to give up power. They have been trained to be leaders of the country. There are over six hundred thousand men in the army, half of them officers. Of course the officers don't do any fighting. It's the poor uneducated privates who get killed. The massive army build-up is justified by the so-called threat from Chile."

You don't have to be long in the country before you realise the hostility that exists between Peru and Chile. It all goes back to the War of the Pacific (1879–83) when Peru and Bolivia quarrelled with Chile over valuable nitrate deposits in the Atacama Desert. In the end Peru lost its southern provinces, Lima was occupied for a time and the country was left bankrupt. But the Peruvians never forgot. Even the children playing on the streets remember. Once I heard a young lad shout after another;

"You're a Chilean."

That's probably the greatest insult you can give. They don't play 'Cowboys and Indians'. I suppose that wouldn't make much sense. Instead they play 'Peruvians and Chileans', and the bad guys are always the Chileans.

My first impression of Lima was that of a very dirty city. The division between the rich and the poor is everywhere. The city is surrounded by vast settlements of *puebla jovens* (young towns). The Indians come to these settlements from the mountains with nothing and set up homes of bamboo. Some of these shanty towns have more than thirty thousand people living in them and the numbers are increasing daily. Living in filth and squalor with no water or sanitation, the Indians descend on the city centre each day to scavenge and steal. I nearly broke my neck one morning on my way to school when I tripped over a manhole from which the cover had been removed. Then I realised that all the covers were missing. The Indians steal them to cook on.

Every window around Miraflores has a sign in the window, '*Se necessita muchacha* (Girl wanted)'. Mostly Indian girls apply. The *muchacha* is a glorified slave. Although she lives in the home she is not treated as part of the family. She does all the housework, cooking, washing, cleaning and looking after the children. She even opens the gate for the lady of the house as she drives her car into the garage. She carries the child's bag to the gate of the school where she hands it over and the poor child has to carry it the rest of the way as the *muchacha* is not allowed to enter the school grounds. If the family goes to the beach, the *muchacha* is there in her white coat, walking behind the family and carrying the picnic baskets for the lunch. She never swims with the family. She can't read or write and speaks only Quechua. All too often she ends up pregnant by the husband or one of the sons and is then promptly dismissed.

In Lima there are poor children everywhere roaming the streets. Some beg, others try to survive as 'shoe shine boys'. They shout the familiar catch phrase, "Shoe shine, Mister?" as they come and sit in front of you with their little stool. The children are experts at stealing and sooner or later you are bound to be caught. The beach is particularly dangerous, as one of our visiting priests found out. He was lying on the beach with all his belongings tucked up tightly underneath his head, enjoying the afternoon sunshine. Soon he dozed off. When he awoke, everything was gone; clothes, passport, money, watch. He was very tall, over six feet six inches, and caused quite a stir as he walked home in his bathing suit. He was thankful that at least he wasn't in his birthday suit!

At the weekends I took the opportunity to visit the sights of Lima. I began with the cathedral, where the head of Pizarro, the Spanish conqueror of Peru, is preserved in a glass case. He founded Lima in 1535 on the banks of the River Rimac. It is known as the City of the Kings because of the date of its foundation (6 January, the Feast of the Magi). It is said that the Indians suggested he build the city here in revenge for his killing of The Inca, as it is a most unsuitable site. There is a constant shortage of water. Pizarro did not live to see the city grow, however, as he was murdered shortly afterwards by one of his generals in an internal dispute. There is a giant statue of him on horseback at the corner of the Plaza beside the Presidential Palace.

Peru has five Saints but the two best known and most popular are St Rose of Lima and St Martín de Porres. Their remains are kept at the Church of Santa Domingo which was the first church built by Valverde, the Dominican monk who accompanied the Spaniards to Peru. The home of St Rose is not far from the church and is a very popular tourist attraction. She planted roses at the back of her home which was very unusual in her day as roses were virtually unknown in Peru before the conquest. In one corner of the garden lies the well where she threw the key of her chastity belt. The well is considered miraculous and people throw in petitions asking for favours. As I had read her life story years earlier I wondered if she was secretly calling me to Peru. I folded my petition and threw it in the well.

St Martín de Porres has a very special appeal to Peruvians because of his colour. His father was Spanish and his mother was a Panamanian slave. He became a Dominican lay brother and devoted his life to the poor. He was also a miracle worker, but his superior forbade him to work miracles until he asked for permission. The story goes that one day when he was returning home he saw a man fall from a scaffolding. He suspended him in mid-air until he went and got permission to save him! He also had a great love of animals; cats, dogs and even mice. Mice first came to Peru aboard the Spanish ships.

St Martin is the patron saint of the poor and is renowned the world over. There is a beautiful shrine in his honour in the Carmelite church in Whitefriar Street, Dublin. I remember one day, shortly after his canonisation, asking a woman on her way into the church if she was going to say a prayer to St Martin.

"No, I gave up praying to him. I used to have great devotion to him when he was 'Blessed'," she replied. (He was referred to as 'Blessed Martin' before being canonised Saint Martin). "Now he's just like the politicians. Once he's got in he's useless!"

In the sixteenth century the Spanish conquistadors set up the Court of the Inquisition in Lima. It was set up to combat heresy, blasphemy and all kinds of sexual deviation. By an extraordinary stroke of good fortune the Indians were exempt from the jurisdiction of the Holy Office, probably because they weren't considered fully fledged human beings. Trials were held in secret and the accused had to be convicted at all costs. Witnesses testified from behind closed doors so they would not be recognised. The first test for the accused was to recite the 'Our Father' and 'Apostles' Creed' by heart. God help him if he made a mistake. If he didn't plead guilty he was brought to the torture room. The sentences included confiscation of property, deportation, the gallows or death by being burnt at the stake. The lucky ones were shot. When the Inquisition was suppressed the people of Lima ransacked and destroyed the building. It has only recently been reconstructed in every detail, even its ghastly torture chambers, for the benefit of the tourists.

It was Lent while I was in Lima and it was preceded by weeks of carnival. As it is in the middle of summer, everyone goes to the beach.

The children celebrate by throwing water and flour at unsuspecting passersby. They get a great kick out of seeing people drenched to the skin or having their clothes destroyed by sticky flour. They also throw water in the windows of the *micros* as they speed along. I couldn't believe my luck one day when a woman gave me her seat by the window. The next minute I was drenched by a bucket of water, much to the amusement of all the passengers.

St Patrick, needless to say, is unknown in Peru. Many have never even heard of Ireland. So I was surprised when I got an invitation to dinner on St Patrick's Day. It came from John Foley, a Kerryman, who had married a Peruvian woman and who lived in the parish. John left Ireland in 1919 and went to work for the American Cable Company. He lived in various countries of South America, eventually settling down in Peru. He married 'into the money' as they say and lived in a beautiful house. Although he had never returned to Ireland, he never lost his Kerry accent and his love for all things Irish. He still followed Gaelic football and was convinced that Kerry would win the All-Ireland Championship again that year. He had invited a large number of friends and relations to the dinner, but John and I were the only Irish people present. John had chosen the menu: bacon and cabbage with lashings of 'spuds'. We drank Irish whiskey from Waterford cut glasses and ate the bacon and cabbage with silver cutlery. Hanging on the wall was a beautiful painting of Glendalough. (This beautiful old monastic site by the lakes in the Wicklow mountains was where St Kevin lived in the sixth century). It had been painted from a postcard by one of John's Peruvian friends.

The following week I was to depart for the mountains to a place called Yauri, where my real work would begin. Everyone kept telling me I hadn't seen anything yet.

"Wait until you get to Yauri," they said, "you will be living in an old dilapidated house with no running water or electricity, not to mention a telephone. The first thing you will have to do is make a bed and then you won't be able to sleep in it because of the altitude and the cold."

I was beginning to wonder if such a place existed. Surely it wouldn't be as bad as they said. I just couldn't wait . . .

3
Where Time Stood Still

The church in Yauri

Yes, there is a place called Yauri, high up in the Andes. It is not well known, even to the people of Peru. You won't find it easily on a map. It is a place where time has stood still for a thousand years. Yauri town has about 7,000 inhabitants and is set in the middle of a vast *pampa* or grassy plain which stretches for hundreds of miles to the snow-covered Andes. The mornings here are bitterly cold, at times reaching temperatures of twenty to thirty degrees below zero. The altitude ranges from 12,000 to 16,000 feet above sea level, almost five times higher than the highest mountain in Ireland!

Yauri is the capital of the province of Espinar which covers an area about the size of Belgium. The whole province is our parish; the highest parish in Peru and perhaps the highest in the whole world. There are over fifty small communities spread out in the surrounding mountains. Almost nothing grows at this altitude: there are no trees, no gardens and no flowers. The Indians try to grow small potatoes, but in general they are a pastoral people with herds of llamas and alpacas (these are members of the camel family and thrive at high altitudes). They also keep sheep, not fat chubby ones as in Ireland, but lean and skinny ones with very little meat. Vicuñas, the sacred animal of the Incas, roam wild in the highest regions. These animals are also of the camel family, but they are not domesticated. They are rare and are in danger of becoming extinct. Their silky wool is among the finest in the world.

The physical characteristics of the Indians have changed little since Inca times. They are short in stature, the men averaging about five feet two inches and the women four feet ten inches. They have a dark brown complexion and their eyes are chestnut or maroon. The women have long black hair. The chest and shoulders of both sexes are well developed. This is undoubtedly due to the size of their lungs which have grown over the centuries to cope with the lack of oxygen in the air. At times the oxygen level can be less than half that at sea-level. No wonder I was constantly out of breath!

The town of Yauri is a desolate place, a huddle of tin-roofed, mud-walled shacks. Up until recently the roofs were all made of *ichu*, but as this had to be renewed every year it has now been replaced with corrugated iron. The streets are just caked mud which turns into a muddy swamp during the rainy season. The Indians go barefoot or wear sandals cut from old rubber tyres. The mud squelches between their toes as they plod along up to their ankles in the mire. The children are quite happy, covered from head to toe in dirt. Western standards of cleanliness and decorum mean nothing here. Everywhere stinks. People go to the toilet any time, any place without the slightest inhibition or self-consciousness. They urinate or defecate in the street or from passing trucks. The women wear no underclothes. They just bob down quite publicly and relieve themselves under their wide hooped skirts.

Indian huts are built in a rectangular shape, consisting of one room with a thatched roof. There are no windows or chimney and the smoke fills the whole hut, gradually escaping through the thatch. The door is just a hole in the wall, low and very small. The fire occupies one corner of the hut during the rainy season, while opposite it are laid some alpaca and llama skins. This is where the family sleeps. They never take off their clothes. It's much too cold for that. The women take off their outer skirt and use it as a pillow. The men use their ponchos. They all sleep huddled together to keep warm, covered with skins and blankets, along with the dog and the guinea pigs. No wonder they are always infested with fleas and lice. There are no tables or chairs in the hut, as the Indians spend most of their day outdoors. There are niches in the walls for placing implements and fetishes. Pegs made from animal bones are used for hanging things. On the floor there is a variety of household equipment, storage jars, pots, baskets, cooking utensils, a grindstone, mats and skins. An extended family occupies other huts arranged rectangularly around a central court or patio. Outside this is a stone-walled corral for the animals.

The Indians live a harsh life, enduring temperatures ranging from the extreme heat of the midday summer sun to the freezing cold of the winter nights. Without a hospital or a doctor there is not much hope of survival if they contract even a minor disease. Half the children die before they reach two years of age and the average life span of an adult Indian is only forty-five years.

☆   ☆   ☆

My first home in Yauri

The loud clang of the church bell rang out from the church tower. Sebastian, the sacristan, was calling the people to Mass. I was already

43

awake; I hadn't slept a wink all night. I heard every sound, every barking dog and other eerie noises which I didn't recognise. However it wasn't the noise that kept me awake, I just couldn't sleep. I looked at my watch. It was half past six on Sunday morning.

The tap in the patio had frozen. It usually thawed out when the sun came up. Anyway it was too cold to wash and shave. I found some water in a bucket and lit the primus stove. Des had warned me to boil the water for at least twenty minutes. (At this altitude it was difficult to get the water to boil at all.)

"There's a little creature like a silvery eel in the water here," said Des, "I saw it once under a microscope in Sicuani."

We had brought some tea bags and little wheaten pats of bread from Sicuani. I was just ready to start when there was a loud banging on the door. As I opened it an old Indian woman put her arms around me and gave me a hug.

Esther

"*Papay Cristobal* (Father Chris), you are very welcome to Yauri. I hope you stay with us for a long time," she said.

She didn't actually kiss me but rubbed her cheeks against me like a hungry cat. Her skin was leathery and coarse with age. Over her shoulders she wore an *inkuna* (a piece of woven material) tied in a knot at the front.

"I knitted you some gloves for the cold," she said, as she offered me a pair of black gloves that were much too small.

"My name is Esther and I have always looked after the priest very well."

As she was about to leave, another old woman appeared at the door. She was smaller than the first and looked even poorer. She was dressed in an assortment of clothes and her grey hair hung down from under an old woollen hat. Most of her front teeth were missing. I had to bend down to give her a hug.

"I am called Trinidad, after the Blessed Trinity," she explained. "I brought you two of my finest *cuys* (guinea pigs) for your dinner."

Trinidad

In Inca times this would have been the offering to The Inca when he visited a village. From a bucket Trinidad produced two slimy pink little bodies and presented them to me. They looked absolutely revolting. They were skinned but complete with head and tail and they weren't gutted. Their little bodies were still warm as she put them into my hands. They were a far cry from the lovely cuddly little animals that we kept as pets at home. I thanked her for her kindness but I'm sure she noticed the look of disgust on my face.

On the way to the church for eight o'clock Mass, everyone stopped to hug me. By now I was getting accustomed to hugging people. The

Indians are so warm and kind. Shaking hands is considered formal to the point of rudeness. So instead you are embraced and hugged. Even the children wanted to say 'Hello'.

The church in Yauri is enormous. They say it took over a hundred years to build. It was started by the Spaniards in 1800, but with the granting of Peruvian independence in 1821 all work ceased and most of the priests returned to Spain. The church wasn't completed until 1900. Like most churches in Peru it is adorned with riches. The high altar is covered with silver from one of the local mines. There are oil paintings on the wall and elaborate shrines all around the church. The various saints are considered personal friends by the people and there are always little groups standing around each statue in silent prayer. Sebastian has to sleep in the church every night with his dog to guard the treasures.

Although there were some wooden benches in the church, most of the women sat on the floor. The children brought their animals to Mass. There were sheep and pigs and a beautiful little white llama. As I raised the Host and said, "Behold the Lamb of God," there were two little lambs looking up at me.

Melchor and me

I said Mass in Spanish and Melchor, the catechist, translated what I was saying into Quechua. The homily was always a two-way affair. You asked questions and everyone answered back. The fact that most of the answers were wrong didn't bother them. They didn't know how to be shy or embarrassed. The women looked on stoically without an expression on their faces. If only I could tell what was going on inside their heads!

After Mass there were eleven couples to be married. They gathered around the altar in a semi-circle, the women in their beautiful coloured skirts and *lliclas* (shawls), the men in homespun trousers and little multicoloured waistcoats. They repeated the marriage vows and exchanged the rings, but they weren't too particular about the finger on which they put the ring. Some of the women had their babies on their backs while the bigger children sat in the front seat. As is the Indian custom they had already lived together before marriage for many years and usually had several children. I noticed that the women were barefoot while the men wore football boots. It must be the local football team, I thought. Afterwards Des informed me that this wasn't the case. The men love to play football and their most treasured possession is their football boots. They were wearing their boots in honour of the big occasion.

Distributing communion at Mass almost always caused a stampede. Everyone rushed up to the altar at once. Men with bultos, women with babies on their backs and children everywhere. They have no sense of forming a queue. A catechist stood on each side of me and they beat the people back with long sticks.

"Go back there and don't be acting like unruly llamas," they shouted.

After receiving communion they simply turned around and bulldozed their way back to their places. It was utter chaos. They had never been trained to receive communion so they didn't know how to put out their tongue. They just bit at my fingers as I tried to give them the Host. As they opened their mouths they pushed a wad of coca leaves to one side to reveal a green gunge covering their whole mouth. It was like looking into the jungle. Even young children joined the throng, thinking I was giving out sweets. It all appeared so undignified but I was soon to learn this is the reality of life in the mountains.

After Mass they crowded into the sacristy for holy water and a blessing. Men, women and children came. Even wild looking young lads with long hair knelt before me and asked for a special blessing. One man asked me to bless his whip which he said he used to keep his children in order! Then came the baptisms. I called out a long list of unfamiliar names and asked them to form two lines down the church.

Mario Rodriguez Machacca
Felicitas Hancco Diaz
Julio César Mendoza Yucra
Yony Roxana Mamani Ccama
Zulema Abigail Quispe Huahuaccapa
Washington Condori Choquepata
Juvenal Puma Tturo
Florentino Machaca Condori, and on and on.

More confusion! I literally had to point to the spot where I wanted them to stand. Father, mother and *padrino* (godfather). As far as the family is concerned, the *padrino* is the most important person of all. He is usually chosen because he has money or power. He buys the clothes for the child and arranges the fiesta. Often he is the mayor, a policeman or the president of the community. The women breastfeed the children during baptism so I have to be careful not to baptise the mother's breast instead of the baby's head! Both boys and girls wear short skirts with nothing underneath to facilitate going to the toilet, which they often do just as they are being baptised. It seems to be the sudden shock of the cold water touching the head. They frequently have diarrhoea. Sometimes the children may be as old as twelve or more and you have to catch them first, before you can baptise them. Afterwards at the door of the church the *padrino* throws sweets to the waiting children.

Des (known as Padre Albanito) said Mass in Spanish at eleven o'clock and I attended to the constant flow of people who came to the parish office. One woman came in great distress. As she could only speak Quechua I had to ask a young boy called Benigno to translate for me.

"My husband was killed by rustlers three nights ago and they stole all my llamas and alpacas. I know where the killers are but I need a lawyer to bring them to court," she cried.

I told her I could put her in touch with the bishop's lawyer in Sicuani. She was overjoyed. She was accompanied by her daughter, Lourdes, who was about eight years of age. She was dressed in simple clothes, her little hands and feet covered in warts. She was a beautiful girl with long black hair and dark eyes. I couldn't help thinking that if she was dressed in fine clothes she could have been a princess. Just because people are poor doesn't make them any less beautiful. I gave them some bread and fruit

Lourdes *(left)* with her mother and friends

to eat. I had brought some chocolate from Ireland and I gave Lourdes a Yorkie bar. She looked at it in amazement but didn't know what it was. I gestured that she could eat it and she put it into her mouth just as it was.

"No, you must unwrap it first," I said, as I showed her how to take the paper off. She had never seen anything like it before.

As she tasted the chocolate, a smile came over her face. Although she was shy, she put her arms around me and gave me a hug.

Sunday is always the busiest day of the week. It is market day and the Indians come to Yauri from miles and miles around. They bring their animals to barter for vegetables and fruit or whatever else they might need. In spite of all the activity, there is a strange air of silence in an Indian market. Nobody shouts or makes undue noise. They believe that when you barter you are exchanging the spirit of the animal for the spirit of the fruit or vegetables; the spirit of the sheep for the spirit of the onions or bananas. The spirits are held in great respect and they must not be disturbed. They spread out their produce in little heaps on the ground in front of them and then they just sit and wait.

When the Indians came to the market they also came to the church and if they needed to arrange a baptism or marriage they had to come to the parish office. For some reason everyone seemed to want a baptismal certificate. Benigno told me that it was the first time that Indians had been given the right to vote in the presidential election, but in order to vote they had to be registered. As these Indians had never been registered at birth a baptismal certificate would be accepted. I thought of how Mary and Joseph must have felt two thousand years ago when they arrived in Bethlehem to register.

An Indian family waiting to see me after Mass

The parish office was beside my bedroom and in the office we had baptismal registers that went back hundreds of years. They were written by hand and in ancient and archaic Spanish. Some were impossible to read. Sebastian normally looked after the office, but as he treated the Indians very badly and constantly shouted at them I decided to give him a hand.

"*Iman su tiki?* (What is your name?)"

This was the first phrase I learned in Quechua.

"Zenon Qquellcca Choqquehuanca," came the reply.

"What?" I asked with surprise.

"Zenon Qquellcca Choqquehuanca," he repeated.

"How do you spell that?" I asked in astonishment, forgetting that Indians can neither read nor write.

He just looked at me with a blank stare on his face.

"What is your date of birth?" I tried.

He kept looking at me as if I wasn't talking to him. Normally Indians don't know when they were born. In fact they usually don't know the days of the week or the months of the year. Everything is calculated by its relationship to some important event in their lives. They will say;

"I was born just before the Feast of All Souls," or "after Christmas" or "during Holy Week" or "just before the big earthquake."

Zenon turned to speak to an old woman who was with him and then he replied;

"I was born just before Carnival."

"What year might that have been?" I asked in desperation. Another blank stare. I really wasn't getting anywhere. I guessed from his appearance that he must be about thirty years old, so I started searching thirty years back. It is not easy to tell an Indian's age by looking at him. When you ask an old woman what age she is, she will normally say she is over eighty and she certainly looks it, but you know she couldn't possibly be, because Indians don't live that long.

I was very excited when I eventually found his name in the book.

"Was your father's name Aparicio Qquellcca?" I asked.

"Yes," he said, wondering how I could possibly have known.

"And your mother's name was Aydee Choqquehuanca?"

"Yes," he replied again in amazement.

"What is the name of your *madrina* (godmother)?"

"Dina Mamani Chino," he replied, pointing to the old woman beside him.

I filled out the form and he went away very happy. Now he could vote for the first time. Zenon was actually thirty five years of age, born on 5 February 1945. He might even celebrate his birthday some day.

The atmosphere in Yauri was still very tense after the events which had occurred in February, shortly before I arrived. The windows of the priests' house still bore the marks of the bullets from the machine guns. Neat precise pencil holes, which didn't even crack the glass, told me what had happened.

Des told me that not long before I arrived in Yauri, people from the entire community had assembled in the stadium for a meeting. A left-wing presidential candidate by the name of Hugo Blanco was the speaker they had all come to listen to. Blanco was a charismatic character, a *mestizo* with a Spanish father and an Indian mother. He became a revolutionary leader by adopting the Inca image. The Indians looked on him as another Inca king. He had a long beard and adopted the Indian lifestyle, always wearing a beautiful red poncho. He had organised the Indians and called several national strikes and land seizures. These revolts had been brutally crushed by the security forces. Blanco had been accused of killing a policeman while defending an Indian woman and her daughter who had been raped by a landowner. He was saved from the death penalty only by an international campaign on his behalf. As a result he was hated by the police.

Everyone waited anxiously for his arrival in Yauri. Time was passing and he still hadn't arrived. The people in the stadium were getting restless. The word was that Blanco had been held up in Sicuani because he couldn't get transport to Yauri and he was going to be late. The people were prepared to wait for him but the police moved in to disperse the crowd. Indians don't move quietly, especially when they don't want to go. The police began to use force and started beating the people, arresting about half a dozen young boys and girls. They manhandled them and dragged them by the hair across the Plaza to the police station opposite our house. There they were thrown into the cells. A large crowd gathered outside, enraged by this show of police brutality. They began to chant for the release of the prisoners. The police, young men in their twenties, were on edge as they formed a cordon around the door. A girl at the back of the crowd picked up a stone and threw it at the police. With that all hell broke loose. The police opened fire on the crowd with machine guns and blunderbusses. Three people were killed instantly and many more were wounded. One young man who tried to escape into the priests' house was shot in the doorway. As he lay dying he said;

"We were only looking for our rights and the police opened fire on us."

That night screams could be heard coming from the cells as the police tortured the prisoners. Des said that they repeatedly asked the youths the same question.

"What is the gringo priest teaching you?"

A truck was seen arriving and crates of beer were carried into the police station. It was the local landowner, Julio Velasquez, congratulating the police on the 'wonderful job' they had done. Later that night the police took the bodies away in a truck and buried them in a secret location. They were afraid of repercussions from the families.

Not long after this the new priest, Padre Cristobal, arrived. No wonder the police weren't overjoyed to see me.

☆   ☆   ☆

Those first weeks in Yauri were like living in a dream. It was as if I was in another world. Yauri is another world. I soon learned to adapt to the primitive circumstances. As we had no proper kitchen or cooking utensils, Des and I ate out in a restaurant in the town. A 'restaurant' is a fancy name for the place but it was where the truck drivers had their meals. There was no menu, everyone ate the same concoction which came from a big earthenware pot. The place took on an added air of respectability when the gringos started dining there. It went from a one-star to a five-star overnight! It was probably just as well we didn't know what we were eating. We ate breakfast and supper at home. This consisted mainly of tea and bread. We had two cups, two plates and a knife and fork each.

The 'kitchen' in Yauri

Something had to be done. I suggested to Des that we go to Sicuani and buy what we needed and maybe look for some chairs and a table. We set off like a newly married couple who had just returned from their honeymoon and were about to set up home, except there were no presents. The most valuable item that we bought was a Phillips kerosene stove. It had a little plastic container that you had to hang high on the wall with a pipe leading down to the cooker. The stove was slow to start but when it heated up it worked quite well. We bought a can of kerosene as well as a couple of gasoline cans and loaded them on the back of the truck. We also got cups, pots, pans and cutlery. From now on I would be doing all the cooking.

On Sundays I sauntered off to the market after Mass with my big basket and bought all that we needed for the week – potatoes, onions, carrots, maize and all kinds of exotic fruit. We set up the 'kitchen' in one of the rooms off the patio until we could build a proper kitchen. However there was something else more urgent than the kitchen. Up until now we were using a hole in the ground outside for the toilet and, apart from not having any privacy, it was extremely cold. I could never get used to going to the toilet anywhere, anytime as the Indians did. Sometimes when I was out there first thing in the morning they came to talk to me.

"*Papay Cristobal*, could you bless my little baby, she is very ill?"

At first I pretended not to hear, but that just meant that they came closer and shouted louder.

"Just a minute," I would say, hoping they would go away, but they just stood there . . . watching.

"*Papay*, I want to confess my sins."

"Can I get married next Sunday, *Papay*?"

"*Momentito*," I would shout again, putting my hand over my face in embarrassment. Indians are not easily embarrassed. I don't think they know what it means. With the colour of their skin it is difficult to see if they are blushing. Going to the toilet for them is the most natural thing in the world. The children never have to be potty trained as they 'go' anywhere and anytime they want. Their little bottoms don't even have to be cleaned. They just roll in the dirt or as they get older they use a smooth pebble from the river. When the children noticed that I didn't urinate in the street they would ask me;

"*Papay*, do you not have to do a pee-pee?"

There was another danger that I had been warned about which made going to the toilet a hazardous operation – the black-widow spider. Not many insects survive at these high altitudes, but people have been bitten by the black widow. Their bite is poisonous and often fatal, especially when you are not near a hospital or a doctor to administer the antidote. This gave added urgency to the need to start building a proper toilet. But nothing gets done quickly in the mountains. Esther suggested that we talk to Mariano. He was good at making adobes and building huts. He was a small man with very dark features, deep set eyes and a few hairs on his chin. His teeth were dark green from continuously chewing coca leaves. He got started immediately on the adobes. These are like cement blocks made from clay and water mixed with *ichu* to bind them together. Mariano, barefooted, with his pants pulled up over his knees, trampled the wet clay until all the materials were well mixed. He then put the clay into an oblong wooden mould and placed it carefully on the ground to dry. This drying process took about a month. When the top part was dry he turned them on their side so that the rest of the block dried and became hard and solid.

"If you turn them too soon, they will crack," explained Mariano, as he turned each one over gently.

Adobes drying in the sun

I drew up a plan and showed it to Mariano, but he wasn't accustomed to following a plan. Everything was in his head. He looked at the plan for a few moments and said;

"You just show me what you want knocked down and what you want built up and I will do my best."

I planned to knock down one side of the patio and build a toilet, a shower, a kitchen and dining room.

"You just have to build three huts together," I explained.

He shook his head, wondering what anyone would do with three huts.

While Mariano could make all the bricks that I needed, I had to get everything else – wood, nails, corrugated iron, wire, water tank, shower etc. As none of these things could be bought in Yauri, I had to make several trips over the mountain to Sicuani. Even in Sicuani there were no toilets to be had and so I had to make one long journey to Lima.

Mariano had never seen a toilet before and wasn't quite sure what it was for. I told him that I would install it, but that proved easier said than done. I had no trouble fixing the overhead cistern and pipes, but when it came to fixing the bowl to the clay floor that was another story – it kept toppling over. I needed cement . . . another trip to Sicuani!

The most wonderful sound I have ever heard was the first time I pulled the chain and it worked . . . heaven! Soon our toilet became a tourist attraction in the town and people came just to look. I thought I could train the children to use it, so I left the door open . . . disaster! They defecated all over the floor and used the toilet to wash their feet!

Shortly after arriving in Yauri I set out with Des to celebrate the feast of *Santisima Cruz* (Holy Cross) at Negro Mayo which is at the most southern end of the parish. May is the month of the *Santisima Cruz* and every community and village celebrates this feast. As Negro Mayo was over seven hours drive away it was bright and early when we drew up outside the only petrol pump in Yauri. A young boy ran out.

"*Allillanchu, Papay* (How are you, Father?)"

He started the generator, unhooked the gasoline hose and began to fill the tank.

"How much?" he enquired.

"Fill it up," I said, as I kept an eye on the meter.

Soon the tank began to overflow and the gasoline splashed all over the ground. Luckily the Indians don't smoke. I was careful to replace the cap myself as they usually forgot.

The feast of *Santisima Cruz*

"There are four main roads out of Yauri," explained Des, as we continued on our way.

"If you take the wrong road you could be going for hours in the wrong direction. All the roads look the same and there are no signposts. The Indians all know where they are going and there are no tourists here."

With that he pulled the old Dodge truck to the right along two tyre tracks worn into the *pampa*. The muddy waters of the River Salado flowed to our left. There were two women trotting along with babies on their backs. The Indian women never seemed to walk but hopped along like turkeys, busily spinning their wool on a spindle. They fed raw wool onto a stick which they then bobbed up and down with their hands. The two women didn't hear the truck until it was almost upon them. They jumped to one side and when they recognised the padres they shouted for a lift.

"Where are you going?" we asked.

"To the market in Tocroyoc," they replied and with that they jumped into the back of the truck.

Llamas and alpacas were grazing on a nearby hill while a line of sheep headed to the river for a drink. Suddenly a family appeared from nowhere; a man riding a bike in front, the woman coming behind carrying a wooden cross and a young girl walking by her side. The cross was painted green and a white cloth was tied across the middle.

"What's that about?" I asked Des.

"They are bringing the cross to the church to be blessed," he explained. "This is their annual penance in honour of the Holy Cross."

"Could we stop for a minute to take a photo?" I asked.

As soon as the man saw the camera he jumped off the bike and took the cross from his wife. He proudly held the cross while the mother and children gathered around. Indians never smile for the camera but rather put on a more serious face than normal.

"*Gracias, gracias, Papay,*" said the man, as he gave the cross back to his wife and picked up his bike.

Just outside Tocroyoc we crossed the river on a rickety old wooden bridge. The bridge swayed as we passed gently over it. We stopped for breakfast at the parish house where Frans and Regina, a German couple, ran a medical post. Frans was an ex-priest who came to the jungle as a missionary and fell in love with Regina. Shortly afterwards they moved to Tocroyoc. They worked a lot with herbal medicine and were greatly appreciated by the community.

Tocroyoc was once a thriving parish with its own resident parish priest and curates. The last priest left here about twenty years ago. There is a beautiful church in the centre of the Plaza, but it is now sadly neglected. Des told me a story about the time the first Carmelite bishop visited Tocroyoc. His reputation had gone before him; how he didn't like plastic flowers or cracked statues. He would ceremoniously take them out and break them. So when they heard he was coming the people hid all the statues. However, there was a 'miraculous' stone and holy well just outside the town which was there from before Inca times and the people had great faith in it. The Bishop considered that it was bordering on idolatry so he ordered it to be destroyed. Four men were chosen to do the job, much against their will. They scattered the pieces in all directions, but as they did the people gathered them up just as quickly and took them back to their huts. The stones were still considered miraculous and were used to ward off all kinds of illnesses. Each of the four men were said to have died in mysterious circumstances shortly afterwards.

Continuing on our way, we descended a steep gorge where the road followed the course of the river as it flowed along the valley. In a short space of time we had crossed the river three times. There were no bridges so we just drove through it. We passed small groups of Indians

The road along the valley

making their way to the market in Tocroyoc. The women were carrying heavy *bultos* on their backs, while the little babies gleefully observed their surroundings as their mothers hopped along. Now and then the mother would swing the baby around to feed it at her breast. Small herds of llamas walked proudly in front, each with its own leader who didn't like anyone to show him the way. A young lad was dragging a reluctant sheep along at the end of a rope. One old man had a pig on his shoulders, its feet bound firmly together to prevent escape. Our truck left a cloud of dust trailing behind as a scorching sun blazed down from a cloudless sky.

Word had reached Ocururo that we were on our way and everyone came out to greet us. They spread out across the road so that we couldn't pass. Des explained that there were divisions in the town about who was to build the new church. The roof had fallen in on the old church some years earlier. Work had already started on the new one but different families wanted to finish it. So it remained half built. We stopped the truck and the crowd gathered around to welcome us. The president of the community stepped forward to speak;

"Padres, it is a great honour that you should visit us today. The people of Ocururo have great faith. Our patron saint is St Francis and we are building a church in his honour. But there is a lot of work to be done. Could you bless our church and we will finish the building."

He picked up a bucket of water and some salt and everyone made their way to the church. Just then another man began to speak.

"Holy Padres from Sicuani; the Mamani family have lived for generations in Ocururo. Our fathers and grandfathers have worshipped in this place. My grandfather built the old church and it is only right that we should build the new one. Our family donated the statue of St Francis which stands here today."

Des nodded to me to bless the water as he began to speak.

"Padre Cristobal and I are very happy to be here with you today and to bless your new church. St Francis is very pleased with you for the beautiful church you are building in his honour. He would wish that every man, woman and child of Ocururo would join together in completing the work. There is plenty for everyone to do – adobes to be made, *ichu* to be gathered, wood to be found. We will come back to say Mass on the feast of St Francis when the church is completed."

With that there was loud applause. We sprinkled the holy water on the four walls and continued on our way.

As we left Ocururo, Des remarked;

"I thought there was going to be trouble back there for a moment when that fellow began to speak . . . It's wonderful – the power of the priest."

The dirt track began to wind its way up the side of a mountain.

"This is called the *Escalera Diablo* or Devil's Staircase," explained Des, "and it is very aptly named."

Higher and higher we climbed, around treacherous hairpin bends. One false move and we would end up in the valley below.

"Look down there near the river," Des indicated, without taking his eyes off the road. I could just make out some wreckage in the distance.

"That's a truck that didn't make it," he continued, in a matter-of-fact tone of voice. "There were over twenty people killed in that crash last year. The steering went and they hadn't a chance."

"What's that?" I exclaimed. A grey rabbit-like animal with a long bushy tail and long hind legs like a kangaroo had suddenly darted across the track. I was always on the lookout for strange birds and animals, but I had never seen anything like this before. As I looked around there were more of them sitting on the jagged rocks, their heads cocked high and ears erect. As we approached they darted furtively behind the rocks.

"Viscatchas," said Des, "the rabbit of the Andes. They live up here on the high mountains. They eat the *ichu* and other little mountain plants. They have very sharp teeth and can give you a nasty bite. That's if you can catch them. They can jump about twenty feet into the air. The Indians eat them. They say they are very tasty, but they are impossible to domesticate."

He must have read my thoughts. I had already made up my mind that one day I would like to keep one as a pet. One last pull on the steering wheel and we had reached the summit. We could see for miles across the snow-capped peaks. Down in the valley there appeared to be a little village. I could just see the church surrounded by huts with a few tin roofs glistening like jewels in the sun. To one side a rock face towered steeply over the entire village. I wondered if this was Negro Mayo.

"Oh no!" said Des, "That's Condoroma, named after the Condor."

Just as he spoke, one of the giant birds glided past us, floating peacefully down to the valley below . . . '*El Condor Pasa*'.

"Condoroma was one of the biggest silver mines in the Inca Empire," explained Des. "All the silver used in the Inca temples and Inca weapons was mined here. The Indians were wonderful silversmiths, using very primitive instruments. If you look closely you can still see the big holes in the side of the mountain which led into the mine."

Sure enough they were clearly visible.

"They even had giant furnaces in which they smelted the ore."

"What did they use for fuel?" I enquired, incredulous, as there was no wood or no trees about.

"They never used wood, as trees don't grow at this altitude. They used *bosta* (llama dung). Llama dung is a great fuel and it was the only fuel they had up here. The Indians gathered it for miles around and they were obliged to bring it to the mine. Travelling from as far away as Yauri and beyond, they gathered the dung up every morning and loaded it onto the llamas. All the llamas belonged to The Inca and no Indian could ever own one. The Inca would kill a certain number of llamas every year for meat, but only the male ones. The females were never killed. Do you know that llamas have some very peculiar habits?"

I was making a mental note of everything he said.

"They all dung in the same place, which makes it easier for the Indians to gather it up. It is all in little heaps."

"You're joking," I said.

"It's true and there is something else that is peculiar to llamas," he continued. "Apart from human beings they are the only animals that mate lying down."

"Really?" I responded, smiling to myself.

"You just watch the next time you see them but don't get too close, you'll get a spit in your eye. They don't like you looking at them . . . just like human beings," he concluded.

I began to wonder if we would ever reach Negro Mayo, but the time passed quickly as we chatted and drove along. There wasn't another village in sight. Finally we turned another corner.

"That's Negro Mayo!" shouted Des, pointing to a mountain in the distance. It wasn't a village at all but a mountain over 15,000 feet high with a huge cross on the summit. "That's where we celebrate the feast of *Santisima Cruz*."

"Why do they want Mass on top of the mountain?" I asked.

"An old Inca custom," replied Des with a smile.

"But the Incas didn't have Mass," I responded knowingly.

"No, but for them every mountain was sacred. It was alive. It had a spirit called an *apu* (lord). The *apu* watched over the whole valley and the Indians had great respect for him. He could make their crops grow or he could destroy them in an instant with a heavy shower of hailstones or kill their animals with a bolt of lightning. Before they sowed their crops of potatoes they made an offering to the *apu*."

"But we are not going to say Mass to the *apu*," I interrupted.

"Not exactly. When the first missionaries came with the Spaniards they explained to the Indians that the real *apu* was Jesus Christ and they placed a cross on the top of every mountain and hill. That is why the Indians have such a great devotion to the Holy Cross and whenever there is a shower of hailstones there is a great demand for Mass."

By now we had reached the foot of the mountain. We passed truck after truck stopped on the side of the track for the feast. This was the main route to Arequipa in the south and the trucks constantly passed this way, laden with people and produce. The truckers too had great devotion to the Holy Cross, and many had *Santisima Cruz* written in bold letters on the front of their trucks.

Hundreds of people were making their way to the top of the mountain.

Many were dressed in their multicoloured traditional costumes, and ponchos of every colour. A band was playing loudly on the summit. Everyone was singing and dancing and in a happy festive mood. In spite of the hot sun there was a cool breeze blowing. They certainly needed their little woollen hats tied under their chins. Four men carried a table for the Mass and I gathered some stones as weights to prevent everything blowing off the altar. Des sang the Mass in Quechua and everyone joined in. As we gave the final blessing and looked out over the waves of mountain peaks it almost seemed as if they were bowing in humble adoration.

Celebrating *Santisima Cruz*

Afterwards we feasted on roast lamb and potatoes. One of the truck drivers had brought a crate of beer. He opened a bottle and filled a single dirty glass. He ceremoniously poured it on the ground as is the custom. The *apu* was always served first.

4
Living with the Indians

The children loved my truck

There was no need to set an alarm clock in Yauri as I could never imagine oversleeping. Anyway, nothing happened by the clock. The Inca Indians still live by the sun. I usually slept for about four hours and then I lay awake the rest of the time waiting for the dawn. As the first rays of light streamed through my tiny window I looked at my watch . . . it was four o'clock in the morning. (We Europeans are slaves to the watch.) Suddenly there was a loud banging at the patio door. I rushed out expecting some emergency, only to be casually confronted by an Indian family.

"*Papay*, could you baptise my *huahua* (baby) next Sunday?" asked the father.

"Is the baby seriously ill or in danger of dying?" I enquired hesitantly.

"No, *Papay*, she is very well," he replied pointing to a little child peering out over her mother's shoulder.

At first I felt like explaining that it was only four o'clock in the morning and could it not wait until a bit later, but before I could say a word he continued;

"We came in yesterday from Corporaque and we are going home on Monday after the fiesta. We have great devotion to Our Lady and we would like Purificación to be baptised during the fiesta. Señor Pachapuma Quispe has agreed to be the *padrino*."

I knew Señor Pachapuma, he was a very popular *padrino*. He was the local judge, a chronic alcoholic who was constantly drunk even when he was presiding at court. This mattered little as his judgements depended more on who bribed him with the most beer rather than the rights or wrongs of the case. It was a very wise move to have the judge as a *padrino*. He might be needed to return a favour in the future. I wrote down the names and told them to come back on Saturday for the preparation.

I had been on my own in Yauri for a couple of weeks now and I was learning fast. Des had gone to Lima for a well-earned rest. When you live at such a high altitude for long periods of time it is recommended that you spend at least two weeks at sea level every six months. Of course that doesn't apply to the Indians who are born and reared here.

Mariano continued to make adobes every day. By now the patio was full and he had already knocked down the wall on one side. He never seemed to eat but every now and then he sat on a stone, took out his little bag of coca leaves and chewed away. All the Indians chew the coca. Not only does it help with the symptoms of altitude sickness, but it also curbs feelings of hunger and cold. Mariano had a daughter of about eighteen years of age called Edelberta and I had asked her if she would help me in the office with the baptismal certificates. As she spoke Quechua and could read a little, she had less trouble looking up the family names. She was very kind to the Indians, especially the older ones, and she never raised her voice. Sebastian, however, didn't seem too pleased with this new arrangement.

A very important addition to the 'family' was Kimichu, an Alsatian dog. Tiny gave me first choice when his own dog had pups. When I saw them on a visit to Sicuani I had no hesitation in picking the one with the

Myself, Kimichu and Benigno

drooping ears. He looked so sad. When I brought him back to Yauri in the truck he suffered from altitude sickness, but he soon acclimatised. He loved coming out with me to the communities and barked continuously at the sheep and the llamas. Whenever he got free he ran after them, but he didn't do them any harm. It was just his nature. He also barked most of the night. Perhaps he too found it hard to sleep. We didn't have any problem choosing a name for him. It seemed to come naturally. We called him 'Kimichu' which is Quechua for sacristan or guardian of the church. Most of the Indians referred to Sebastian as Kimichu. This led to some very amusing incidents when they came looking for Kimichu.

"Is it the dog or the sacristan you are looking for?" I would ask jokingly. Indians don't get jokes. They just put on a blank stare. I was reminded of the story of the parish priest in rural Ireland who kept a prize bull. The farmers came from miles around, at all times of the day and night, to borrow the bull. The housekeeper would put her head out the top window and shout;

"Is it the parish priest or the bull you want?"

☆   ☆   ☆

I also made many mistakes in those early days on my own, like the time when I decided to put a notice on the door of the patio. It read;

OFFICE HOURS
Mornings. . . . . . . 8 am – 12 pm
Afternoons . . . . . 2 pm – 5 pm
Baptisms . . . . Sundays
PLEASE DON'T KNOCK ON DOOR BEFORE 8 am

At dawn the next morning there was a loud banging on the door again. I had forgotten that the Indians couldn't read or write and they never knew what time it was. I decided to leave the patio door open. But this meant that they just came straight across the patio and into my own room. The fact that I was in bed didn't bother them. The Indians should never be judged by our standards of behaviour. They would never knock on the door before entering my room. They usually just stood in the patio and shouted;

"*Papay, Papay . . .*"

If you happen to be talking to someone else they will just interrupt immediately with their request, without as much as "Excuse me". Eventually the only bit of privacy I had was when I went into the toilet and shut the door.

Another thing I learned the hard way was never to say "No". Your initial response to any request, no matter how impossible, must always be "Yes". I had arranged to celebrate the fiesta of The Birthday of Our Lady in Pichigua on the following Tuesday. However, this was the same day Pedro and his committee from Huisa Ccollana wanted me to celebrate their fiesta of *Santisima Cruz*. I explained;

"I won't be able to go to your fiesta next Tuesday because I have already arranged with Pichigua to celebrate the feast of The Birthday of Our Lady."

As soon as I said "I won't be able to go," I could see the expression on their faces change. I continued;

"The president of Pichigua came in last week and arranged their fiesta for next Tuesday. They have everything organised. They are expecting me at ten o'clock. They have even killed the sheep."

By now Pedro is not even listening and as soon as I stop talking he says;

"But won't you be able to come to Huisa Ccollana?"

I might as well have been talking to the wall.

"I would be able to come on Wednesday," I suggested helpfully.

"Our fiesta is on Tuesday. We always celebrate our fiesta of *Santisima Cruz* after the full moon in May and that is on Tuesday. We can't change it. You don't want to come," he suggested sadly.

"Of course I want to come," I interrupted, "but as I explained I'm already committed to Pichigua." He wasn't listening again.

It was a hard lesson to learn but the only solution was to say "Yes", even though you knew you couldn't go.

What would happen when I didn't arrive? Although I was dreading the consequences, I needn't have worried. They continued with their fiesta on the Tuesday and when the padre didn't come, they made an excuse for me.

"*Papay* must have been held up somewhere and he couldn't come." The important thing as far as they were concerned was that I had said "Yes". It meant that I had really wanted to go.

I drove around the back of Yauri church and headed down past the *beaterio* where some women still lived in community like nuns. They called themselves *beatas* and they wore a type of brown habit, but they were not really nuns. The *beaterio* was founded by some rich hacienda owner to carry on an old tradition of the Incas who used to have Virgins

A beata

of the Sun. In Inca times these women would have lived beside the Temple of the Sun and looked after it, weaving fine tapestries and preparing the meals for the priests. When the Spaniards first came across them in Cuzco they referred to them as the 'Nuns of The Inca'. Most of them escaped into the mountains to Machu Picchu. Those who stayed behind didn't remain virgins for very long after the soldiers arrived.

At one time there were more than ten *beatas* in Yauri, but in recent years they were down to three. A drop in vocations it seemed, although I think it was less a vocation than an escape from the drudgery of living on the *campo* (countryside). Of the three *beatas* who remained, Isabel was a teacher, Timotea played the organ in the church and Mercedes was a catechist and did wonderful work in the communities preparing the people for the sacraments. All three were reluctant to leave the *beaterio* and so they had brought their mothers and other members of their families to live with them.

I passed by Sebastian's home – a mud hut where he ran a little huckster shop, keeping it stocked up with what he could get from the church. People respected him because he slept in 'God's house'.

Ducks were paddling in the river, only rising into the air at the last moment as I splashed across in the truck. There was no bridge. A few women were washing clothes a little further up while little children played in the dirt. I was on my way to Chalki to celebrate the feast of St Isidor. I tried to remember what Des had told me about taking the right road, but what do you do when there is no road at all? I asked a young boy who was minding some sheep if this was the way to Chalki.

"It's *pura pampa*," he said, pointing straight ahead.

This was a phrase I was to become very familiar with in time. *Pampa* is an Aymara word meaning 'open space' and it described perfectly where I was heading. The Aymara Indians were another tribe that inhabited all of this region before they were brought under Inca control. Many of the placenames around Yauri come from the Aymara language.

As I drove closer to Chalki people began to appear from nowhere. Not a hut was to be seen, yet small groups of Indians were hopping along in their festive attire. They were all headed in the same direction, towards some white-looking hills in the distance. As I approached I could just make out the shape of a white chapel which blended almost invisibly into

The church at Chalki

the background. This was Chalki and it was easy to see that it got its name from the chalk-coloured hills surrounding it. A band was playing at the church door. They immediately came towards me when they saw the truck. Kimichu began to bark. A young Indian girl ran forward and put a garland of coloured wool around my neck. An older man took my Mass kit and followed behind. The band was made up of drums, pipes and whistles and struck up a happy tune as we all marched to the church.

In front of the church the Indians had assembled about twenty yoke of oxen with long wooden ploughs. The oxen were covered with multicoloured blankets and had feathers sticking out of their necks. The townleaders were dressed in old army uniforms resurrected from some ancient war. These men would all march in the procession around the church after the Mass.

This was the feast of St Isidor, the patron saint of farmers, who in paintings is often depicted walking behind two oxen and guiding a wooden plough. He lived in the sixth century just outside Madrid and worked on the land. The Incas had great respect for the land which they called *Pacha Mama* (Mother Earth). All their food came from the earth and it was in the earth that their bodies were buried when they died. This made the earth sacred and they had many ceremonies and customs to give thanks to the earth, like pouring the first glass of beer on the ground for the *apu*. The Spanish missionaries were quick to adopt these

70

customs and christianise them. Hence the importance of the feast of St Isidor.

Normally the churches in the parish were so small that I celebrated Mass outside, but the church in Chalki was bigger than most. It had thick adobe walls and the roof was covered with a heavy thatch of *ichu*. The floor sloped towards the door with a table at the higher end for the altar. Behind the table stood a large adobe altar covered with plastic flowers and hundreds of burning candles.

As the people crowded in, I prepared the altar for Mass. Kimichu slept underneath the altar as was his custom. Just as I was about to begin the Mass, the *alferado* (the person responsible for organising the Mass) rushed up to me and said;

"*Papay*, can I bring the holy souls to the Mass?"

I looked puzzled, but remembered that the important thing was to say "Yes".

"Certainly," I answered, not knowing what he was going to do.

He disappeared and returned a few moments later with a *bulto* on his back. He proceeded to empty the contents on the ground in front of the altar. Out fell the bones of his ancestors which he had dug up from the nearby graveyard. With that Kimichu came to life and ran off with one of the bones . . . there was uproar! The *alferado* ran after the dog and was followed by other members of his family.

After a while they came back with the bone and placed it with the others. I began the Mass. I prayed for the living and the dead, especially those dead here present.

After the Mass the *alferado* approached me again.

"Would you accompany the souls to their resting place, Padre?" he requested.

"Certainly," I replied.

We formed a little procession and proceeded to the graveyard beside the church. There we placed the bones in the freshly dug grave from which they had just been removed before the Mass.

"May they rest in peace," I prayed, as I sprinkled them with holy water – at least until they are once again disturbed for the next feast of St Isidor!

Yatmani Churata Ccama, the local photographer, came to see me one day with a problem. I knew him well because he was always in the church for every wedding and baptism. His was the only camera in Yauri and he did a 'roaring trade' clicking the little babies being baptised and the solemn-faced married couples with their children after the wedding. Today he was accompanied by a young boy from the *campo* called Lenin. They wanted to take a solemn oath on the Bible. Yatmani explained what had happened.

Lenin was his godchild who lived in the community of Huayllunca out beyond the copper mine at Tintaya. The boy always stayed with his *padrino* when he came to the market in Yauri. This morning when Yatmani woke up his camera was missing. The only other person in the house was Lenin so he must have taken it. Lenin protested;

"I never saw your camera. I don't know anything about cameras. What would I want with your camera?"

"Who else could have taken it?" argued Yatmani, raising his voice.

"What about all the people who came yesterday to collect their photos? Any one of them could have taken it when you weren't looking," ventured Lenin calmly.

"I had the camera last night before I went to sleep," replied Yatmani.

"I was asleep before you and when I went out to do a pee-pee this morning you were already up. When could I have taken the camera? I don't even know where you keep it," protested Lenin.

"Alright, alright, that's enough," I interjected. "So you would like to take an oath on the Holy Bible?"

"Yes," they replied in unison.

"An oath is not to be taken lightly," I explained, "It means that you are solemnly swearing before God that you are telling the truth. Do you understand that?"

"Yes," they both replied confidently.

I took a red-covered South American Bible from the shelf. First I asked Yatmani to put his hand on the Bible and declare before God that he would tell the truth. He put his dirty hand on the Bible. His long nails had begun to curl inwards. He began;

"I swear before Our Father in Heaven that I had my camera last night and this morning it is gone."

Then Lenin put his hand on the Bible;

"I swear by Almighty God and my father and mother that I didn't steal my *padrino's* camera." As he took away his hand I could see its sweaty imprint on the cover.

I turned to Yatmani;

"Well, now at least you know that it wasn't Lenin who took your camera. Someone must have stolen it during the night," I suggested.

They went away happy, chatting together as the best of friends. I felt relieved that at least I had solved one problem.

The following Sunday I met Yatmani outside the church. He was busy clicking away with his camera.

"I'm delighted to see that you got your camera back," I said curiously. "How did you catch the culprit?"

"Oh, I knew it was Lenin all the time," he said, "I found it in his *bulto* before he left. He admitted taking it in the end."

I couldn't believe my ears. I had learned another important lesson. Truth is relative for the Indians. Very often they tell you what they think you would like to hear. For them that is the truth.

And they do the same with God.

Most of the communities in the parish can be reached by truck but there are some higher up in the mountains that can only be reached on horseback. Totora Alta is one such community and that was where I was going. I was able to drive the truck as far as the bridge at Santo Domingo. This meant taking the main road for Santo Tomás, past a graveyard on the right. Over time I had noted carefully every little landmark to point me in the right direction because once out of town everywhere looked the same. When I say 'main road' I mean it more in relation to traffic than the condition of the road because that never changed. It was always *pura pampa*. Whenever I found myself behind a big lorry, which was very seldom, I just took a wide berth into the *pampa* to avoid the dust. Normally I had the whole countryside to myself.

On the way to Santo Domingo there was a big lake which attracted some very exotic wildlife in the rainy season. As I passed by there were a number of long-legged birds, like storks, standing motionless in the centre of the lake. There were ducks everywhere. This was a seasonal lake and in a month's time it would disappear until the rains came back

The bridge at Santo Domingo

next year. In the distance I could see the bridge at Santo Domingo. The last time I was approaching this bridge I saw a tragic sight. Just as an Indian was leading his flock of sheep across, a giant Volvo truck drove towards the bridge from the opposite side. The leading sheep took fright and instead of turning back it just jumped over the side of the bridge into the river over a hundred feet below. Five more sheep followed before anyone could do anything – a kind of sheep kamikaze!

I didn't need to cross the bridge on this trip, so I left the truck beside a mud hut on the bank of the river. Two Indians were waiting for me on the other side with horses.

"*Allillanchu, Papay,*" they greeted me shyly.

They were not accustomed to talking to the priest and they didn't really know what to say. Anyway they spoke very little Spanish and they realised that I wouldn't understand much Quechua. They loaded my bag onto one of the horses while I threw my leg over the other horse, only to land unceremoniously on the ground on the other side. The two Indians burst out laughing. It's not often they saw the padre lying on his backside on the ground. I dusted myself off and climbed onto a nearby rock as the Indians brought the horse alongside. They had placed a poncho on its back as there was no saddle. My feet just dangled down on each side. There was no bit in the horse's mouth. A rope had been tied around his nose just so that I would have something to hold on to. When I say 'horses' I am

74

On horseback to Tortora Alta

speaking in a general sort of way. At least they had four legs. They were small sturdy animals that could be better described as mules. I doubt if ordinary horses could negotiate the steep mountainside at this altitude.

My two Indian guides led the way as we set off up the mountain. As we climbed higher and higher I had to lean well forward so as not to slide off. Looking back over the *pampa* I could see the dim outline of Yauri in the distance, the bell tower clearly visible. As I reached the top there was a herd of animals grazing on a nearby mountain. They were like llamas but smaller in size with a shorter neck. Shouting to my companions, I asked what they were.

"Vicuñas," they shouted simultaneously.

So these were the famous vicuñas that I had heard so much about. Each year the Indians rounded them up in communal drives and sheared them of their prized silky wool. It was this wool that would have been used to make clothes for The Inca and tapestries for the temple. It was reputed to be the finest wool in the world. When the Spaniards first saw the Inca tapestries they were amazed at how finely woven they were – much more beautiful than anything they had seen in Europe. It was said that The Inca never wore the same clothes twice but gave them to one of his relatives. Large quantities of wool would have been needed as all his bedclothes were woven from this fine vicuña wool. The Spaniards brought back some of these blankets for the bed of Don Philip II, the king of Spain. Vicuñas are not domesticated and are a preserved species in Peru today. There is a twenty-year jail sentence for killing one. That is not to say that the Indians never kill them, but the law is difficult to enforce in the mountains. I could just imagine how valuable a coat made from vicuña wool would be.

By now we had reached a plateau and much to the horse's relief we continued on a more level, winding path. Even at this height there was a large number of people – men, women and children picking potatoes. The men hacked the hard ground with a kind of small pick while the women and children followed behind gathering up the marble-sized potatoes. The Indians make their potatoes into what they call *chuños* to preserve them. This is done by leaving the potatoes for three days in the extreme night frost of July and August. They are then trampled underfoot to squeeze out all the juice. Finally they are left out in the hot sun for a week until they are as hard as stones. The Indians then pile them in little heaps outside their huts to be used as needed. By simply pouring some water on them they become potatoes again. The Inca Indians have been preserving potatoes like this for centuries, long before Cadburys ever discovered 'Smash'.

Sorting the potatoes

Suddenly we were at the edge of a steep canyon where the path descended almost vertically to the river below. We had begun to descend before I had time to jump off the horse. My two guides would never think of warning me. They never even glanced behind, but presumed that gringos were experts on horseback. By now I had a sore backside and my 'John Wayne adventure' was losing its glamour. How I didn't go head first out over the horse's head I will never know. I was hanging on to his mane for dear life! Once at the bottom we had to cross the river which luckily wasn't very deep. As we struggled to the top of the mountain, the community of Totora Alta came into view.

Groups of Indians had gathered around the tiny thatched church. Everyone had come from miles around to celebrate the feast of The Visitation of Our Blessed Lady. There was no question of saying Mass inside the church. There was barely enough room for the statues and the banners for the procession. The *alferado* came to greet me and told me that there would be three weddings and about fifteen baptisms. The papers for the weddings had been arranged in Yauri but the baptisms had to be registered today. This meant that I had to write down a long list of impossible Indian names and it was a long and arduous process. Luckily some of the young people could speak Spanish and Quechua fluently.

In Inca times people didn't use surnames. The parents just gave their child any name that appealed to them. It could be the name of an animal or a place. Typical boys' names included: Strong, Happy, Crystal, Hawk, Condor and Jaguar. The girls were called Pure, Star, Gold, Egg, Coco etc. Nowadays the Indians pick the most extraordinary names for their children, especially foreign ones that they don't understand. The parents in Tortora Alta had a great liking for American presidents. So I found myself writing:

> Washington Champi Saraya
> Roosevelt Mamani Chura
> Julius César Roa Cuyo
> Purificación Aguilar Diaz
> Gisella Churata Yucra
> Lourdes Pampa Ttito

One family wanted to call their child 'Hitler'. I was completely taken aback.

"Do you know who Hitler was?" I asked.

"We heard he was a great leader and we would like our boy to grow up to be a leader of our people too," said the father.

"I don't think you would like him to grow up like Hitler," I said. "He was an evil man. What do you think of the name 'Pedro'? He was another great leader." They agreed.

"Pedro Sumire Orosco," I wrote.

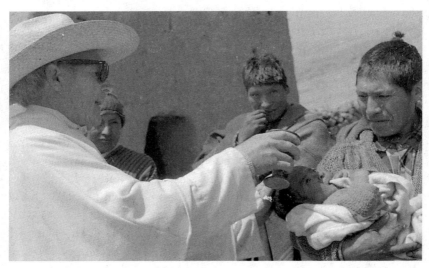

I was relieved to baptise this baby 'Pedro' and not 'Hitler'

After the Mass we went in procession around the church carrying a large statue of Our Lady. The little band of flutes, whistles and drums played festive music as the people sang and danced. Afterwards the *alferado* invited me to come to his hut for a meal. There was a big brown pot on top of a fire of animal dung. Women were running in and out busily getting the meal ready. An old woman ladled out a bowl of piping hot soup from the pot. The husband placed a poncho on a rock and gestured to me to sit down. As I sat eating my soup and looking in wonder around me, I couldn't help thinking that I could be in the middle of the fifth century here. It was like going back in time.

"*Papay, Papay,* come quickly!" shouted Benigno, as he ran into the patio. "They are bringing a dead man in on a horse."

The dead man on the horse

I went to the window and saw a group of women with babies on their backs and some men leading a horse with a dead man tied across its back, cowboy style. The dead man was a typical Indian, dressed in short homespun woollen trousers and jacket. He hands and feet were tied and there were drops of blood dripping from his mouth. The women were crying as they hitched the horse to the flagpole outside the police station. Four policemen came out to inspect the body and immediately ordered everyone into the station. A large crowd of people gathered around to observe the scene. Benigno went into the station to see what was going on. He soon returned with the news.

"Three of the women killed the man," he said excitedly. "They caught him stealing some wooden sticks that they had bought to thatch their huts and they beat him to death with them."

With that he rushed back out to gather more news. I went back to the window. The four policemen had returned to the horse where they proceeded to untie the dead man. The body was completely stiff and when they laid him on the ground his hands and legs cocked up in the air. As men, women and children looked on, two policemen stood on his shoulders while the other two pulled at his feet. You could hear the sound of the bones breaking as they stretched him out. It was a terrible sight to witness. They tied him up in a blanket and brought him into the station. Benigno came running back.

79

"They killed him two days ago and were afraid to bring him in until now. It was his family who insisted that they go to the police. The women are denying everything. They have all been put into the calaboose for the night," he explained.

Benigno was a young boy of about ten years of age when I first met him. His father was dead and his mother could be seen regularly on the side of the road, out of her mind. She was a chronic alcoholic and would drink anything, even the kerosene that we used in the cooker. Benigno had long given up on her and had decided to fend for himself. He was extremely streetwise. He hated school and when he discovered that there was always something to eat at the new gringo priest's house, he came regularly. He could speak Spanish and Quechua fluently and he soon became my official interpreter. Whenever a family came in from the mountains I would shout for Benigno.

"Benigno, come here. Ask them what do they want."

"*Bautisachiytan munashani huahuayta imacunatac necisitacunri?*"

"They want to have their child baptised. What do they need?"

"Tell them that the baptisms are on Sunday after the Mass. Both parents must be present along with the *padrino*. They must come to the preparation on Saturday afternoon. They also need a candle and if they have a birth certificate they should bring that too."

"*Jamunayqui sabado unchayta preparacoq. Jamunayqui ccosayquihuan, warmayquihuan, y oq' padrinopuyan. Chaymanta apamunayqui oq' partida de nacimientotahuan inscribinapac. Apamunayqui velacunatahuan,*" said Benigno, and they went away happy.

After a while Benigno didn't have to refer back to me at all. I would just stand there while he did all the talking. Then the people would leave, without my having to say a word.

"Benigno, what was all that about?"

"Oh, they just wanted to know what they needed for baptism (or marriage or a burial etc) and I told them." He had become more important than the parish priest!

Benigno loved coming with me on my journeys to the *campo* for the different fiestas. Each morning he would greet me with;

"Where are we going today, *Papay*?"

Melchor *(left)* and Benigno *(right)* with others out in the *campo*

I'm sure he learned more on those trips than he ever could have learned at school. I know that I learned a lot from him. He also knew everything that was going on in the community. He could tell me everything about everyone we met along the way, together with their family history. Returning home one day from one of our trips he casually remarked;

"*Papay*, do you know that Melchor didn't translate exactly what you said at the Mass today."

"What!" I exclaimed in surprise. I had always wondered how Melchor could talk for about ten minutes translating one of my sentences.

"What did he say?" I asked.

"Well, he started off by saying that Padre Cristobal was a very nice man, a very holy man and that he was very good to have left his country to come and live with us. But he doesn't really understand our customs yet. And then he began to tell them what you really meant to say."

"What was that?" I enquired.

"How they must always remember their glorious past; always stick to their old customs and traditions, work hard together on the land so that *Pacha Mama* will give a good return. How *padrinos* should look after their godchildren and how we should respect and work for our *padrinos*. When lightning strikes your llama it's because God is angry with you."

As we reached Yauri I began to realise how much I still had to learn and one of the first things I must do is learn Quechua.

An Indian family

Every culture has its own particular characteristics, its own particular customs and its own particular way of doing things. So it was with the Indians in the Andes. Very often the directions they gave me to a particular community were impossible to follow. They had no idea where a truck could or couldn't go. I never had any trouble getting out of Yauri town as there were only four ways you could go. But it was when I was out in the middle of the *pampa* that I got lost. Sometimes I would try to note on my compass the general direction in which they were pointing.

So it was that I was heading due west on my way to Huisa Ccollana. This was the community to which I couldn't go on the day they wanted (I had gone to Pichigua). When I hadn't arrived they had carried on with the fiesta and simply arranged another day for the Mass. I found myself driving up a long valley with mountains on either side. I was completely lost! The valley was beginning to look like a dead end and I was just about to turn back when a number of Indians on horseback appeared on top of the mountain. It was like a scene from the wild west. My imagination began to run riot. The Indians were about to attack. I was the only cavalry around. For a moment I found myself back home sitting on the wooden benches in the cinema on the Fairgreen in Rathdrum, Co. Wicklow. The horses came galloping towards me. It was a friendly delegation from Huisa Ccollana to lead me to their community. I left the truck where it was and joined the others on horseback.

The tiny chapel was perched on the far side of the mountain. There wasn't a hut to be seen for miles and yet a large crowd of people had gathered for the Mass. Most of them would have walked for hours to get there. They appeared more shy and primitive than the people of Yauri. The children kept their distance. They had probably never seen a gringo priest before. Many of the children had brought little lambs that were abandoned by their mothers.

It was easy to preach the Gospel to these poor people. The Gospel was written especially for them. When Jesus spoke of the Lost Sheep he was speaking to people like these. They knew what it was like to lose a sheep, a llama or an alpaca. The little shepherd boy or girl who leads out their sheep, llamas or alpacas in the early morning, knows each one by name. If one is lost they spend all day looking for it. They dare not return home without it. And when I spoke of the seed that fell on rocky ground and wouldn't grow, they just had to look around them. It was so difficult to grow anything at this high altitude.

After the Mass there was *chicha* (a home-made brew made from fermented maize) for everyone, served from a *tomin* (large earthenware jug). The women had prepared a meal of soup and potatoes. There was no meat, just two fried eggs. As the Indians don't use knives or forks I had become an expert at using my fingers, but I had yet to master the art of eating fried eggs that way.

In the Bible Jesus speaks about a blind beggar sitting at the side of the road in Jericho. Yauri has a blind Indian beggar. His name is Tomás and he loves to go to all the fiestas in the surrounding communities. How he gets there God only knows. But he is always waiting for me when I arrive. Before I can open my mouth he greets me with;

"*Allillanchu, Papay.*"

Tomás loves to sing at the Mass and he accompanies himself by placing some stones in a tin can and rattles them to the rhythm of the tune. Everyone loves him. As I was about to leave Huisa Ccollana Tomás asked me if I would give him a lift to his community. He didn't have a white stick, but he had no difficulty walking beside me as I made my way back to the jeep.

"How long did it take you to get to Huisa Ccollana?" I asked.

Tomás, the blind man

"I walked most of the night," he said, "the dark doesn't bother me. For me it's always night."

"Do you have any family?"

"My mother abandoned me shortly after I was born," he said, "she couldn't cope with a blind child."

"How did you survive?" I wondered.

"The community looked after me. Everyone was very kind. They even built me my own hut."

"Do you prepare your own food?"

"Most of the time," he replied. "The community give me plenty of potatoes and *chuños* and *choclos* (maize). But I love coming to the fiestas. I never go hungry," he added, tapping the *bulto* on his back which the people of Huisa Ccollana had given him.

I opened the door of the truck and he sat in beside me. I turned the truck around and headed back up the valley. Soon we were travelling in the wide open *pampa*. After a while Tomás shouted.

"Stop! This is where I get out."

I looked around and there was nothing to be seen for miles. I opened the door and Tomás got out.

"*Gracias, Papay*," he said, as he gave me a big hug.

"See you in Apachaco for the feast of St Francis," and he began to walk into the distance. I looked after him dumbfounded. How did he know when to get off? How did he know in what direction to go? Where was his community? And I needed a compass!

☆   ☆   ☆

The church and ruins at Apachaco

Apachaco was once a bustling town, but it now lay in ruins. Built in a rocky valley the ruins still remain because the walls had not been made of adobe but from the local stone. Although it is a ghost town it still has a beautiful stone church. The church was built by the Franciscans and was dedicated to St Francis. Apachaco was once the capital of the province of Espinar until it was struck by a terrible plague sometime in the eighteenth century. The whole town was wiped out. The capital of the province was moved to Corporaque and then in 1917 it was moved again to Yauri. Apachaco has no drinking water and I wondered if that may have had something to do with the devastating effects of the plague.

Although the town of Apachaco was no more, the Indians who lived nearby never forgot the feast of St Francis. The church was as big as a cathedral and it was packed for the occasion. The inside was cold and damp with very little light penetrating through the tiny open windows. The floor was paved with stones. There must have been over a hundred young people gathered around the altar. The children who had come from the surrounding schools did not appear shy and everyone was eager to talk during the homily. The gospel was the story of the feeding of the five thousand with the five loaves and two fishes. I read it in Spanish and Benigno told the story in Quechua. It proved particularly appealing to the children. They listened as if they had never heard it before, and most likely they hadn't.

"Wasn't that an extraordinary miracle that Jesus did?" I said.

"*Ari, ari* (Yes, yes)," came the reply.

"Could you do that?" I asked.

"*Manan, manan* (No, no)," they shouted.

"Could your teachers do that?"

"*Manan, manan*," they laughed, turning to look at their teachers who were standing behind them.

"Could the padre do that?"

"Yes, he could if he wanted to," came the reply, quickly translated by Benigno. Now all eyes were on me. Where was I to go from here? Now the teachers were laughing.

"Did you ever see the padre perform a miracle like that?" I asked hesitantly.

"*Manan*, but the padre takes God's place and God can do everything." Benigno smiled. He felt very important in front of the other children.

"How many baskets were left over?" I asked, quickly moving on.

Everyone wanted to answer. I pointed to a little girl.

"*Chunka iskayniyoq*," she replied confidently. (*Chunka* means 'ten', *iskay* means 'two' and *niyoq* just means 'and'.)

So numbers in Quechua are formed by adding the various numbers together. I always found the Indian children extremely intelligent; if only they had a chance. They learned very little at school and most could neither read nor write.

After the Mass a man came to ask me if I would come and bless his little daughter.

"Certainly," I said, "Where is she?"

"We had to leave her at home, she is too ill to travel," he explained.

"Is it far?" I enquired, knowing that I couldn't walk very far.

"No, it's not far," he assured me, "just over the hill."

I was about to learn yet another very important lesson. "Not far" for an Indian is a very long way for me. We walked for about an hour with no sign of his hut.

"Wait, wait," I said, as I sat down on a rock. "I have to take a rest."

"Are we nearly there yet?" I asked breathlessly.

"Just behind the hill," he replied.

"That's what you said before. Which hill?"

When we had walked a little further he pointed to a cluster of huts in the valley.

"There it is," he said, "it's not far."

The opening into the hut was so small that I didn't know whether to put my head or feet in first. In the end I crawled in on all fours. Inside was the most beautiful little girl I had ever seen, cradled in her mother's arms. Her mother was sitting on the ground. The child's long black hair was matted together for want of combing and mucus oozed from her nose. She was chewing a crust of bread. Her beautiful dark eyes lit up when she saw me and a little smile came over her face. I put my hand on her head to give her a blessing. She began to cough, a terrible cough, and she coughed and coughed and couldn't stop. All she needed was a little medicine, but I had nothing to give her. I knew that she would be dead in a few days, like so many more here in the mountains. The graveyards are full of little white crosses. The smile of that little child still haunts me because I was there and I could do nothing.

5

On the Inca Trail

"*Papay, Papay, Papay . . . ,*" came the shouting from the patio. I was still in bed as the first rays of light appeared through the tiny window in my room. My face was almost numb with the cold but otherwise I was warm and comfortable, tucked up in the sleeping bag I had brought from Ireland. It was guaranteed to keep you warm even at twenty degrees below zero. I was really putting it to the test.

"*Papay, Papay,*" I heard again, amid the barking of Kimichu. I opened the door and looked out. There in the patio was an Indian in a red poncho and *chullo*. There was a large *bulto* on the ground beside him.

"*Allillanchu, Papay,*" he said, turning towards me, his breath forming little puffs of steam as he spoke. In spite of the cold there were little beads of sweat on his forehead.

"*Allillanmi,*" I replied, trying to remember the greeting in Quechua. Even in English it would have been difficult at this hour of the morning.

"I'm Luis Phoccohuanca from Huayhuawasi. Will you be going to Cuzco soon?" he asked, coming towards me and giving me a hug.

"Cuzco," I thought for a minute. "Yes, I'm going next week for the celebrations of *Inti Raymi* (The Festival of the Sun)."

"I'll come with you, *Papay*. I want to visit my wife who is in prison there," he added. "In the meantime I'll stay with Melchor in the parish centre."

When we finally set out on the long journey to Cuzco, Luis told me his story.

"My wife and two other women are in prison in Cuzco for murdering a man about a month ago in Huayhuawasi," he explained.

"Was that the man they brought into Yauri on a horse?" I asked. The image of the police stretching him out on the ground like a dog will stay with me forever.

"Yes," he said, "That is the murder they are accused of, but they didn't do it. They are innocent."

"Did they not catch him stealing some sticks and then beat him to death with them?" I asked.

"No, that is the story his family made up, but everyone knows that it was his brother who killed him. My wife wouldn't hurt anyone, *Papay*. She is a simple, ignorant Indian. She doesn't even know the letter 'a'," he added.

"Where is the man's brother now?" I asked.

"He bribed the police and now he has gone to Arequipa. He killed his brother for the land. Everyone in the community knows it," he replied.

"Luis, do you have a family?" I asked.

"Yes, I have three children. The baby is with her mother in the prison. She is still feeding the baby at her breast. I left the other two with neighbours. My children wanted to come to see their mother, but there was no way I could bring them," he said sadly.

"Where are you going to stay in Cuzco? Do you have any family there?" I enquired.

"No, *Papay*, but a woman in the community told me I could stay with her sister."

"What are you carrying in the *bulto*?" I asked, knowing that Indians always liked to talk about everything. They never felt offended if you asked them a question.

"Mainly food," he replied. "I sold three sheep in the market on Sunday and bought a primus stove, potatoes, maize, rice and some clothes."

In Peruvian prisons the government does not provide any food. Everything must be brought in by the family, otherwise the prisoner just goes hungry. Luis was bringing food for all three women from his community.

"How long will you stay in Cuzco?" I asked.

"As long as my wife is in prison," he answered simply, "and that could be years. I hope to get some work in Cuzco and visit my wife and child every day."

"Have you been to Cuzco before?"

"I have never even been to Sicuani," he explained. "I have lived all my life in Huayhuawasi. I come to the market in Yauri from time to time."

In Inca times it was the custom to live and die where you were born, never to move outside your community, except to serve in the army. Nowadays many families move to the cities in the hope of finding work and they usually end up in worse misery.

Luis was observing everything as we drove along and reacted like a little child seeing things for the first time. As we approached Sicuani he saw his first eucalyptus trees.

"Look, they're moving," he exclaimed, as they swayed gently in the breeze. "They must use plenty of *abono* (manure) to grow them so tall," he added.

From Urcos the road was paved so we glided along calmly without bouncing up and down. Luis began to sing to himself. It reminded me of the yellow brick road on the way to the Wizard of Oz. I thought that it could hardly have seemed less amazing to Luis as we sped into the unknown. I could see that he was gradually getting more nervous and anxious. Would he know the way? Would he be able to find work? Where would he stay?

He didn't voice any of these fears but I imagined that they must have been going through his mind. Surely there was one thought that gave him great courage – soon he would be with his wife and child again.

I drove right up to the great door of the women's prison in Cuzco. Luis got out and just stood looking up at it. He took his *bulto* from the back of the truck, went up and knocked on the prison door and then walked straight in.

☆   ☆   ☆

Cuzco was crowded for the festival and I was very lucky to get a room at the Hotel Ollanta. I just couldn't wait for one thing . . . a shower. I never thought a shower could feel so good. I just wanted to wash away months and months of dust and dirt. There was a lot to be said for civilisation. It was wonderful too to see Cuzco without suffering from altitude sickness. Tourists had come from all over the world, as well as natives from many parts of Peru, to celebrate *Inti Raymi*.

In Inca times the year was divided into twelve months, each with its own name and festival. There were four principal feasts related to the Sun and the greatest of these was *Inti Raymi* which was celebrated at the end of June, during the summer solstice. These Inca festivals had been revived in recent years by a group of people in Cuzco called the *Indigenistas*, mainly to promote tourism. Their aim was to bring the descendants of the Spanish face to face with the Indian tradition they had ignored and tried to destroy. The main interest of this group was in the art and culture of the Indian, but not so much in the poor Indians themselves, who were still considered second class citizens in their own country. In a recent speech the leader of the *Indigenistas* said;

> We, the people of Cuzco, are proud to be a society with a past; a society whose origins are lost somewhere in America's most fertile legends. America is synthesised in Cuzco. When we walk in the streets of Cuzco and remember our ancestors, we realise we have a glorious past. It's a past we have to strengthen, not disregard. Cuzco was the capital of Indian America.

Nevertheless the *Indigenistas* found it hard to identify with the real Indian. Instead they identified more with the romantic Indian of long ago. They forgot that the Indians that were still being exploited were the real heirs to a glorious past. They preferred to go back to pre-colonial times and to capture the spirit of the Incas in the ruins and monuments that abounded in the city. They had documented all the Inca remains in Cuzco which were too massive to be destroyed by the Spaniards. One of the most awe-inspiring of these was the ancient fortress of Sacsayhuaman, overlooking the city. Tourists refer to it as the 'Sexy Woman' because that's what it sounds like in Quechua. It is a megalithic construction of huge rocks, some weighing over two hundred tons, fitted together without the use of mortar. It dates back to The Inca, Pachakutek, who reigned during the late fourteenth and early fifteenth centuries. Much of the original structure still remains, having survived the centuries and the many earthquakes which affect this region.

It was here that the festival of *Inti Raymi* was to take place. Thousands flocked to the summit from early morning, many dressed in their national costumes. They drank large quantities of beer and *chicha* and everyone was quite merry. There was music and dancing everywhere. Dancing and drinking were also the two favourite pastimes of the Incas and this was one tradition that the people liked to continue. I took a *micro* from the Plaza and joined the happy throng on their way to the top. There was one-way traffic as the *micro* wound its way up the spiralling road. Whole families went together and brought their lunch to have a picnic in the ruins. I brought my wide-rimmed cowboy hat to protect myself from the burning midday sun. As I made my way up on to the ramparts on top of the rocks I had a wonderful view of the natural amphitheatre below me.

The festival of *Inti Raymi*

The pageant began. The Inca was carried shoulder-high on his litter by his subjects to the accompaniment of music and dancing. All were dressed in the authentic costumes of the period. He was flanked on either side by his warriors carrying shields and spears. All proceeded to an altar which has been erected in the centre of the arena. The Inca ascended the giant steps. A beautiful white llama was brought to the altar where it was sacrificed to the Sun. The Inca cut its throat, catching the blood in a golden goblet from which he drank. A fire was then prepared and The Inca lit the fire from the rays of the sun, using a magnifying glass. In Inca times this fire would have been guarded by the Virgins of the Sun in the Great Temple. For a moment we were all transported into a glorious past and the mysteries of the Inca Empire. The huge blocks of stone in Sacsayhuaman seemed to guard and keep the real Inca soul.

☆　　☆　　☆

From the first moment I arrived in the Andes I had become fascinated by the customs and beliefs of the Indian people. In many ways it seemed that little had changed here for hundreds of years, going back to the time of the Inca Empire and beyond. The Indians were a spiritual people and religion played a very important part in their lives. It was evident that this was not something that suddenly happened with the coming of the

Spaniards and the Christian missionaries. Determined to find out more I decided to go 'on the trail of the Incas'.

There was nothing written about the Incas before 1532 and even then most of the accounts were written from a Spanish point of view. These were written by chroniclers who observéd and interviewed the Indians. Many of the chroniclers were priests and members of religious orders. I was astounded by the similarities to the Christian faith which I found in their ancient religion.

The Incas believed that everything they could see around them came from one source – a provident God. This supreme God they called *Viracocha* (Creator). Once he had created everything, he left Peru, walking across the waters of the Pacific. This was why the Incas thought that Pizarro was *Viracocha* returning across the waves. Even to this day, white men are referred to as *Viracocha*. Apart from the supreme God there were many other lesser gods, each of which took on special importance at particular times. The Incas saw the world as being made up of three parts: *hanaq pacha* (the world above), *ukhu pacha* (the world below) and *kay pacha* (this world). Each of these three worlds was thought to be inhabited by supernatural beings.

Viracocha inhabited the 'world above' where he was helped by other lesser gods or sky deities. These were the Sun and the Moon which the Incas called the sister and spouse of the Sun. Above all, the Incas were worshippers of the Sun, which gave light and warmth and life to the vegetable world. I didn't have to live long in the Andes to realise that without the sun it would be impossible to live at these altitudes. This was why so many religious festivals were in honour of the Sun. They built great temples dedicated to the Sun and sumptuously adorned them with gold which they referred to as 'tears wept by the Sun'. The Moon was worshipped to a lesser degree. The stars were the Sun's heavenly train. Venus was the page of the Sun, a youth with long curling locks. The rainbow was a beautiful emanation from the Sun, sent to show his pleasure. Thunder and lightning were his dreaded ministers, sent to punish and castigate.

The Incas studied the astrological bodies for agricultural purposes. They probably knew the length of the year, but little is known of their calendar. Like the Indians of today, they were not interested in dates or days of the week, but instead went from new moon to new moon. The twelve lunations were 10.9 days behind the solar year, so in three years the Incas would have been a month out. They must have readjusted this in some way. The year began in December with the rainy season and the monthly festivals were connected with agricultural activities. They timed their planting season with the blooming of a certain variety of cactus.

'This world' was inhabited by *apus* or spirits of the mountains. *Pacha Mama* was the fruitful earth from which things grew and *Mama Cocha* was the sea which gave a plentiful supply of fish. There were also *wacas* (sacred objects or places which have to be worshipped). Springs and stones were the most common *wacas*, but hills, caves, roots, quarries, forts, bridges, palaces, prisons, houses, meeting-places, tombs and historical sites could also be included in this category. There was another kind of *waca* called *anapachita* where a traveller placed one stone on top of another on the side of the road and prayed for his safe return. This custom is still practised today by the truck drivers in the mountains. The 'world below' was inhabited by the *supay* (evil and destructive creatures). These evil spirits went around tempting people.

The Incas practised their religion by means of rites and rituals. They had rites in which they asked God for protection against the elements, or to purify their sins or heal their sick. They also had festive rites which celebrated important dates in the calendar like *Inti Raymi* and the coronation or death of one of The Incas.

There were other rites for the celebration of important stages in the life of the person such as birth, adolescence, marriage and death and various offerings were made to the Gods such as food and drink, especially coca. Llamas and guinea pigs were sacrificed by cutting their throats. Albino llamas were especially favoured for sacrificial use and they also practised human sacrifice. Boys and girls of about ten years of age were brought to high mountains and sacrificed to the Gods. These children had to be physically perfect and were feasted beforehand. All these rites showed that the Inca had a belief in a superior being that could help them. All life was sacred and the sacred touched the most important areas in their lives.

The Incas' approach to religion was more emotional than intellectual and they had numerous superstitions. Comets, eclipses and meteors foretold the death of The Inca. The howling of a dog or the hooting of an owl also foretold a death. (I was reminded of the crying of the banshee in Ireland which was said to foretell the death of someone.) Seeing certain animals in the house such as snakes, spiders, lizards, worms, moths or frogs was a very bad omen to the Incas. If they met a snake in their path they could only avoid the bad omen by killing the snake and urinating on it.

Their religion was organised through a hierarchy of priests, both men and women. As well as taking part in the ceremonies, the priests heard confessions, interpreted dreams, offered sacrifices, made intercessions and cured the sick. In ancient Peru, there were no churches as we know them. All the ceremonies were performed out-of-doors. Only the priests and high officials entered the Temples. The most important ceremony took place in the Great Square opposite the Temple of the Sun in Cuzco. This temple, known as the *Coricancha*, was the most important shrine in the Inca Empire. A magnificent and lavishly furnished building, it was used mainly as a repository for sacred objects, an altar, idols of the principal deities and the bodies of the deceased Incas. Many great religious objects of solid gold hung on the walls, the most important of which was a great disc of the Sun in the form of a human face with rays emanating from it. During these fiestas in the Great Square in Cuzco, the bodies of the deceased Incas were brought out to take part in the sacrifices. There was dancing and the drinking of *chicha*. The Spaniards, who saw only idolatry in Inca worship, destroyed the Temple of the Sun and built the church of Santo Domingo on its foundations.

Beside the Temple of the Sun were housed the Virgins of the Sun. It is said that these Virgins numbered about three thousand. They took perpetual vows of chastity. It was no wonder the Spanish thought they were nuns. No man could enter the convent although some of the chroniclers speak of eunuchs who acted as servants and doorkeepers and also as confessors to the Virgins. These virgin women tended to the needs of the priests, prepared their food and wove their garments. They also wove the imperial garments, the finest cloths made in Peru and probably the finest in the world. Some of these textiles required a year of work to make.

I was very surprised to learn that confession played an important part in the Inca religion. I also found the similarities with the Sacrament of Confession extraordinary. The Incas believed that sin made the gods angry and impelled them to punish the sinner with bad luck in this life and condemnation to the underworld in the next life. Their concept of sin was different from ours. Offences against neighbours such as murder and theft were condemned, but disobedience to The Inca's wishes and neglect of festivals was also sinful. An illness or misfortune was considered to be the result of sin. It was not necessary to confess sinful thoughts. The priest heard all the members of a particular community and confession was generally heard by the side of a stream. More serious sins had to be taken to priests of higher rank. Confessions were made in secret and were not to be divulged. The priest gave a penance which was usually a period of fasting or praying or both. The penance was in inverse proportion to the priest's fee! Then the sinner washed in the stream and the sin was borne away. Or they might spit on some straw and throw it in the river.

The Incas also believed in the resurrection of the body and the existence of the soul after death. They did not embalm the body as the Egyptians did, but disembowelled it and left it to dry in the hot sun. They usually buried people with some of their belongings as well as utensils and treasures. This led to many of the ancient burial sites being plundered for their treasure over successive centuries. The burial ceremony of an important person was completed by sacrificing his wives and servants to keep him company and to serve him in the other world.

After death came judgement. The spirits of the Inca dead went to 'heaven' or 'hell', although some were believed to hang around their old home to annoy the living! 'Hell' was the centre of the earth where the wicked had to expiate their crimes with hard labour. It was always cold there and they only had stones to eat. 'Heaven' was with the Sun, where the good enjoyed a life of tranquillity and ease and where there was an abundance of food and drink. The Inca king automatically went to heaven when he died.

The Inca Empire was ruled according to a very strict code of ethics. This code concerned the observance of the laws of worship and the welfare of the group. The most famous are the three commandments which are so often quoted and so little practised today;

> *Ama kella* (Don't be lazy)
> *Ama sua* (Don't steal)
> *Ama llula* (Don't tell lies)

Apart from these, others were;
>Don't kill,
>Don't commit adultery,
>Don't be effeminate (homosexual),
>Don't get drunk,
>Don't attack travellers,
>Don't be dirty,
>Don't be abusive.

There were regular tribunals of justice in the towns and communities and it usually took five days to determine a case. The laws were few but severe, and had to do mainly with criminal matters. Blasphemy against the Sun and The Inca was punishable by death. Also burning a bridge meant death. Other offences like removing landmarks, turning water away from a neighbour's land or burning a house, were all severely punished.

The Incas considered themselves descendants of the Sun. They had a Divine as well as a human origin and these origins were steeped in legend. The Sun sent two of its children, Manco Capac and Mama Oclla to gather the people into civilised communities. They were both brother and sister, and husband and wife. They emerged from Lake Titicaca and set out together in search of the perfect place to found their kingdom. Wherever their sword freely entered the earth, that would be the place. After travelling for a long time they came across a beautiful valley where they tried to plunge their sword into the earth. It entered freely and is said to have remained there to this day. They called the place Cuzco. Manco Capac was the first Inca and he taught the men the art of agriculture. Mama Oclla was the first *Coya* (queen) and she taught the women the art of weaving. The Incas gradually overcame their neighbours and exerted superiority over the surrounding tribes. This was at the beginning of the twelfth century.

This fable was probably fabricated very cleverly by the later Incas to give themselves a celestial origin. The Inca king was the son of the Sun, he was both God and man. Cuzco became a holy city with its great *Coricancha* and the centre of a flourishing monarchy. There was only one Inca at any one time, descending from father to son and the lawful queen was usually selected from one of his sisters. The Inca had complete power; he was emperor and God. A despot, he was educated by wise men, especially in military matters.

The Incas didn't know how to read or write. They didn't even know the wheel. However, they were such good administrators and builders that they have been called 'the Romans of South America'. Although they have left no written records, they have left lasting monuments in stone, temples, fortresses and terraced mountains as can be seen at Sacsayhuaman and Machu Picchu. How they constructed these stone monuments without the wheel remains a mystery to this day.

The name 'Peru' was unknown to the natives. This name was given to the country by the Spaniards. The Incas called their land *Tahuantinsuyu* (Four corners of the earth). The Empire was divided into four sectors, through which ran four great roads, each converging on Cuzco. (Cuzco means 'navel' or 'bellybutton'.) Each sector had its own national costume and its own governor, who normally resided in Cuzco. There was a form of Inca nobility called *curacas*, who served as territorial officers. The Incas adopted many customs that were there long before their time. Everything was based on the *ayllu*. This was a clan or community of families greater than a tribe, a kind of 'family of families', living together in separate dwellings and depending on each other. The *ayllu* was united in three ways: relationship, government and work.

1. Relationship: All the members of the *ayllu* were called brothers, related to a common ancestor.
2. Government: Each *ayllu* had a *curaca* who was the chief of the *ayllu* and responsible to The Inca. In times of war he appointed a *sinchi* to take charge of training the young men for battle.
3. Work: The *ayllu* had to work the land in order to survive. The land was not just economically useful but it was also sacred – their dead were buried in it. Work was obligatory and collective. Their motto was 'Don't be lazy' and idleness was a crime in the eyes of the law. Industry was rewarded. Only the children, the old and the sick were excused.

There was three forms of work: *ayni*, *minca* and *mita*.

A. *Ayni:* This was working the land of the *ayllu* collectively. Each family was given a plot of land sufficient for a husband and wife, with an additional portion for each child – twice as much for a boy as for a girl. This was renewed each year and either increased or decreased.

B. *Minca:* This involved working the land of The Inca collectively to pay taxes. The work also included building houses for newly married people. Their motto was 'Today for you, tomorrow for me".

C. *Mita:* This was working for the benefit of the state to support the temples, ceremonies and the priests.

The people had to cultivate the state lands first. Then they tilled the land of the old, the sick, the widows and those soldiers who had gone to battle. Then they tilled their own land and finally the land of The Inca. The task of tilling was performed with great ceremony by the whole population. They were called early in the morning from the highest vantage point. All came – men, women and children, dressed in their gayest clothing and singing the praises of The Inca. Later the Spaniards put some of these tunes to music and they exist to the present day.

The Inca divided the people into numerical groups for the purpose of collecting taxes. It began with the *puric* (chief of the family). Ten families were governed by a *chunca camayoc*, one hundred families by a *pachaca camayoc*, one thousand families by a *huaranga camayoc*, and ten thousand families by a *huno camayoc*.

The *curaca* collected all taxes for The Inca. He was responsible to The Inca and had access to him at all times. There were immense flocks of llamas throughout the empire which were appropriated exclusively to the Sun and The Inca. The male llamas were sent to Cuzco every year. The female llamas were sheared and the wool deposited in magazines around the province. From here it was shared out to each family according to its needs. The women were experts at spinning and weaving. All the mines belonged to The Inca. A small proportion of the community was instructed in mechanical arts to make gold and silver ornaments. A register was kept of all the births, deaths and marriages throughout the country and exact returns of the population were made to the government each year. They also kept statistics of soil fertility and the nature of the products.

Although they could neither read nor write, the Incas had an ingenious method of communication called the *quipu* (a system of knots). When the Spaniards first saw it, they thought it was a system of writing, but now we know that it was really a method of counting. It consisted of one

The quipu system of communication

horizontal cord and hanging from it were many smaller cords of different lengths and colours with knots at intervals. The *quipu* could also be used to send messages and record history. Each *quipu* had a person called a *quipu camayoc* to interpret it. A yellow cord signified gold or maize, a white cord signified silver or peace and a red cord represented blood or war. Shepherds also used the *quipu* to count their flocks. They were experts and surprisingly accurate.

Part of the agricultural produce of the empire was brought to Cuzco and the surplus was stored throughout the province to be used in times of drought and scarcity. The Spaniards found these *tambos* (buildings or storehouses) filled with maize, coca, quinoa, woollen and cotton clothes of the finest quality as well as vases and utensils of gold, silver and copper. They were amazed that the *quipu camoyoc* could tell at a glance, by means of a few knotted cords, the exact amount of the goods stored. In the time of the Incas no one could become rich and no one could become poor. Everyone was looked after according to their needs.

The Incas also built an extraordinary system of roads through the Andes and constructed suspension rope bridges across ravines, rivers and gorges. These ropes were made from a type of flax-like plant called *maquez* and were the thickness of a human body. The more tranquil rivers were crossed using balsa rafts. Like the Romans, the Incas needed roads for the transport of supplies. But because they had no wheels they did not need well-paved or wide roads. They frequently built steps on steep slopes. The Spanish were amazed at the Inca roads. Like the ideal Roman road they followed a straight line where possible and then zig-zagged up the steep slopes. Goods were transported on the backs of people or by llama train.

All along the roads they built *tambos* for The Inca and other travellers. These were spaced about ten miles apart. Some were used as fortresses and were filled with grain, weapons and munitions. Many wars were fought in the name of religion, the worship of the Sun. The Inca weapons consisted of bows and arrows, lances, darts, battle-axes and slings. Their spears and arrows were tipped with copper or bone (those of The Inca were tipped with gold or silver). On their heads they wore helmets made of wood or the skins of animals and their defensive armour was a shield. When another tribe was conquered they were introduced to the worship of the Sun and temples to the Sun were built in the conquered territory. The new labour force was used to work the lands of The Inca. They didn't see the necessity to abolish the habits, customs or local traditions of the conquered tribe. Unlike the Spaniards who tried to destroy every semblance of the Inca religion, the Incas did not destroy the other tribe's gods but removed them to Cuzco to be put in the temple for the lesser gods. After a conquest, the Incas would also remove the *curacas* and their families to Cuzco to learn the Quechua language and customs. When they returned to their place of origin they had to leave their eldest son in Cuzco as a guarantee of good behaviour. Unruly tribes were transplanted in their entirety to a distant part of the province, never to return. Every citizen of the Inca Empire had to wear the costume of his or her native province.

The Incas had a wonderful system of communication and transportation called *chasquis* (a form of state mail). The *chasquis* were Indian runners who carried messages from place to place, such as dispatches for the government. These were either verbal or in the form of *quipus*. The runners also brought fish from the sea to Cuzco for The Inca, or game or fruit from the jungle. They say that the fish arrived fresher in Cuzco in the time of the Incas than it does today by plane. The *chasquis* had their own special dress and they stayed in *chucllas* (little huts) along the road. They worked in pairs so that while one slept the other kept watch in case a messenger came.

Although the Inca culture was just one of many highly developed cultures that existed in ancient Peru, by the end of the twelfth century all of these had been conquered and absorbed into the Inca culture. The Inca Empire lasted for nearly four hundred years and reached its golden age at the end of the fifteenth century just before the arrival of the Spaniards.

Shortly after the Spaniards discovered the 'South seas' (which we know as the Pacific Ocean) rumours circulated in Panama of the existence of a 'City of Gold'. A *curaca* by the name of Biru was said to possess a vast kingdom with great riches of gold and pearls. The search for El Dorado began. After many failed attempts, Pizarro and a small group of men landed at Tumbes on the north coast of present-day Peru, in July 1532. The name 'Peru' is a mispronunciation of the *curaca*, Biru, whose name was given to all the lands to the south of Tumbes. Pizarro learned that the 'City of Gold' was farther inland and higher up in the Andes.

The Spaniards had arrived at a time when there was a split in the Inca Empire. There was a dispute going on between two Inca half-brothers, Atahualpa and Huásar, as to who was the rightful heir. Atahualpa had gained some notable victories against Huásar and was on his way to Cuzco to assume his imperial throne when he heard of the arrival of the Spaniards in Tumbes. He presumed that Pizarro and his soldiers were the creator god *Viracocha* and his demigods, returning across the water as had been prophesied by old legends. Atahualpa decided to await their coming, thinking that they would help him against his brother Huásar.

Pizarro set out from Tumbes with one hundred and eighty soldiers, both infantry and horsemen. The journey across the desert was unbearable. The heat, the thirst and the bright rays of the sun made the journey hazardous. Pizarro encouraged his men with the promise of vast quantities of gold. But worse was yet to come. Soon they were climbing the steep mountainsides and suffering from the extreme cold and the effects of the high altitude. Finally they arrived at Cajamarca on 15 November 1532. This was a stone city with a square just like any in Europe. When Pizarro learned that The Inca was camped nearby with his followers he sent messengers to invite The Inca to dine with him. Atahualpa accepted the invitation for the following night. He entered the Plaza in Cajamarca carried on his golden litter and accompanied by a large band of warriors with which he hoped to capture the foreign invaders. But the Plaza was empty as the Spaniards were hiding in the surrounding buildings. Two lone figures walked across the square, a priest and his interpreter. The priest was a Dominican friar, Vincente de Valverde, who was chaplain to the Spanish expedition. The Inca beckoned them to approach. Through his interpreter the friar began to speak.

"I bring you good news of an unknown God, a Holy Pontiff who lives in Rome, and a great Emperor in Spain."

This was the formula that the Spanish always used to intimidate their enemies. Atahualpa wasn't having any of it. He asked;

"Where did you come by this information?"

Valverde produced the Bible he was carrying.

"This holy book contains the word of God," he claimed, presenting the Bible to Atahualpa who looked at the book, but didn't understand a word. He then put it to his ear to hear what it had to say. Hearing nothing he threw it to the ground in disgust and shouted to the Dominican;

"Go back to your long-bearded friends and tell them to return all they have stolen on their way here."

He said it with such anger that Valverde took fright and ran trembling towards where Pizarro and the others were hiding.

"Attack, attack!" he shouted, "Atahualpa is a Lucifer and he will massacre us all."

With that, the Spaniards attacked by shooting their blunderbusses and waving a white flag in the air. The horses ploughed into the Incas who had their weapons concealed under their tunics and couldn't take them out in time. There was utter confusion. The Spanish blew their trumpets and continued to attack. The Indians retreated towards the Plaza wall which collapsed under the pressure. Pizarro made straight for Atahualpa sitting on his litter and killed the bearers. Atahualpa was taken prisoner.

That night the Spaniards gathered around to look at The Inca by torchlight. He was an Indian of about thirty-five years of age and although defeated he still maintained an air of majesty. Dressed in fine clothes, a little tattered after the battle, he looked fierce and intelligent with a bright light in his eyes. Atahualpa, fearing that Pizarro might

The capture of The Inca

depose him in favour of his half-brother Huásar, secretly sent orders that Huásar was to be killed and this was done immediately. Atahualpa then offered to fill his cell as high as he could reach with gold objects, as the price for his freedom. Pizarro accepted the offer and The Inca dispatched messengers to all parts of the empire commanding that gold be brought to Cajamarca. A short time later it began to arrive, transported by Indians with great *bultos* on their backs and by llama train. A large part of it came from the Temple of the Sun in Cuzco.

Soon the room was filled to the stipulated height and The Inca, although officially declared free, remained, 'for the welfare of the country', under guard with the Spanish. (The great heap of gold ornaments, fashioned laboriously by artistic Inca craftsmen, was melted down into bars. Nine forges were employed in the process. The Spanish crown received one-fifth of the treasure while the rest was divided up among the soldiers.)

The guards found Atahualpa very intelligent and began to teach him how to read and write. They would write a word on the palm of his hand and when he showed it to different soldiers they all pronounced the same sound. Atahualpa found this fascinating. Once they wrote the word *'Dios'* (God) on his hand but when he showed it to Pizarro, he didn't know what it meant. Pizarro could neither read nor write. It was said that The Inca lost all respect for the Spaniard from that moment on. The Inca also had another problem with Pizarro. The Spaniard hadn't washed since he left his ship and he was filthy and covered with lice. The Inca couldn't bear the smell and advised Pizarro to go and wash himself in the nearby Inca baths.

The Inca's presence soon became an impediment to the plans of the Spanish and many called for his death. Pizarro at last consented and Atahualpa was brought to trial on numerous charges including usurpation, the murder of Huásar, idolatry, adultery, incest, polygamy, embezzlement and planning an uprising against the Spanish. He was convicted and sentenced to be burned alive in the main square of Cajamarca. As the wood was being ignited, Atahualpa was told that his sentence could be changed to strangulation if he accepted Christianity. He agreed and was baptised against his will and then garrotted in front of Pizarro and a large crowd of onlookers. So it was on 29 August 1533 that the last Inca Emperor died. With the execution of Atahualpa, the whole empire collapsed because all power rested with The Inca. In destroying the head, the Spaniards succeeded in bringing down the whole system.

The garrotting of Atahualpa

With the collapse of the Inca Empire came the colonisation of the country and in this the Church had a major role to play. In the initial stages, the unity between the interests of the State and the interests of the Church was absolute. The early years of the Spanish conquest were marked by violence against the native population. The reasons for this have been ascribed to the greed of the invaders and the belief that the native people were living in ignorance and idolatry and could only be saved by receiving the message of the gospel, whether they liked it or not. The great work of converting the pagan Indians began immediately. Everything was done to baptise the largest number of people in the shortest possible time. Many of the Indians accepted baptism out of fear or simply to be left in peace.

The Spanish conquistadors always claimed that their conquests were 'for God and for King'. There are many versions of how the Church was an accomplice in the conquest of the Incas. Certainly missionaries came with the conquistadors and the order to put Atahualpa to death was given by the priest, Valverde. However, evangelisation was soon to separate itself from the conquest. Not long afterwards the same Valverde, as the first Bishop of Cuzco, became one of the most energetic defenders of the Indian against the abuses of his fellow countrymen. Gradually bishops were appointed who distanced themselves from the conquest. Further improvements came with the arrival of religious orders – Dominicans, Augustinians, Franciscans, Mercedarians and Jesuits. Religious houses sprung up, particularly in the cities, and local vocations began to emerge. Progress in the studying and teaching of Quechua, particularly by the Jesuits, also contributed to the improvement.

The Church gradually built a new nation while the Spanish soldiers plundered for gold. The second Bishop of Lima, St Toribio Alfonso de Mogrovejo, created the first Centre of Theological Studies and published the first book in Latin America, which was the Catechism. He organised his archdioceses, forming the basis of what would later become the political division of Peru. Just fifty years after the arrival of Pizarro, the whole country was divided into parishes, each with its own church, parochial house and land for the support of the clergy. At the same time the mendicant missionaries, especially the Dominicans and the Franciscans, penetrated the Andes and even entered the Amazon jungle ahead of the Spaniards, many never to return.

The Incas had seen the wisdom of imposing the Quechua language on the entire empire: it united the people. In the same way the Church saw the need to study the language and traditions of the Indians. The priests learned Quechua and translated the sounds into writing, producing catechisms, dictionaries and grammars. The priests and religious were now the ones nearest to the Indians. When in 1550 the Crown ordered that all Indians must speak Spanish instead of the native language, the Church opted to teach Christianity through Quechua and this led to a conflict between Church and State. In 1613 at the Synod of Lima, priests were ordered to preach their sermons in Quechua. The Crown in turn issued new orders in 1634, and later in 1685, for everyone to speak Spanish. Some Spanish priests didn't want the Indians educated at all and one Spanish bishop said that 'an educated Indian was a lost Indian'. They were regarded by many as little more than animals. In 1635 a Dominican, Fray Bonaventura de Salinas y Cordoba, preached in the cathedral in Cuzco. For the first time he said that the Indians were 'our brothers and fellow countrymen'. The bishop denounced the Dominican to his superiors and a book that he was about to publish was cancelled. Later he was diplomatically expatriated to Rome.

With the expulsion of the Jesuits at the end of the eighteenth century there was much less emphasis on the Quechua language and the real campaign to make Spanish the official language began. The Indians became more and more marginalised from the rest of the country and suffered terrible abuses at the hands of the Spanish. Some Spaniards kept fierce dogs to attack and kill the Indians. As recently as 1989 a notice appeared on the door of the Spanish Embassy in Lima:

> Pups (two months old), guard dogs to defend people and property, height 80 cm, weight 80 kilos. These are the famous dogs of the Spanish conquest called 'Indian eaters', and are very popular with the Spanish nobility. Their parents were imported from Leon (Spain). Can be seen. Documents in order.

Peru eventually gained its independence from Spain. After the final victory over the Spanish at Junin, Ayacucho in 1824, hundreds of priests and all the principal bishops went back to Spain. Some left voluntarily while others were forced out. A great vacuum was left in the Peruvian Church during the formation of the new government. As a result there was a complete collapse of pastoral work, not only from the lack of clergy but also because of the quality of those who remained. Nowhere was this vacuum more keenly felt than among the Indian population of the Andes. Many churches were deserted and numerous parishes were left without a priest. Today, over four hundred years after the death of Atahualpa, little has changed for the Quechua Indians. The Spanish and Indian descendants have never been united as one nation, still less as one people. Spanish civilisation is superimposed on that of the Indians but there is no exchange between the two. During a recent international assembly on education, a Peruvian senator gave the percentage of the population who could neither read nor write. When a bishop intervened to correct the figure, the senator explained;

"Ah, well, of course if you include the Indians, the percentage will be much higher."

One major outcome of the Spanish conquest was that the Indians were converted to the Christian faith. Their pagan temples and symbols were replaced by Christian churches and crosses. In processions the saints are now paraded in much the same way as the Incas would have paraded the bodies of their dead rulers. With the invasion of the Spanish many Indians fled to the higher regions of Peru and formed a kind of resistance that was no longer based on military strength, but on their difference of language and on the remains of their religious beliefs.

In the Indian practice of the Christian faith, there still remains to the present day many customs and traditions from their Inca past. Nowhere is this more evident than in the communities in the mountains around Yauri.

6

Shine On, Inca Girl

Preparing food on the patio

"What is the one thing that you couldn't survive without?" I asked Des one morning when there was no milk for the tea.

"Water," he replied without a moment's hesitation.

"There's no doubt about it, you couldn't survive here long without water."

There had been no water in the tap in the patio for about two weeks now. But we weren't the only ones affected. The whole town was cut off. We had to go in the truck to the spring at Corporaque where we filled up cylinders and every available vessel with water. We lost most of it on the way back with all the bouncing up and down. The River Salado flowed nearby but the water was salty and it was contaminated by the mine at Tintaya. Des went down to see the mayor at the council office in Yauri and was assured that they were investigating the situation and the water would be restored as soon as possible.

"That means they are doing nothing!" commented Des on his return.

Most of the people in the town had resorted to drinking the local beer. The fact that there was no water didn't seem to bother them. It never ceased to amaze me how calmly Indians accepted hardship and misfortune.

"That's Huisa Ccollana again," sighed Benigno who had just dropped in for breakfast. He always came early in case we might be going out to a fiesta.

"What does the village of Huisa Ccollana have to do with Yauri not having water?" I asked, thinking he didn't know what we were talking about.

"The water for Yauri comes from that community ," he explained. "The council piped it in about two years ago. The whole town helped to lay the pipes, but during the dry season the people of Huisa Ccollana break the pipes and divert the water to their land to sow potatoes. Nobody admits doing it because it always happens at night under cover of darkness."

"Does the council know that?" I enquired.

"Of course they do, but they haven't any new pipes to fix it. They are waiting for them to come from Arequipa."

Just then a family arrived to have their baby baptised. They had walked all night from Pichigua because the baby was dying. As the mother took the little child from her back it was gasping for breath. I could see the baby didn't have long to live. It wasn't much bigger than my hand. I took some of the precious water and asked them what name they had chosen for their child.

"Felicitas," they replied, "it's a girl."

"Felicitas, I baptise you in the name of the Father and of the Son and of the Holy Spirit. Amen."

About five minutes later she died. The parents didn't show any emotion. They wrapped Felicitas in a cloth and that night when it was dark they buried her in the graveyard. It is the custom that Indian children cannot be buried during the day. The father produced a little white cross and asked me if I would write 'Felicitas' on it.

As I wrote the letters I thought how 'Felicitas' meant happiness. She certainly didn't have much happiness during her brief stay in this world. Please God she was happy in heaven. The parents were happy that they had arrived in time for her baptism.

"Gratisllan kanca, Papay," they said, thanking me as they left.

Mornings began early in Yauri. We had many visitors before the Mass at eight o 'clock, which meant about an hour after they heard the bell. They would have left their huts at the sound of the church bell. The Indians in the town came to Mass almost every day and if the Mass was for the soul of a member of one of the communities the church was usually full.

Usually the family of the dead person sat in the front seat and they all held lighted candles during the Mass. They also placed a little table in front of the altar and covered it with a black cloth. They put a candle at each corner and placed some of the dead person's clothes on the table as well as meat, eggs, maize and potatoes. I couldn't believe my eyes the first time I saw it. I knew that in Inca times it was the custom to bury the dead with clothes and food for the next life. It was one custom that the early missionaries adapted to Christianity, where it became an offering to the church on behalf of the dead person. It was one custom that the Indians loved and they wouldn't let me start the Mass until everything was in place. Afterwards the table had to be blessed with holy water. I still think the Indians believed that the soul wouldn't go hungry if they put plenty of food on the table. I always used to take an egg or potato and console myself with the thought that it wasn't of much use to the dead person. The living needed it more.

A woman came to me before Mass one morning carrying a skull in her hand.

"Would you say Mass for this Holy Soul?" she asked, as she held up the skull.

"Who is it?" I asked, staring at the beautiful white teeth which were still intact.

"I don't know," she replied, "I found it as I was passing the graveyard and I thought, poor soul, I'm sure you would like a Mass."

"But maybe it's not even a Christian," I suggested.

"It doesn't matter," she answered, "it's better not to take any chances."

She placed it on the altar during the Mass. Afterwards she returned it to the graveyard and buried it. At least it wouldn't haunt her for passing by and taking no notice.

Sometimes there was a problem to be solved during the Mass. They interpreted literally that part of the gospel where it says that if you have anything against your brother, first of all you must try to be reconciled with him. If he won't listen you must go the authorities. If he still won't listen you must go to the priests of the church. On one occasion it was a stolen bicycle. Pablo stood up after the gospel;

"*Papay*, my bike was stolen last week when I went to the market in Corporaque. My cousin told me that he saw Justiniano Mamani from Corporaque riding my bike the following day."

With that Justiniano Mamani stood up.

"I didn't steal his bike. I have my own bike which I bought in Sicuani over a year ago."

"How is it that no one saw you with a bike until last week. I know my bike. One of the pedals is bent," explained Pablo.

"I use my bike very little. I keep it at home and both pedals are perfect. My bike is almost new," replied Justiniano.

The two men were on opposite sides of the church and a large number of family and friends were gathered around them to give support. Everyone wanted to speak.

After much discussion someone suggested that they take an oath on the Bible.

"I don't think that is necessary just yet," I suggested, knowing that wouldn't clarify anything. I turned to Justiniano;

"Could you bring your bike next Sunday and we will examine it. Also if you have the receipt from the shop in Sicuani bring it too."

Everyone agreed that we would continue with the problem next Sunday after Mass.

☆   ☆   ☆

Peru declared its independence from Spain on 28 July 1821. Each year Independence Day is celebrated with great pomp and ceremony and today we were also celebrating the installation of our new president, Fernando Belaúnde Terry. He was returned to power with a landslide victory and after twelve years of military dictatorship, Peru was again a democracy. The Indians who were able to vote for the first time voted for Belaúnde because of his commitment to the building of roads and public works. His election symbol was a spade.

This was Belaúnde's second time to be president. In 1968 General Juan Velasco had taken power in a military coup d'état, taking Belaúnde out of the Presidential Palace while still in his pyjamas and sending him by plane into exile. Velasco had broken with tradition and set up an agrarian reform which divided up all the big haciendas and redistributed the land among the Indians. Many of the *hacendados* (large landowners) around Yauri had resisted this reform and now they looked forward to recovering their lands with the election of the new president. As a result there was an increased state of tension between the landowners and the Indians in the mountains.

The celebrations began with a special Mass of Thanksgiving at ten o'clock, attended by all the authorities in Yauri. The sub-prefect is the highest civil authority in the province and is appointed by the Government. The *alcalde* (mayor) and the town council are elected by the people of the community. Although Church and State are separate in Peru, all the authorities are obliged by civil law to attend Mass on Independence Day. During the Prayers of the Faithful the *alcalde* said a special prayer. He prayed that the authorities and the priests of the parish might get on better together. It appeared he was trying to tell us something.

Christianity first came to Peru on the side of the powerful and the rich and until recently it has been the domain of the upper classes. It is very difficult to preach 'love' with the sword. Today there is a new emphasis in Latin America and the Church has become the church of the poor. The reality is that the majority of Indians live in a situation of inhuman and degrading poverty. The Church is committed to the construction of a new society, more just and fraternal.

However working with the poor can mean trouble. The upper classes, mainly conservative Catholics and supporters of the Church, see their interests being threatened and react immediately. To speak of justice, equality and brotherhood is, in their opinion, to preach communism. These respected citizens, landowners and business people consider this type of religion subversive and dangerous. However, they have the power – political, social and economic. They can count on the state apparatus, such as the legislature, the military, the police and the media. With all the enthusiasm of the crusaders of old, they attempt to stamp out 'communism', save the so-called 'Christian society' and defend democracy and freedom. In doing so, these 'pillars of the Church' often resort to repression, torture, murder and other kinds of violence,

apparently without any qualms of conscience. They respect no one –
neither bishops, priests, men, women nor children. This is the reality of
the situation, particularly in the mountains of Peru.

All the authorities in Yauri are from the 'upper class'. The poor Indians,
most of whom can neither read nor write, could never aspire to such
positions. To an innocent gringo priest the hierarchy of importance that
exists among the various groups in the town can be confusing, especially
when you are trying to treat everyone equally. I was left in no doubt
about the importance of those few of Spanish descent who held all the
positions of authority. At the top are the sub-prefect, the *hacendados* and
the *alcalde*. Next come the *mestizos*. These half-Spanish, half-Indian
people run the small businesses in Yauri. Because they can read and
write some of them are on the town council while others are teachers.
Then there are the merchants. Although most of them are pure Indian,
many have given up their Indian ways. They have little huckster shops in
town and sell everything in small quantities. Once when I asked Benigno
to buy me some tea he came back with only one tea bag. I asked why.

"They only sell one at a time," he said.

The merchants also sell fruit, vegetables and dyes in the open market
on Sundays. Some have trucks and can bring supplies from Sicuani,
Arequipa or the Amazon jungle. The women merchants wear distinctive
tall white hats which give them an extra air of importance.

I soon began to realise that the people who lived in the town
considered themselves much more important than the *campesinos* who
lived in the outlying communities and there seemed to be an inbuilt
rivalry between the two. The further out from the town the Indians lived
the less important they became. And of course the Indians who lived
higher up in the mountains were considered little more than the llamas
and alpacas.

Usually when I speak of Indians I am referring to the poorest of the
poor. Many of these also lived in the town and while those living in the
town usually spoke Spanish they all knew Quechua as well. One of the
ways of not being an Indian is not to speak Quechua. In Peru today to
attain any kind of material success or to climb the social ladder you have
to deny everything Indian.

The first Mass on Sunday was in Spanish and was normally attended by
the townspeople. They occupied the seats while the Indians felt more

comfortable sitting on the floor. The second Mass was in Quechua and was attended by the poor Indians living in town and the *campesinos*, who would have come to Yauri for the market. Some of the wealthier townspeople think that the church is theirs and that the priest is there mainly for them. Then a gringo priest arrives who seems more interested in the poor Indians and they become suspicious. (In the past the wealthy landowners and the authorities would have worked hand in hand with the priests, who depended on them to a large extent for support. The *hacendado* had his own private chapel on the hacienda and could call on the priest to perform a wedding or baptism at a moment's notice.)

Some of the bigger haciendas extend over an area of thousands of acres and they use the Indians as slave labour. The Indians refer to them as *gamonales*. They say that this is an animal that lives by sucking the blood from other animals. The worst insult you can give to anyone is to call him a *gamonal* and the Indians sometimes paint this word on the sides of the landowners' houses.

Then there are the *mistis*. These are the Indians who have done well and given up their Indian customs and traditions. They go to work in Lima or Arequipa and then come back wearing European clothes. They often look on their own culture and background with contempt. (It was the *mistis* who became the go-betweens with the colonial power for the collection of taxes.) Needless to say none of these different groups like gringo priests who work with the poor Indians and defend their rights. They don't like to see us going out to the communities to celebrate the fiestas and we are frequently called 'communists'. (To work with the poor Indians was to be a communist.) We had to take precautions. For instance we had to remove all the red covers from our books! The police would often search for red-covered books, thinking they must be about communism, especially if they were written in English. I even had to tear the red cover off my Bible.

However, these weren't the only problems. On the day before the General Election, an incident occurred which was to have far-reaching consequences for the whole country and especially for me. Five hooded figures walked into the office of the registrar in a little village called Chuschi in the Province of Ayacucho, just outside Cuzco. They tied up the registrar and burned the registration book and the ballot boxes. Many dismissed it as an act of vandalism. But in this one small incident the

Sendero Luminoso (The Shining Path) had declared war on the Government of Peru and in the next fifteen years, thousands of Peruvians would lose their lives at the hands of this extreme terrorist group.

☆   ☆   ☆

Trinidad came to visit me every day. She usually rummaged through the rubbish looking for food.

"For my *cuys*! "she would say, but I knew she ate most of it herself. She was always filthy, yet she insisted on giving me a big hug. Although extremely poor, she had a certain air of nobility about her. Esther told me that Trinidad was from a well-to-do family who abandoned her when she was a child. She certainly had a very generous heart in spite of her poverty and was always bringing me little gifts. Once when I returned from a trip to another parish, she presented me with an old hen in the bottom of a bucket. She had cooked it, feathers and all. She hadn't even cleaned it out!

"I brought you a chicken," she said, "because I know you don't like my *cuys*." I accepted it with thanks, wondering where she had stolen it from. Trinidad loved to tell me that she was named after the Blessed Trinity. She always spoke about the Trinity as if it was some friend of hers. In the church in Yauri there was the most extraordinary representation of the Blessed Trinity I have ever seen – three identical men, sitting together,

The Blessed Trinity in Yauri

all dressed exactly the same, with large wide-rimmed black hats. The Indians had great difficulty with the Unity and Trinity of God. On Trinity Sunday these three characters were taken out of their glass case and paraded around the Plaza.

Trinidad always took pride of place at the head of the procession. Everyone liked Trinidad and she returned a broad toothless smile as they wished her a happy feast day.

I will never forget the day that I had a misunderstanding with Trinidad.

"*Allillanchu, Papay,*" she greeted me as she entered the little door to the patio and came forward to hug me.

"*Allillanmi, Trinidad,*" I replied, "How are you today?"

"Oh, I'm not well at all, *Papay*. I never slept a wink all night," she complained with a moan. Then she added, feeling her stomach;

"*Estoy totalmente constipado* (I am completely constipated)." I was very surprised to hear that because it was not a normal complaint in the mountains. If anything it was usually the opposite. (I suffered constantly from diarrhoea while living here.) I felt sorry for her and wondered what she had been eating. Then I remembered that among the medicines I had brought from Ireland to cover all eventualities, were some Ex Lax bars which I had never used. With the way my insides were going, I never would. They look like bars of chocolate and taste like chocolate too.

"Trinidad," I suggested, "I have the very thing to cure you."

I gave her the lot. She was very grateful and ate a bar straight away.

"Take more tonight," I advised her, "and tomorrow you'll be fine."

That evening Tiny arrived from Sicuani on his way to the parish of Santo Tomás. During supper I was telling him about Trinidad and how she had a bad dose of constipation, and how I had given her the Ex Lax bars. He burst out laughing.

"*Estoy constipado* doesn't mean what you think," he explained. "In Spanish it means that her nose is all blocked up. She has a heavy cold."

Poor Trinidad! Next morning when she arrived at my door she looked pale and gaunt.

"How are you today, Trinidad?" I asked, trying to keep a straight face.

"Much worse," she replied, "that medicine you gave me was no good. It was very strong!"

☆   ☆   ☆

We set out at dawn on the long journey to Santo Tomás. Tiny had asked me to accompany him there for Confirmations. His old Ford truck was laden down with supplies for the Franciscan priests living in Santo Tomás. We were also carrying four cylinders of fuel as there were no garages on the way. The road as far as Santo Domingo was familiar to me, but beyond that it was unknown territory. It took us hours to reach the border of the parish of Yauri. At last Tiny pointed to a little church between the hills to our right;

"That's Oquebamba!" he said, "The last church in your parish."

Working with the *chakitaklla*

All along the way the Indians were digging the barren ground and sowing the little potatoes. It was now springtime in the mountains. The men were using a very primitive implement called a *chakitaklla* (foot plough). It literally means 'foot only' and is a type of wooden spade with a piece of iron at one end. As the men plunged it into the ground the women pulled back the sod with their hands. The ground was rock hard. Two oxen with a wooden plough came behind them to break up the sods. The whole community worked together – men, women and children.

"There is a whole ceremony attached to sowing the potatoes," explained Tiny. "They first elect a 'priest' to direct operations. He dresses in priestly robes. Then he performs a symbolic wedding of a young boy and girl. Everyone celebrates with music and dancing and the drinking of *chicha*. Water is brought from the river and sprinkled on the ground as a kind of blessing. They then implore *Pacha Mama* to produce an abundant harvest. The whole ceremony is a type of religious rite, like that of the Benedictine monks who pray as they work in the fields."

To me it seemed it would take a miracle for anything to grow on this barren mountainside.

A fox ran across the road in front of us. He looked savage and scared as he turned and bared his teeth before disappearing behind the rocks. There were viscatchas everywhere. Perhaps that's what the fox was after but he would have to jump very high to catch a viscatcha. More likely he was after a sheep when the shepherd boy was not looking.

As we reached the top of a steep hill I could just see the outline of a tiny threadlike track in the distance, winding its way between the mountain peaks as far as the eye could see.

"Where does that road lead to?" I wondered aloud.

"That's the road to Santo Tomás," explained Tiny, "that's where we're going. We're not half-way there yet." It was after midday.

In the early afternoon we reached the parish of Velille, an old stone village alongside a river with a quaint little stone bridge across it. The locals eyed us suspiciously. Obviously they weren't accustomed to visitors. They had a dour and serious look as they rode along on their mule-like horses. Velille looked more primitive than Yauri, if that was possible.

"This is 'cowboy country'," explained Tiny, "they deal mainly in livestock."

I saw the church with a parish house alongside it and Tiny suggested we should call to see the parish priest, Julio César Mendoza, one of the few Peruvian priests remaining in the prelature.

"He came here about ten years ago when he left Corporaque," recalled Tiny. "He must be nearly seventy years old by now. The people of Corporaque were so happy to get rid of him that they gave him one of the village maidens when he left."

I wasn't quite sure what that meant, but all was soon to be revealed. A young woman came out to greet us when she heard the truck coming.

"*Allillanchu, Monseñor*," she said, with a child in her arms and two more alongside her.

"*Allillanmi, Cecilia*. Is Padre Julio at home?" enquired Tiny.

A village in the *campo*

"No, he is away on business in his lorry. I expect him back tomorrow or the next day," she replied. (It's hard to be precise in the mountains.) "Come and have something to eat."

We were so tired that we gladly accepted the invitation. I shook the dust from my clothes as I got out of the truck.

"This is Padre Cristobal," said Tiny, introducing me. "He is working with Padre Albanito in Yauri."

"*Allillanchu, Cristobal*," she said, trying to give me a hug without squashing the baby.

I was going to ask her where the toilet was until I remembered it was out the back . . . anywhere! Cecilia began to prepare some soup in a big pot on an open fire, while the children played on the ground.

"They're his children," whispered Tiny in English. Not that she would have understood even if we spoke in Spanish but we always tried to avoid speaking English in the presence of Indians. It's not polite.

"How are the children getting on?" enquired Tiny, as the oldest one peed on the floor.

"They are getting on very well now, Monseñor," she replied. "We lost our baby two years ago with diarrhoea, but we were lucky to have another one. Padre Julio says he will baptise Rosa at Christmas. The mayor has agreed to be her *padrino*."

I was trying to eat my soup with my eyes shut so as not to notice what might be in it. I just had to hope for the best. The bishop gave Cecilia and her children a blessing and we were on our way again.

"What was all that about?" I asked, as we crossed the bridge and turned left for Santo Tomás.

"It's an old Inca custom," answered Tiny, smiling. "These unfortunate men were sent out from Cuzco to the back of beyond and forgotten about. They were young and virile. The Indians don't understand celibacy. In Inca times a boy of twenty-five and a girl of eighteen had to be married. According to Indian custom you are not a man unless you are married and have children. The only trouble with Julio is that he had a woman and children in every parish and he always left them behind when he was transferred. He has certainly proved his manhood whatever about his sense of responsibility."

"Does Rome know about this?" I wondered.

"I'm sure they do!" replied Tiny, "they have been told often enough. But of course there is little they can do about it. Julio never really goes through any marriage ceremony, he is too cute for that, so he is not legally married."

As we bumped along on the never-ending road to Santo Tomás, Tiny recalled an episode from the time the Carmelites first came to Sicuani. He was superior in Lima at the time and it was decided that the Carmelites should start a monastery in the most primitive part of the prelature. The Order wanted to get back to the spirit of Mount Carmel. Santo Tomás was chosen as the ideal place because it was primitive and isolated. Three North American Carmelites were sent to start the new foundation and take charge of the parish, but it proved a fiasco. One of them wrote from Santo Tomás at the time:

> Communications are so poor that telegrams to and from Sicuani take three days. There is no other means of communication. There is no electricity. Water must be boiled, filtered and then iodised. There are no banks, no drugstores and no hospitals. Both the Indian and the white man of the sierra live predominantly in the past. They fear change. All vital decisions are made by consulting their immediate family. In such a closed society, foreigners are not readily accepted. We were unable to stay there for periods longer than a few weeks at a time. Besides boredom and respiratory problems, all building materials and most foods had to be

purchased in Sicuani or Cuzco. Every six months called for an altitude leave. All thirty eight of the parish villages are accessible only by horse and some only after three days' travel. One third of the town speaks exclusively Quechua and the ratio is the reverse in the villages. The common tongue for all is Quechua. The educated man in the sierra is well revered. In the eyes of the Indian, the white priest is so much superior to him that he is unapproachable. Such a relationship in a parish causes an extreme sense of uselessness.

The experiment lasted less than a year. The Carmelites left Santo Tomás and the three priests returned to the United States.

It was late in the evening when we reached Santo Tomás. The sun was just disappearing behind the surrounding peaks, spreading a bright orange glow on the sleepy town in the valley below. The climate is warmer here and the first thing I noticed was the beautiful palm-like trees that were growing everywhere. We stopped in the Plaza beside the most beautiful church in the whole prelature – a magnificent structure with a great dome like St Peter's in Rome. It was built by one of the former parish priests who came from a very rich family. He put all his wealth into the church as a memorial to his family.

Children on the hillside

We were given a great welcome by all the people of the town. The parish is run by three Franciscans, two priests and a lay brother. One of the priests was a jet pilot during the war and the other, Brother Antonio, fought with the US marines in the Pacific against the Japanese. He was wounded and later converted to the Catholic faith and eventually joined the Franciscans. He said being a marine was a wonderful preparation for life in Santo Tomás!

During the next few days Brother Antonio showed me around the parish. High up in the hills in one of the communities there were hot springs where I washed and relaxed in the wonderful waters. In the early morning I watched the children descending the little mountain tracks as they made their way to the local school. Almost all spoke Quechua.

There were fifteen young men between the ages of seventeen and thirty for Confirmation. There were no women. I don't know why Confirmation doesn't happen automatically like in Ireland. Here it is a matter of personal choice and requires weeks of preparation. I was delighted to see that all the altar servers were girls. Tiny looked majestic towering above them with his bishop's mitre and crosier. He could almost have been an Inca. We celebrated long into the night with music and dancing. I wasn't looking forward to the long journey back to Yauri.

On the way home Tiny told me the story of the 'Sicuani Pulpit' riot. A few months after the opening of the Carmelite monastery in Santo Tomás another event took place, this time in Sicuani, which almost cut short all Carmelite involvement in the mountains. In November 1967 the Carmelites began to clean up the Cathedral of the Immaculate Conception and put up an altar facing the people. In the course of the reconstruction, the old pulpit fell down. Word spread quickly around the town. A group of people accused the Carmelites of stealing their prized treasures. A mob entered the cathedral and physically attacked one of the Carmelite priests, Father Geaney. This incident sparked five days of anti-American riots in Sicuani.

"I innocently walked into the church that morning," recalled Father Jim Geaney, "to see what was the matter. I ran into this mob. Next thing I knew, a two-by-four piece of wood came flying by my head. That's when I started running. I called the police and they got the people out of the church. Then a crowd estimated at between eight hundred and a thousand people gathered in the Plaza.

One of our cars happened to be parked in the Plaza, so they broke into it and started pushing this 'symbol of Americanism' around the streets. They tried unsuccessfully to blow it up, and they were just about to throw it in the river when the police stopped them at the last minute. The priests locked themselves up in the parish house in fear of their lives. People were standing outside with rocks in their hands. The riot was finally broken up the following Sunday when troops came in from Cuzco with rifles and tear-gas."

Father Geaney later wrote;

> The occasion of the riots was the changing around of the church according to the new liturgical reforms; the cause of the riots was the agitation of a few leaders in the town, mainly communist politicians, who really whipped up the people to a riot pitch – which wasn't too difficult, given the ignorance of the people, the devaluation of the money at that time, and their deep-seated resentment against the United States in general as the cause of all their woes, economic and otherwise.

I was learning fast about the dangers that lurked beneath the surface, especially amongst the townspeople. My own troubles were yet to come.

As I sit here all alone in the peace and quiet of my room, I have much time for thought and reflection. It is eight o'clock at night and there is not a sound to be heard except the odd bark from Kimichu. The people of Yauri have long since retired for the night. Darkness falls here shortly after six o'clock every evening. It never changes. Summer or winter it is always the same, there is hardly any twilight. Outside a beautiful moon shines down and a million stars illuminate the sky. It is a stargazer's paradise. No wonder these heavenly bodies played such an important part in the lives of the Incas. Soon I will snuggle up in my sleeping bag for the night. It is the only place to keep warm in this cold and freezing night air. My only light, apart from the moon, is my Petromax, a pressurised kerosene lamp which uses up most of the oxygen, and soon I find it hard to breathe. Eventually sleep comes.

Mariano is still making adobes. It seems a never-ending task. His daughter Edelberta has decided to leave the parish office and return to school. The fact that she is eighteen doesn't bother her. It is never too late to learn how to read and write. The following Sunday I found a girl in the choir who would replace Edelberta. She had just arrived from Cuzco with her newborn baby. She had been a *muchacha* to a wealthy family, but the husband had constantly raped her and as soon as the baby arrived she was immediately dismissed. She told me her name was Maria and she would love to work in the parish office.

She had no trouble speaking Spanish and Quechua, but she couldn't read or write. I made a bargain with her. I would teach her how to read and write if she would help me with my Quechua. We began the next day. She would copy a hundred lines a day. Soon she could copy a baptismal certificate and write up a marriage form. Next I put her working on an index of all the baptisms going back over thirty years. All the names were put in alphabetical order. Now it would be possible to find a name in a couple of minutes instead of searching for hours. Sebastian was needed less and less in the office and gradually Maria looked after everything on her own.

Hardly a day goes by in Yauri but something happens which moves me deeply and makes me think. I can never take for granted the extremes of poverty, hunger and misery. When a little child dies of hunger or for want of a little medicine, I am moved to tears. Very often stealing is their only way of surviving. It just becomes a way of life. On one occasion some money went missing from Des's room. I decided to try and find the culprit. Benigno was the first suspect. He denied all knowledge of it, but suggested that it might be Aurelia. He had seen her in the market buying some bread and according to Benigno that was most unusual because she never had any money. Aurelia is the daughter of one of the women who helps in the parish centre. She is about ten years of age, dresses in rags and has long uncombed black hair. She goes barefoot and seems to suffer from a perpetual cold with green mucus coming from her nose.

One day when Des had gone to visit a distant community I was having dinner alone. Aurelia was playing in the patio.

"Aurelia, come here a minute. I want to ask you some questions," I called.

"Did you ever go into Padre Albanito's room?" I began.

"*Manan*," she replied, "the door is always closed."

"Are you sure you didn't take some money from his desk?"

"*Manan, manan*," she repeated, looking at my dinner on the table. She looked so innocent, her dark eyes staring out from a dirty face. She began to cry. Suddenly I realised what I was doing and I felt ashamed of myself. I will never forget the sight of that little girl standing before me. She was obviously hungry and would be lucky if she got a few potatoes before the end of the day. She would most likely go to bed hungry like so many other children of her age. What right had I to question her about money? What difference would it make if she stole all the Inca gold in Peru? I got another plate and shared my dinner with her. As she sat beside me devouring the potatoes on her plate I asked her what was the name of that game she was playing.

"Finding the treasure," she answered, "you have to hop along on one leg with your eyes shut."

She smiled as she wiped the mucus from her dirty face with the back of her little hand.

Emmanuel ran a little medicine shop at the corner of the Plaza. He wasn't a doctor but all the Indians consulted him about their illnesses. He could lance a boil, bandage up a wound and cut out an ingrown toenail. In his little room upstairs he would pull a tooth without anaesthetic, muffling the roars with a heavy blanket. He was a kind man of small stature and he always waved as I passed by in the truck. His wife, Josefina, was a big woman and rumour had it that she was the boss. He was devoted to her, but he also had a certain fear of her. Whenever she asked him to do something he was quick to obey. They had a large family, most of their children having survived the first two critical years of their lives.

Emmanuel came to see me one day with tears streaming down his face.

"Josefina went to Arequipa to buy some supplies," he sobbed, "and she hasn't returned."

"When was she due back?" I asked.

"Three days ago," he replied, "she should have taken the train to Sicuani and come up by lorry."

"Maybe she has been delayed," I suggested, trying to console him.

"I heard on the radio that there was a train crash outside Arequipa and I'm afraid she was on it. She has our little baby, Geovanna, with her. I will have to go to Arequipa to look for her."

"Wait another day," I said, "perhaps she will come tomorrow."

The following day Emmanuel set out on the long journey to Arequipa. He learned that two trains had crashed head-on about two miles outside the town. Thirteen people had been killed and there were many injured. He went immediately to the morgue. There among the corpses he found Josefina. She had been killed instantly. Everything she had was stolen, even the shoes from her feet and the wedding ring from her finger. Emmanuel was heartbroken. He put his arms around her and gave her a final hug. She felt terribly cold.

"Where is the baby?" he asked, as he turned away.

"What baby?" said the attendant, "there's no baby here!"

"Perhaps it was injured and is in the hospital," suggested a woman standing nearby.

Emmanuel went to the hospital. He visited all the injured, but no one had seen Geovanna.

"I heard there was a baby saved," said a nurse as he was about to leave.

"Where is she?" asked Emmanuel anxiously.

"I think one of the rescuers is caring for her in his home," she replied.

Shortly afterwards Emmanuel found Geovanna in the house of one of the rescuers. Apparently she had been asleep in her mother's arms when the accident occurred and was flung headlong through an open window. She was eventually found safe and well by the side of the track. Emmanuel took her into his arms and in spite of his sorrow he was overcome with emotion. Tears of joy and sadness were streaming down his face.

There was great rejoicing in Yauri when Emmanuel and Geovanna arrived home. Although five people from the town had been killed in the crash there was much celebrating because a child had been miraculously saved. It was just before Christmas. There is a custom in Yauri that a newborn baby is chosen each year to be the child Jesus in the crib. They carry the baby around the Plaza in a procession before placing it in the crib in the church. That year they chose Geovanna. The fact that she was a girl didn't bother them.

The following Christmas Emmanuel came to me to ask me a great favour.

"*Papay Cristobal*, I would like to have Geovanna baptised," he said, "and I would consider it a great honour if you would be her *padrino*."

"I would be delighted," I replied, without a moment's hesitation.

I baptised Geovanna on Christmas Day with all her family present. Little was I to realise the profound influence this little child was to have on me during my time in Peru. As I poured the water on her and said;

"Geovanna, I baptise you in the Name of the Father and of the Son and of the Holy Spirit, Amen," she looked up at me as if to say;

"*Gracias, Padrino.*"

Geovanna had become very special. She was 'my little Inca girl' and a special light seemed to shine from her. In this dark corner of a forgotten place another star was born. The gospel has a recipe for everyone. No one is overlooked. There is guidance for the gifted, opportunity for the energetic, development for the rugged and the strong. But for the frail and the weak, for the puzzled and the poor there is also something. No one is forgotten. We are all part of the plan. It is the weakest of God's children that need our deepest interest and our tenderest care. "Suffer the little children to come to me."

So I say "Shine on, Inca girl," symbol to me of the thousands like you who brought the Son of God to earth as a little child to smooth and bless your weary anxieties and your smiles. Come to me, often in your barefoot poverty and look at me with your dark brown eyes. Never let me forget your presence, stay with me and be my dream. Then I will always know why I came to Peru. Shine on, Inca girl.

7

Where There is no Santa Claus

Waiting outside the church

One of the things I have learned while working here is the ability to see and observe things as a little child again. What a wonderful discovery when we realise that no matter how old we are, deep down inside us there is a beautiful little child.

Children don't have a little child inside them. They are already a little child on the inside and on the outside. That is why Geovanna didn't have to pretend. She just had to be herself. She didn't see me as an adult or a gringo or a priest, but just as a friend. With Geovanna I was able once more to look at things around me with a childlike sense of awe and wonder. How terrible it is to grow old; old in the sense of no longer being filled with wonder, no longer looking at the world with the eyes of a child; no longer being amazed at the marvels of this world, the earth, the animals, the sun, the moon, the stars and the mountains.

"Look at the baby alpaca," remarked Geovanna one day.

"Maybe it's a llama," I suggested, not being able to tell the difference between one and the other. To me they both look the same.

"Don't you see its long woolly coat," she said, "a llama's coat is much shorter."

"Will we stop and say 'Hello'?" I asked.

"No!" she replied, "its Mama is with it and she will spit in my eye if I go near it. She doesn't like you looking at her baby."

Then after a long silence she said, "My Mama is in heaven, looking down at me."

Kimichu began to bark.

"Kimichu, you are a bad dog, you shouldn't bark at the alpacas, you will frighten them and they are not doing you any harm," Geovanna scolded.

Kimichu had his head out the back of the truck and continued to bark.

"That's a killichu!" Geovanna exclaimed suddenly, as a little hawk-like bird rose from the *pampa*.

"What do killichus eat?" I asked.

"Other little birds," she replied. "They like to have meat for their breakfast."

"Just like Geovanna!" I smiled, "Geovanna likes lots of meat."

I was about to have one of my many lessons in Spanish from a little girl who was only learning to speak herself. The Spanish word for meat is *carne*, and it is pronounced with a deep guttural sound. I could never get my tongue around it properly.

"It's not car-nay," she laughed, "it's *carne*," as she imitated my feeble attempt to pronounce the word.

"Carrh-nay," I repeated, and again she laughed. I tried to explain.

"Geovanna, my mouth is accustomed to speaking English and in English the word for carne is meat and I have no trouble pronouncing meat. I find it difficult to speak Spanish, not to mention Quechua."

With the Indian custom of never listening to an explanation and a child's capacity to know everything, Geovanna wasn't really listening.

"Well, in the English of Yauri it's *carne*," she said, "and you are not saying it right."

She was silent for a moment and then asked, "What is English?"

"English is another language that uses different sounds to speak, like Quechua," I explained.

"But Quechua is the sound that comes out of the mouth," she said.

(The Incas didn't call their language 'Quechua', but simply '*Runa Simi*'. *Runa* means 'people' and *simi* means 'mouth'.)

"Why do different sounds come out of the mouth?" she wondered.

"Because there are different people in the world," I replied, "Chinese, Japanese, Spanish, Irish, English."

By now I had lost her.

"Show me your hand," I said. She held up her tiny little hand.

"How many fingers have you?" I asked.

"*Uno, dos, tres, cuatro, cinco,*" she counted in Spanish.

"And in Quechua?"

"*Huk, iskay, kimsa, tawa, pichqa,*" she said quickly.

I held up my hand and said; "One, two, three, four, five."

Then I showed her my other hand and continued.

"*Aon, dó, trí, ceathair, cúig* (one, two three, four, five in Gaelic)."

She looked at my big hands and then at her own tiny fingers. She was totally confused.

"The word for meat is *carne,*" she insisted, smiling.

After a while she asked, "Teach me some English."

"Mary had a little lamb," I said.

"Mery hadda likkle lam," she repeated, almost perfectly.

"Whose fleece was white as snow," I continued, explaining the meaning in Spanish.

"Like the snow on that mountain!" she said, pointing to the snow covered peaks in the distance.

"And everywhere that Mary went, the lamb was sure to go."

"Did Mary bring the lamb to church?" she asked.

"Yes," I said, "just like the children in Yauri."

"But the lambs in Yauri are not white!" she exclaimed, pointing to some sheep in the *pampa* that were a dirty brown colour.

"That's because they haven't washed themselves," I joked; "just like Geovanna," I added, laughing.

"What was the name of Mary's lamb?" she asked, trying to change the subject.

"I don't know," I said, "I don't think it had a name."

"It must have a name," she insisted. "Everything has a name. Let's call it 'Marisol' after my sister."

I soon found myself keeping lots of animals in Yauri. Apart from

Kimichu, I had two lambs, a calf, a little llama and lots of rabbits. I grew up among rabbits in the Wicklow hills and spent most of my youth shooting them for dinner. I could never kill the rabbits that I reared in Yauri. I would give them away to the Indians under one condition, that they killed them out of my sight. Geovanna came to see my animals every day and gave each one a name.

☆　　☆　　☆

One day on my way home from Pichigua I was stopped on the road by a man and his son waving frantically. As soon as I stopped, the man presented me with two eggs and began to plead with me.

"*Papay*, come and bless my mother who is dying . . . please *Papay*."

As it was almost dark, I knew I couldn't go very far. It was rocky terrain so there was no way I could take the truck. I had made a resolution, having been caught out many times, never to walk to a hut unless I could see it in the distance. 'Very near' can turn out to be 'very far'.

"Where is your house?" I asked.

"Just down there, behind those rocks," he replied, indicating some huts in the valley. I could just see a wisp of smoke rising in the cold evening air.

"Where the smoke is?" I asked.

"Yes," came the reply.

The man and his son led the way on foot over the rough ground.

"Has she been sick for long?" I enquired, as we stumbled along.

"She is very old, *Papay*. She hasn't eaten anything for some days now."

It was almost dark as we reached the hut. There were two llamas with their heads in the door of the hut. As I approached I realised they were keeping the old woman warm with their hot breath. She lay on the clay ground with a few blankets thrown over her. A younger woman lit a candle as I knelt down to speak to her.

"*Allillanchu, Mamay*," I said.

The old women opened her eyes and stared at me, but she couldn't speak. She caught me by the hand and held it tightly and her little wizened hand was frozen with the cold. She looked about ninety but she could hardly have been much more than forty. She knew who I was. I gave her absolution and anointed her with the Holy Oils. I asked for a little water to moisten her parched lips. The boy quickly filled a bowl from a nearby bucket and I put a few drops to her mouth. We prayed together for a while. As I left, the boy led the llamas back to the door. I was sad and upset as I made my way back to the truck. I tried to understand the deep wound in the hearts of these poor, forgotten, lonely and oppressed people. Surely a dog should die with more dignity than that which I had just seen.

There are many wounds in the hearts of the people of Yauri. They have lived for centuries under the yoke of oppression. They were once the rulers of this beautiful land – a land of gold and silver and many other treasures. The biggest copper mine in the world is just a few miles down the road in Tintaya. The local community was driven off the land and the mine is now exploited by the government and an international mining company. The poor Indians get no benefit from it. But perhaps the greatest source of injustice is the land. The *hacendados* have vast tracts of land on which the Indians work as little more than slaves. Over the years they have been driven higher and higher into these barren mountains where they try to eke out a miserable existence. How often have I thought, 'What in the name of God has brought them here?' The answer is quite simple – they have nowhere else to go.

This injustice and oppression brings with it other deeper wounds. Many have lost their dignity as human beings. They think the world is made up of 'superior' and 'inferior' people. One day a girl called Luzmila

Luzmila and me

133

was sitting with me on the stone step outside my door. She often came to play volleyball with the other children. She was about twelve years old, with long black hair and lovely Indian features. A true Inca maiden.

"You have beautiful white skin," she said, staring at my hand. "That's because you have good blood," she added. "Look at my hand, it is brown and dirty because I have bad blood."

I was shocked and speechless. What could I say to a young girl who thinks like that. What a deep wound lay inside her little heart. I thought of all the time I spent on the beach at Brittas Bay in Ireland, trying to get a tan . . . just to look like Luzmila.

☆ ☆ ☆

Last night I dreamed that I was back home in Ireland during the Christmas rush. I was being carried along by the vast crowd of people down O'Connell Street in Dublin. Turning into Henry Street I could hear the traders shouting out the advantages of their wares.

"Get your Christmas decorations . . . get the last of the holly and ivy!"

"Five balloons for ten pence . . . only a couple left!"

"Buy your fairy lights and Christmas crackers . . . two pounds a packet."

"Get your Mickey Mouse and Jumping Jack!"

Thousands of gaily coloured lights flicker in the night drizzle, casting rainbows on the damp pavement below. The huge Christmas tree glistens in the moonlight while all around there is the rattling of collection boxes while little urchins hold out their begging hands . . . "Spare a penny for the poor?" The shops are full of last minute shoppers laden down with parcels of all shapes and sizes, others with turkeys and some with the odd goose tucked under their arm.

At home in Wicklow all is almost ready. The plum puddings are long since made and the Christmas cake just needs the final decoration. A few forgotten Christmas cards are hurriedly dispatched in the hope they will arrive by Christmas Eve. Children can hardly contain themselves with excitement as they look forward to the coming of Santa Claus, with his sacks of trains, planes, dolls, tanks, guns, games, walkmans and tape recorders. Christmas is really a celebration for the children. Christ was born as a little child on Christmas day. I could hear a choir of angels singing 'Silent Night' in the distance.

"Mary gave birth to a Son and wrapped him in swaddling clothes and laid him in a manger because there was no room at the Inn."

I awoke suddenly to the barking of Kimichu outside my window. I was brought back to the stark reality of life in Yauri; another time, another place. Everything was calm. In Yauri there is no Christmas rush, no Christmas lights, no trees, no cakes, no cards, no plum puddings, no toys and no Santa Claus. Yet Christ is born again among the poor in all the simplicity of Bethlehem. For weeks now the children have been preparing their songs and making their simple home-made instruments. They fashion little pipe-like containers and half-fill them with water so that when they blow into them they sound like birds singing. A beautiful crib is prepared in the church with llamas, alpacas, sheep and lambs.

Coming to the crib

The coming of Christ at Christmas was also a time of sorrow and sadness. Herod decreed that all male children of two years and under be put to death. Virtually every family in Yauri mourns the death of a child – there are thousands of 'Holy Innocents'. It's as though the prophecy of Jeremiah is being fulfilled to this day.

> A voice was heard in Ramah (Yauri)
> Sobbing and loudly lamenting.
> It was Rachel weeping for her children
> Refusing to be comforted because they were no more.

Outside the church before Midnight Mass there was a wonderful air of joy and celebration. The children were all dressed in their colourful costumes, each carrying a star and a candle. I carried an image of the child Jesus and placed it on the altar. After Mass everyone came forward to kiss the child Jesus with awe and reverence. Many of the old *mamitas* (women) return again and again. The children enter the church singing a joyful Indian tune.

> Haku waguellay purirusun Belente
> Kusisunkilla chayaykusun portalmari
> Killa kashagtin riruyukusan intita
> Chaupitutatag kay pachapi kaanchay.

> Let us go on our way to Bethlehem
> Carrying joy in our hearts
> In the moonlight we will see the sun
> At midnight there, we will see the LIGHT.

Christmas Eve night is called *Noche Buena* (Good Night) and is beautiful in its simplicity. In Yauri everything happens in a simple and sincere way. Surely there was never a more authentic celebration of Christ's birth since He was born in Bethlehem. As I retold the simple story of Joseph and Mary and the child Jesus being born in the poverty of a manger, it must have sounded quite luxurious to them. Most of these poor Indians would have been born in far poorer and more inhuman circumstances. Little barefoot children gathered around the altar to sing.

> To conquer poverty, Christ is born
> For the poor who suffer, Christ is born
> That all men should be equal
> Every day Christ is re-born.

For weeks beforehand I had tried to explain to Geovanna the meaning of Santa Claus. It was difficult to transport a gringo custom to the world of Yauri. I was reminded of the problem that the Anglican missionary, Thomas Bridges, had in conveying moral ideas to the Yamana Indians in Tierra del Fuego. Concepts of 'good' and 'beautiful' are meaningless unless they are rooted in concrete things and experiences. He had decided to look at their lives to find metaphors to explain abstract ideas.

So 'monotony' was understood as the 'absence of male friends', 'depression' was that vulnerable time when a crab leaves his old shell and waits for another to grow, 'laziness' was epitomised by the jackass penguin who just seems to sit around all day doing nothing and 'adultery' was represented as a small hawk that flits here and there, hovering motionless over his next victim.

Where was I to begin with Geovanna?

"Geovanna, do you remember the day that you picked some cactus flowers in the *pampa* and brought them home to your papa? Why did you do that?" I asked.

"Because I wanted to give him a present," she explained.

"Well if you are a very good girl, a kind man called Santa Claus will come on Noche Buena and bring you a present."

"Who is Santa Claus?" she asked.

"A good man who wears a long white beard."

"Where does he come from?"

"He lives at the North Pole where there is always snow and ice. He has a sleigh and reindeers and on *Noche Buena* he comes to all the good children and brings them presents."

I wasn't prepared for all the questions that followed, as Geovanna didn't understand a thing I said. She was however a very intelligent young girl.

"What is a beard?"

"It's long white hair that grows down from his chin," I explained, as Indians don't have beards.

"What is a sleigh?"

"It's like a truck without wheels that glides through the snow."

"What are reindeer?"

"Reindeer are like llamas except they can fly through the air, pulling the sleigh with Santa Claus and lots of presents."

"Just like a *lata pichinchu* (aeroplane, literally 'tin bird')," she said.

She seemed so incredulous by this stage that I wondered how I could ever have believed in such things myself. But the sheer joy of awakening on Christmas morning to find presents at the end of your bed was something that I wanted Geovanna to experience.

"How does he know where I live?" she wondered.

"Santa Claus is very clever and he knows where all good girls live."

I had to leave out the part about him coming down the chimney because Indian huts don't have any chimneys.

On my last trip to Lima I had brought back some presents, including a lovely doll. I had arranged with Emmanuel that after Midnight Mass, when all was quiet, I would call to his house. Geovanna was fast asleep on the floor, covered with some blankets. She had her arms around Marisol. I quietly left presents for both of them at their feet.

I will never forget the look of sheer delight in Geovanna's eyes early next morning as she came running to me, shouting;

"Padrino, Padrino . . . he came, he came. That kind man you told me about came and look at what he brought me . . . a gringo doll."

She showed me the doll's blonde hair, blue eyes and white skin. I hadn't been able to find an Indian doll. I suppose Indians are not supposed to buy dolls. Where there is no Santa Claus maybe there is no demand. (The Indians do make their own dolls, however, and in the excavation of Inca burial sites, many dolls used by little girls have been found.)

On Christmas Day Des and I had arranged a party for all the old people of the town. Word soon spread that the padres were having a fiesta and they came from all directions – the blind, the lame, the sick. They came to the parish centre where we had a meal. There were potatoes, maize, rice and a little meat – all prepared in the traditional way, on a fire of *bosta.* We also had a big pot of drinking chocolate and of course plenty of *chicha.* Everyone just sat around on the ground with their little bowls of food and drink. Soon there was music and dancing. In spite of their poverty they love to celebrate and for a moment there was joy and happiness that Christ was born again among the poor in Yauri.

It was after five o'clock by the time Des and I sat down to our Christmas dinner. The Irish Columban fathers in Lima had sent us a turkey which I had roasted in the kerosene stove. Just as we were about to start I looked out to see Trinidad rummaging through the rubbish. The sight almost put me off my dinner. I filled a plate with turkey, potatoes and vegetables.

"Trinidad, come and join us for dinner," I shouted.

"Gracias, Papay," she replied, "I'm just looking for something for my *cuys."* She came in and sat on the floor. Although she had very few teeth, she soon cleared the plate, picking everything up with her fingers.

"That's lovely meat!" she exclaimed, "I have never had that meat before."

Suddenly there was a load banging on the door. I went to investigate.

"Could I have my baptismal certificate?" asked a little man, as he removed his *chullo*.

"Where have you come from?" I asked.

"Sukitambo," he replied, "I have been walking since yesterday."

"*Iman su tiki?*" I asked.

"Pastor Mamani Huillca," he replied.

He didn't even know it was Christmas Day.

The 'rainy season' has started. I never realised what this phrase meant until I came to Yauri. It rains almost every day from December to March. None of your 'mist that lies on the bog' here, but real rain that comes down in bucketfuls. The day usually starts off bright and sunny, but by around four o'clock in the afternoon the sky darkens, the heavens open and the rain comes down in torrents. It continues until about three o'clock the next morning. Some of the bridges and roads are washed away as the rivers flood. In no time at all the streets of Yauri turn into a quagmire, with the mud squelching between the people's toes as they hop along up to their ankles in the stuff. Not a week goes by without news of an accident – trucks careering off the muddy roads into the valleys below. Hundreds of people are killed every year. This is not surprising considering that up to a hundred people can cram into the back of a Volvo truck. Life is cheap in the mountains, especially Indian lives.

Normally we can't go out to the communities during the rainy season. However there is one exception. Huayuilla celebrates the feast of the Child Jesus on the day after Christmas. I set out with Kimichu before seven o'clock in order to be home before the heavy rains came. It was a bright and sunny morning as I took the road to Apachaco. There had been heavy rain during the night and I knew that my first problem would be the river just outside the town. It is normally a little stream that doesn't present any difficulty but today it was a river. I stopped for a moment on a hill overlooking the river to survey the scene and I wondered would it be wise to cross.

It was not very encouraging to see the road disappearing underneath the water and I wasn't quite sure how deep it was. I decided to take a run at it. A great spray of water came up over the windscreen and the truck seemed to stall for a moment but when the water cleared I was on the other side. Steam rose from under the bonnet, but I kept going. If I stopped now I might never get started again. I decided to make a new track through the *pampa* instead of following one of the existing muddy ones. My directions were to turn right at the huts on this side of Chalki. The *alferado* from Huayuilla, Marcelino, would be waiting with two horses on the bank of the river Apurimac. (Yes, I would have to cross the river on horseback and I was dreading the thought.) Suddenly I arrived at the top of a cliff looking down into a valley below. The flooding river had already covered half the valley. By the end of the rainy season the valley would be completely covered. In the distance I could just see two horses on the edge of the water. Kimichu began to bark with excitement. Perhaps he too had foreseen the danger. I drove along the cliff looking for a place to descend into the valley and finally made my way down to meet them.

"*Allillanchu, Papay,*" Marcelino greeted me, as I got out of the truck.

"*Allillanmi,*" I replied, but I must confess I could have felt better.

"We are lucky it is not raining," he said, looking up at the sky.

"What about the river?" I asked, "It looks very dangerous to me."

By now it was about three hundred yards across and was fast flowing in the centre.

"No problem!" he assured me. "I have just come across with the horses a short time ago." No problem for him maybe, but it could be a big problem for me. The Indians always overestimate the capabilities of a gringo, especially a gringo padre. I looked at the horses – no saddles and no bit in the mouth. They could go exactly where they pleased.

"This one is yours," he said, pointing to the bigger of the two.

"You must take off your shoes and put them around your neck and pull up your trousers above your knees."

While I was taking off my shoes Marcelino took off his trousers and tied them around his shoulders along with the Mass kit. He placed a rug on the back of my horse.

"Could you put a rope across his back with two loops for my feet," I asked, "so that I can balance myself going across?"

140

"No problem."

"*Vamonos*," he said, as he led his horse into the water.

I followed tentatively. Kimichu was reluctant to enter the water at first, but when I called he quickly followed.

We proceeded slowly at first as the horses picked their way through the stony bed of the river. Gradually we were getting deeper and deeper and I could feel the freezing water on the soles of my feet. Suddenly the horses were swimming. Marcelino's horse was being gradually swept downstream with the current. Kimichu was following close behind me. Only his head appeared over the water. Every now and then he gave my horse a little nip in the tail as if to make him go faster. As he did, the horse rose in the water and kicked his legs behind him. I held on for dear life and began to wish that I had left Kimichu on the other side. By now we were being carried faster downstream. If I fall off now, I thought, God knows where I will end up. At last the horses were walking again and we reached the far side of the river at least five hundred yards further downstream from where we had entered.

Once on the other side I pulled down my trousers and put on my shoes. We proceeded to climb the other mountainside and soon reached a beautiful little chapel with crowds of people gathered around. They were all dressed in multicoloured costumes, worn especially for the fiesta. The band led us in triumph to where I would celebrate the fiesta. During the Mass I couldn't concentrate. I was never so distracted in all my life. How would I ever get back across that river which was rising by the minute?

Almost everything comes to a standstill during the rainy season, so I decided to avail of the opportunity to do a refresher course in Spanish; Quechua would come later. As the Indians who speak only a little Spanish speak it very badly, I found that since I had arrived in Yauri my Spanish had deteriorated instead of improving. Des told me about a language school in Cochabamba in Bolivia run by the Maryknoll Fathers which he had attended some years earlier. I would have to go to Cuzco to catch the 'Transturin' bus to La Paz and from there take a plane to Cochabamba. Bolivia is only about two hours away from Yauri as the condor flies but it would take me over two days by road. Although the

Catechists studying the bible

bus to La Paz came through Sicuani I went to Cuzco to be sure of getting a ticket. Leaving Cuzco in the evening the bus travelled through the night, arriving in Puno the following day. It was impossible to sleep as we bounced along the dark mountain road.

The early morning sun was rising as we arrived at the shores of Lake Titicaca. The lake looked majestic as the rays of the sun glistened on its still waters. There was something awe-inspiring and magical in the atmosphere. Little wonder that it was from the depths of this lake that the mythical Gods of the Sun had arisen to found the Inca Empire. Lake Titicaca forms the boundary between Peru and Bolivia and is the highest navigable lake in the world, at 12,506 feet above sea level. It is one hundred and thirty miles long and forty-one miles wide. It has no drainage system; its waters just evaporate into the desert. The road followed the lake for miles and the view was breathtaking with the snow-capped mountains on one side and the still waters of the lake on the other.

This was Aymara territory. Although the Aymaras were conquered militarily by the Incas they never lost their own customs and traditions which continue to this day. Like the Incas the Aymara gods had their origin in this beautiful lake. When the Incas conquered another tribe they imposed the Quechua language on them as a means of bringing them into submission. They never really succeeded with the Aymaras and the Aymara language is still spoken widely today especially around

Lake Titicaca. It is not just a different dialect of Quechua but a completely separate language. Both Aymara and Quechua function on completely different grammatical principles from European languages which is why they are so difficult to learn.

In 1610 when the Spanish Jesuit, Ludovico Bertonio produced the first Aymara dictionary he discovered that the language had no irregular verbs or exceptions to the grammatical rules. It is the best thought-out language in the world. Once you have learned the principles, everything follows the rule. The Aymaras refer to their language as *haque-aru* (human speech).

To escape from the Incas many of the Aymaras took refuge on higher ground and in the reed islands in the centre of the lake. As we passed I could see whole families paddling along in their *totora*-reed boats called *balsas*.

It was here that Thor Heyerdahl had his reed boats made for his famous Ra expeditions. In 1947 he sailed from Peru across the Pacific Ocean to Polynesia on his *Kon-Tiki* expedition, named after a legendary Inca Sun god. He wanted to test his hypothesis that aboriginal Peruvian Indians could have negotiated this vast expanse of ocean in their primitive sailing rafts and populated the islands of the Pacific. His raft was made of nine thick logs of Peruvian balsa wood lashed together with hemp rope. No metal was used. Two masts supported a large rectangular sail and a bamboo cabin was built near the raft's centre. The *Kon-Tiki* was set adrift fifty miles off the Peruvian coast with a five man crew. Ninety three days later Heyerdahl and his crew sailed past the island of Puka Puka, east of Tahiti. Eight days after that the *Kon-Tiki* crashed onto a reef in the Tuamotu Archipelago. The sailors waded ashore to an uninhabited island and were rescued a week later.

We stopped in Puno for breakfast before continuing along the lake to the ferry that would bring us to Guaqui in Bolivia. The *M.V. Ollanta* had been built in England. The ferry parts were brought by ship to Peru, by truck to Arequipa and then by train to the lake where it was reassembled. Before we could get on the ferry we had to go through a rundown Peruvian customs post just outside Puno. We queued up in single file to have our passports checked. A fat customs officer dressed in navy uniform with shiny buttons and a peaked cap sat behind a table. He looked bored and yawned loudly without embarrassment. The two top buttons of his tunic were undone, revealing a silver chain around his neck. He stamped the passports automatically – German, Japanese, French. He took my passport without looking and was about to stamp it when suddenly he looked up at me.

"Are you resident in Peru?" he asked abruptly.

"Yes," I replied, "I'm working in the parish of Yauri, in the province of Espinar". I could see by his reaction that he had no idea where Yauri was and anyway he wasn't interested in details.

"Will you be returning to Peru?" he asked.

"Yes," I responded, "in about six weeks' time. I'm going to study Spanish in Cochabamba." He obviously couldn't care what I was going to study.

"Where is your white paper?" he demanded.

"What white paper?" I asked.

"As a resident in Peru, you need a white paper with your passport to exit and enter the country."

The people in the queue behind me were getting impatient.

"Where can I get this white paper?" I asked.

"In the Banco de la Nación in Puno," he replied.

"But how can I go back to Puno now?" I protested. "Anyway the bank is not open at this hour." He just shrugged his shoulders.

I quickly took some dollars from my pocket.

"Can I pay you here?" I asked, waving a fifty dollar bill in his face. He looked at the money as though hypnotised and quickly put it in his pocket.

"I'll make an exception this time," he said, "but in future make sure your papers are in order." He stamped my passport with an officious thump.

☆　　☆　　☆

The boundary between Peru and Bolivia passes through the centre of Lake Titicaca. Bolivia separated from Peru when it achieved its independence on 2 April 1825 at the express wish of its liberator, Simon Bolívar, after whom the country is named. (Prior to this it was called Upper Peru.) Bolivia is a landlocked country, the combined size of France, Spain and Portugal. It has a population of only about six million people, mostly Quechua and Aymara Indians. Although it maintains an active navy it has no sea as it lost its Pacific sea-coast to Chile during the War of the Pacific.

I knew very little about Bolivia before I arrived other than that Che Guevara was shot in the mountains of Bolivia and the outlaws Butch Cassidy and The Sundance Kid met their end there, or did they? I knew also that Bolivia had at least one revolution a year. In over one hundred and fifty years of independence it had seen almost two hundred presidents, the present one coming to power the previous July after yet another revolution.

It was snowing as we eventually made our descent into La Paz. The city is approached from a high plateau descending into a canyon which has been carved out of the mountain by the La Paz river. It is the highest capital city in the world at 12,000 feet above sea level. It was founded by the Spaniards in 1548, on the site of an old Inca village, as a way-station along the caravan route from the famous silver mines at Potosi to Lima. It provided a welcome shelter from the harsh climate of the *Altiplano*. La Paz was named after Our Lady of Peace because of the peaceful conditions at the time. Who could have imagined its future turbulent history?

I made my way to the church of Our Lady of Pompeye where the Maltese Carmelites have a parish. I was given a great welcome by the parish priest, Fr José Cilia, a lovely man. José was delighted to have my company for a few days.

"You were lucky to arrive before the curfew," he said, looking at his watch. "It begins in five minutes time at eleven o'clock and lasts until six in the morning."

José lived on his own and did his own cooking. He had learned, like me, that an Indian cook can be more of a hindrance than a help. He kept a lovely little pet monkey which was his constant companion. The monkey immediately made friends with me by sitting on my shoulder.

"I am very busy here," he explained, "with many Masses and funerals every day. The present government is hated by everyone. They govern only by force and out of fear. People are killed every day."

The monkey jumped on to the table and took a banana from the bowl, peeled it and proceeded to eat it. I was fascinated by the cleverness of the little animal and decided that I must get a monkey one day.

"A funny thing happened last week when I was down the town with the monkey," recalled José. "I met the priest from the next parish who had an urgent problem. 'José, I'm happy to see you,' he said, 'I have two funerals at the same time. Could you say one of the Masses for me?' I told him I'd love to, but asked him what should I do with the monkey. 'Leave it in the sacristy,' he suggested, 'and shut the door.' I reminded him that the monkey would tear the place down. 'You don't mean to tell me that you can't say Mass because of a bloomin' monkey,' he replied. 'Maybe I could put it under my jumper,' I said. 'Put it where you like,' he replied, 'but say the Mass.' In the end I put the monkey under my jumper and put on the vestments. I said Mass before a packed church, and afterwards prayed over the coffin. I was on tenterhooks all the time in case the monkey would make a sudden appearance and give the congregation his blessing!"

That night I was awakened by the sound of gunfire. The next morning José told me that nine people were shot dead in a house down the road while holding a meeting. One of them was from the parish. That evening I concelebrated the funeral Mass. Thousands of people attended. José preached an elegant sermon on freedom, justice and martyrdom. In the sacristy afterwards he remarked;

"We'll be lucky if we are not both in prison before the night is over."

He had had a lucky escape just six months previously. It happened one evening as he was coming home from a sick call wearing his Carmelite habit. Suddenly a car pulled up beside him. Two masked men jumped out, hit him over the head and bundled him into the car. They brought him up the mountains above La Paz and stripped him of all his clothes. His hands were tied behind his back and he was left shivering and blindfolded. He could smell the burning of his habit and expected to be shot at any moment.

Then there was silence. After a while he freed himself and took off his blindfold. There was no one there. He was freezing with the cold. He made his way down to the river and followed it back to the city. In the early morning he found himself on the outskirts of La Paz . . . naked! Finding an old cement bag on the side of the road he wrapped it around him and made his way to a friend's house. As the woman opened the door he fainted into her arms. He spent the following week in hospital recuperating from his terrible ordeal.

On the second day in La Paz, José asked me if I would say Mass in a private house where the husband had died. As I reached the house there were lots of cars parked outside. It was a beautiful mansion situated in its own grounds. "These are certainly not Indians," I thought. Everyone was elegantly dressed and obviously of Spanish descent. The coffin was placed in the centre of a large sitting room. The lid was left open and there were flowers placed all around the room. People were sobbing. The widow, who was dressed in black, was standing beside the coffin with her two children. I offered her my sympathy and began the Mass. One of the children read a lesson. I gave a homily on death and sadness, family life and the hope of resurrection. The family thanked me profusely as I left.

That evening at supper José casually remarked;

"How did you get on at the funeral Mass?"

"All went very well," I replied, "the widow was very upset."

"It was a very sad case," he said. "He was the manager of one of the biggest banks in La Paz. His wife went off with another man and took the children with her. She also took the credit cards and spent thousands and thousands of dollars, all drawn from his bank. He couldn't meet the repayments and finally, in despair, he committed suicide by shooting himself."

"What!" I exclaimed in disbelief. "Why didn't you tell me?"

"If I told you, you wouldn't have gone," he said.

☆   ☆   ☆

It's just twenty-five minutes by plane from La Paz to Cochabamba, the 'city of eternal spring', a beautiful town situated in a narrow steep-sided valley in the centre of Bolivia. Once part of the Inca Empire the Indians here speak Quechua. Further south lay Argentina and Chile, right down to Tierra del Fuego (Land of Fire). All the Indians to the south of Bolivia are now extinct, killed off by the greed of the white man. The sheep farmers offered one pound sterling for an Indian's ear because they were stealing their sheep. Later when they realised that the Indians were surviving the loss of their ears, they changed it to their testicles.

Darwin described these Indians as the most curious spectacle he had ever witnessed – "I couldn't believe the difference between savage and civilised man. It is greater than that between the wild and domesticated animal."

Threshing the primitive way

The land around Cochabamba is very fertile and produces large quantities of maize, wheat and potatoes. Coca is grown on three quarters of the farmland and is the country's leading source of foreign exchange (although it is illegal to export it). The economy of the country relies completely on contraband and in the traffic of drugs. Once when I went to the bank in Cochabamba to get some dollars, they politely told me that they had been out of dollars for a couple of days;

"There is an important drug transaction taking place tomorrow, so if you come back after that there will be plenty of dollars."

The language school in Cochabamba had been the German Consulate during the war and the centre of Nazi intelligence in South America. Many Nazis escaped to Bolivia after the war and were now living peacefully around Cochabamba. Shortly before I arrived, a large cache of arms was discovered at the bottom of a well in the grounds of the school. The Maryknoll Fathers first came here in 1947 and opened a school for their own students. In 1954 it was opened up to everyone and to date over 3,000 missionaries from thirty-eight countries had attended the school.

The school was a vast complex known locally as 'Gringoland', with all modern conveniences including a swimming pool and tennis court. Some of the younger, more idealistic students were inclined to criticise it for being too luxurious for the Third World. After Yauri I wasn't

148

complaining and I thoroughly enjoyed my daily swim and game of tennis.

The teaching was on a one-to-one basis and you advanced according to your own level. The teachers came from all over South America and rumour had it that some of the lady teachers were keen to marry a gringo and emigrate to the United States. It had been known to happen. My teacher was an elderly woman from Argentina called Lucia. She was from Rosario, outside Buenos Aires, and had gone to school with Che Guevara. She spoke of him in glowing terms. He was from a middle-class background and received a good education. He became a revolutionary in Guatemala when he experienced the terrible injustice and poverty there. Then he moved to Cuba and joined up with Fidel Castro. When he heard of the situation in Bolivia he thought that another liberator like Simon Bolívar was needed. He arrived at a particular time when an army general called Barrientos had become a dictator in Bolivia through a military coup.

Like Peru, Bolivia is a paradise where the poor Indians live as beggars. It has the greatest resources of tin and copper in the world. While the military were buying large houses and driving around in Mercedes Benz cars, the poor Indian miners were dying of hunger. They had not been paid for months. News came that there was a guerrilla in the mountains. Many ordinary Indians thought that the guerrilla didn't exist, that it was a ploy by the government to massacre more people. 'White massacres' they called them when the military threw the corpses on the public roads. There were many 'white massacres'.

Che Guevara wrote in his manifesto;

> Since the government remained in power by force, the working people needed arms to defend themselves. Power must be given to the working people to change the system of exploitation; to create a more just system, more humane, without hunger, misery, lack of food, without injustice. The miners gave an ultimatum to the government; pay them or they would go to the mountains and join the guerrillas. They would rather die in the mountains than in the mines.

The army renewed its efforts to track down Che Guevara and kill him. In 1967 his small band of guerrillas was defeated by Bolivian forces near Santa Cruz and Che Guevara was captured and executed. Many people didn't even know he was in Bolivia until a photograph of his corpse appeared in the newspapers.

☆   ☆   ☆

It was while in Bolivia that I had the most embarrassing experience of my whole life. I was playing tennis one afternoon when I pulled a muscle in the back of my leg. I could hardly walk.

"What you need for that is a good sauna," advised Gerry McGrane, the school director. "There are very nice sauna baths just a short distance away."

I decided to take his advice so I hobbled up the road to a sign that said 'Sauna'. I entered through an archway of bamboo to a patio where a beautiful young Bolivian girl of about eighteen was sitting behind a desk. There was no one else around.

"*Buenas tardes, Señorita,*" I said, "Is this the entrance to the sauna?"

"*Sí, Señor,*" she answered, "You change in the cubicle and the baths are on the other side of the patio."

I gave her five Bolivianos (about a dollar) and asked for a towel.

"You don't need a towel, Señor. We don't have towels."

I entered the cubicle and undressed. Then I wondered how I was supposed to get from the cubicle to the baths. I would have to walk across the patio past the young girl. Ah well, she must be used to it. Maybe it's the custom in Bolivia.

I opened the door of the cubicle and walked as quickly as my pulled muscle would allow across the patio while at the same time trying to hold my hands as discreetly as possible. I entered the sauna and through the steam saw two girls in bikinis looking up at me. 'Good God!' I suddenly realised that I was supposed to wear my bathing suit. I sat down quickly on the bench behind them, hoping that they wouldn't scream out. They started giggling uncontrollably. After a while they left. How was I going to get back to the cubicle? I peeped through the door. The girl was not there. The coast was clear. Now's my chance. My pulled muscle suddenly seemed to have made a rapid recovery!

8

Storm Clouds Gather

Pablo *(standing left)* calling a meeting in Yauri. Tiny *(on radio)*,
Julio *(standing on Tiny's right)*, Sebastian *(far right)*

Early one morning Pablo Ccahuana Chura came to see me from
Mullacahua. He was president of his community and he was
accompanied by four others. Melchor had let them in by the back door
through the parish centre.

"*Allillanchu, Papay,*" they said in unison.

"*Allillanmi,*" I answered.

"These are the members of my committee," said Pablo, naming them
one by one.

"Marco Zavalla Quispe, secretary; Wilber Parra Condori, treasurer;
Casildo Guzman Ttito, responsible for law and order and César Agusto
Ramos Ccama, responsible for the water supply." As he introduced
them, each one gave me a big hug.

"We would like to talk to you confidentially about a very important
matter," he continued.

"That is why we didn't come in past the police," added Wilber.

I brought them into my temporary kitchen and we sat around the table.

"Last week we had a general meeting of all the communities in Yauri," began Pablo, "and it was decided that one of us should run for *alcalde* at the next local election. I was nominated as the most suitable candidate as I was the only one who could read and write in Spanish. When I was young my parents sent me to my uncle in Arequipa to go to school."

"Since they changed the law on voting," said Marco, "we could easily win if everyone voted for Pablo." (Up to now only those who could read or write could vote, which meant that all the Indians were excluded. But with the Presidential Elections last year the law was changed and now everyone had a vote.)

"What do you want me to do?" I asked. "You realise that priests can't get involved in politics."

"We don't want you to get involved but we had to talk to someone," said César, "and you are our friend."

"We knew you would give us good advice," added Casildo.

"Do you think I should run, and if I was elected, would I be able to do a good job as *alcalde*?" asked Pablo.

"Of course you could," I replied, "but you do realise it won't be easy. You certainly won't get any co-operation from the *hacendados* or the merchants in the town. They will do everything they can to interfere with your work."

"We know that, *Papay*," they said, "but we will have all our own people behind us."

"You will be the first Indian ever to be elected mayor in Yauri," I explained. "It has always been a rich landowner. They will bribe some of the Indians to vote for them. It is very difficult to refuse money when you are poor."

"We want to give our people back their dignity," said Pablo. "They have trampled on us for too long. The last straw came last year when the police shot down our young men like animals."

"We want to follow in the footsteps of our great hero, Tupac Amaru II," interjected Casildo.

"Who was he?" I asked innocently.

"He was a great leader of our people," said Pablo. "He was a direct descendant of the last Inca from whom he took his name."

Pablo went on to tell me that Tupac Amaru was born on 19 March 1740, in a place called Surimana, just outside Combapata. Proud of his noble origins, he became a great leader and gave his life trying to free his people from Spanish oppression and injustice. At first he tried to win freedom by peaceful means and when that didn't succeed he began an armed revolution. Thousands of poor Indians rallied to the cause. The first great battle took place in Tinta, on the road to Cuzco. He had many famous victories before he was finally defeated in a fierce battle outside Combapata.

He escaped to the mountains, but he was betrayed to the Spanish by the people of Langui. They also captured his wife and two sons. (At the mention of Langui I saw in my mind the 'Swiss Chalet' village by the lake.) A great crowd gathered in the main square in Cuzco to witness the executions. They cut out the tongues of his two sons and then they hanged them in front of their father and mother. They tried to garrotte his wife but her neck was too thin and a soldier had to choke her with a rope instead. They tied ropes to the hands and feet of Tupac Amaru and four horses pulled in different directions. But he was too strong and they couldn't dismember him. Finally they cut off his head and sent it to various towns to be displayed before the people.

"When it came to Sicuani nobody came to look at it," said César.

"He died on 18 May 1771," said Pablo, "a day that every Indian remembers with pride."

"I'm sure you will be a great leader of your people too," I said.

"With God's help," he replied, as he knelt down for my blessing.

"*Gracias, Papay,*" they said, as I showed them out the back door, "say a prayer that we succeed."

In Peru all elections take place on Sundays. The Church made an agreement with the government that there would be no religious services during the hours of voting, between 8 am and 5 pm. I had asked Sebastian to ring the bell at 5.30 am and at regular intervals until 6.30 am, when I would celebrate Mass. That would give me plenty of time to be finished before voting began.

Everyone from the parish had come to Yauri to vote and the town was packed with people. The atmosphere was electric as no Indian had ever

Yauri church with a local 'taxi' in the foreground

challenged the landowners for the office of mayor before. Pablo had received many threats as he went around the communities canvassing for votes. The landowners commandeered all the trucks and fitted them out with loudspeakers. Their booming voices could be heard canvassing for miles around. Pablo went around quietly, speaking to the Indians in Quechua on market days.

The Indians made their way to the church at the sound of the bell. They believed that God was on their side and they had come to ask Him for a last minute intervention so that all would be well. Pablo and his group arrived early and took up the front seat. None of the landowners came to church. They didn't need God. They had Mammon on their side and he hadn't let them down yet. Anyway it would be beneath their dignity to mix with the peasants. As I entered the church I noticed little groups around each statue and shrine praying out loud. There was a large crowd around the Three Persons of the Trinity. They were praying to each Person individually.

"*Dios Yayac* (God the Father) watch over our Pablo today."

"*Dios Churic* (God the Son) come again to help us."

"*Dios Espiritu Santoc* (God the Holy Spirit) fly down and hover over us."

"*Suntimpi* (Amen)."

I put on the green vestments of the Blessed Trinity and approached the altar to begin the Mass. Suddenly there was a loud commotion at the door of the church where a large group of Indians had gathered. The *teniente* (chief of police), accompanied by two policemen with machine guns, was barging his way up the central aisle of the church. This young man had been sent to Yauri from Cuzco last year after the riots, to try to bring some law and order to this lawless town. He was ruthless in his dealings with the Indians and was detested by all except the landowners. As he got nearer I could see he had removed his pistol from its holster and was brandishing it around. The church had taken on the air of a wild west saloon. He entered the sanctuary and his companions turned to face the congregation, their machine guns at the ready. As he came towards me he shouted;

"What do you think you are doing?" He was pointing his pistol menacingly in my direction.

"I'm just about to begin Mass," I said calmly.

"Don't you know that Mass is forbidden on election day," he retorted.

"I know Mass is not said during voting hours between 8 am and 5 pm but as it is now only 6.30 am I will be finished in plenty of time."

"You are forbidden to say Mass today," he said, interrupting me.

I inadvertently placed my hand on his shoulder to try to reason with him.

"Do not touch me!" he shouted angrily, pushing my hand away. "I will have you arrested and put in jail for assaulting a police officer."

"Señor," I said, "you have no authority to come into this church. You certainly have no right to enter the sanctuary which is reserved for the celebration of Holy Mass. Would you be kind enough to leave immediately."

He reluctantly moved outside the sanctuary with his two companions.

I then turned to the congregation who were looking on in amazement.

"My dear people of God, this man has no authority to come into our church armed with these dangerous weapons. This is the house of God, it is a place of peace. I will denounce him to his superiors in Cuzco. But in the meantime I am not prepared to argue with machine guns, so we will postpone the Mass until tomorrow. When you have finished your prayers you can leave peacefully."

The *teniente* stormed off with his two bodyguards without saying a word. I immediately contacted Tiny in Sicuani by radio and told him what had happened. He had just celebrated Mass in the cathedral. He could hardly believe what the *teniente* had done.

"It must have been at the instigation of the landowners," Tiny suggested. "They must have thought that you were going to tell the Indians how to vote." He assured me that he would go personally to Cuzco and denounce the *teniente* to his superiors.

Days later as I was about to go to the church for Mass, the *teniente* paid me a visit.

"Padre Cristobal, Padre Cristobal," he shouted from the patio. When I looked out and saw who it was I was sure he had come to arrest me. This was the first time he had ever passed the door.

"*Buenas tardes*," I said, walking towards him.

"Padre Cristobal," he said as he put his arms around me and gave me a kiss on both cheeks. This took me by surprise, but I could smell that he was obviously drunk.

"Padre Cristobal," he blubbered again, not wanting to let me go, "you are my best friend in the whole world."

What a difference a few drinks can make, I thought to myself, but I had to excuse myself to say Mass.

"Very good," he said "but you are my best friend and tomorrow I will come again and we will have a drink."

I began to think that I was better off when he was my enemy. The next day he arrived with a crate of beer and dropped it on my doorstep.

"Padre Cristobal," he repeated, "you are my best friend and I want to drink to your good health."

I don't particularly like beer but just to be polite I thought it best to have a glass with him.

"Thank you very much," I replied, "I will get some glasses and a bottle opener."

"No need," he retorted, as he opened a bottle with his teeth and began to drink from it. I got a glass for myself.

"Come on," he urged, "let's celebrate our great friendship." With that he filled my glass.

"Drink up," he said, "there is plenty more where that came from."

I pretended to drink a little.

"You are a wonderful man to leave your beautiful country and come to the mountains of Peru," he said. "The United States is a great country."

"I don't come from the United States," I explained, "I come from Ireland." There was a long silence.

"Ireland is very poor," he said, "the people are dying of hunger."

"Not now," I explained, "that was during the Famine, a long time ago."

"But I heard on the radio last week that someone died of hunger in Northern Ireland," he persisted.

"That was Bobby Sands," I said. "He was on a protest hunger strike. He refused to eat."

"Margaret Thatcher is your president."

"No!" I said, "she is Prime Minister of Britain."

"It said on the radio that she was President of Ireland," he argued.

"The radio says a lot of things," I replied.

I could see that the situation could easily get out of hand as he drank bottle after bottle of beer, opening each one with his teeth. He spat out the caps like bullets from a machine gun. He began to get more and more incoherent. The conversation had ceased to make any sense and by now he couldn't stand up. I went to the door and called two policemen who were on duty next door. They came and carried him out, together with the crate of empty bottles.

About a week later a jeep pulled up outside the door and four police officers from Cuzco got out. One was carrying a typewriter. They were looking for Padre Cristobal. I invited them in. They were most courteous and polite.

"Are you the padre who complained about the *teniente* on election day?" asked one, introducing himself as the head of police in Cuzco.

"Yes," I said, "I'm Padre Cristobal."

"I believe he gave you some trouble by going into the church and forbidding you to say Mass."

"That's right!" I said, "but the *teniente* says that I am his best friend, the best friend he ever had." The police officer smiled. Then it dawned on me.

"Did the *teniente* know that you were coming today?" I asked.

"Yes," he replied, "we notified him last week that we were coming to investigate his conduct."

So now I knew the reason for the crate of beer and the kissing on the cheek. What a hypocrite! The Indians have a wonderful name for it in Quechua. They call it *iskay uya* (two faced).

I made a long statement about everything that had happened, while the police officer typed it out in detail with two fingers.

"We have a list of accusations a mile long against him," he said. "I thought Yauri might cure him."

As they left they expressed their deep regret for everything that had happened.

"He should never have entered the church with machine guns," they said. "He will be dealt with very severely."

Within a week the *teniente* was gone. The last I heard he was guarding a copper mine out in the mountains, somewhere near Santo Tomás.

Pablo came back to thank me on the night of the elections.

"Now that I am *alcalde*," he asked, "what am I supposed to do?"

"I'm sure you'll think of something," I replied, giving him a big hug.

☆   ☆   ☆

Stuck in the mud on the way to Cuzco

I hadn't slept a wink for about a week now with toothache. The altitude seemed to make it worse. As there was no dentist in Yauri I was hoping it would simply go away. Each day it got worse. There was an abscess inside my tooth, so gradually the side of my face was beginning to swell. There was nothing for it but to make the long journey to Cuzco. I set out with Des one afternoon in the midst of a downpour. I knew it was not wise to travel during the rainy season but it had to be done. The road was completely washed away in places, and where it did exist it was only visible as a river about two feet deep.

"We'll go by Yanaoca," suggested Des, as we came to the fork in the road above the lake at Langui. Des had been stationed in Yanaoca some years earlier so he knew the place well. It is much smaller than Yauri but has a beautiful church. There is a police station as you leave the town and they have a barrier across the road where all trucks are checked for contraband. This usually means that you bribe them beforehand and you sail through. The padre is normally waved through without checking but today was different. Four policemen surrounded the truck with their guns and ordered us into the police station. It was still raining heavily.

"Where are you going at this time of day?" demanded the chief behind the desk.

"We're on our way to Cuzco, to the dentist," said Des, pointing to my swollen jaw. The chief glanced in my direction without any sign of sympathy.

"Why don't you go to the dentist in Sicuani?" he asked.

"We've come from Yauri," explained Des, "it is shorter this way."

"Do you have luggage?" he asked.

"Yes," I replied, "I have a small case with my personal belongings."

"Bring in the case," he ordered, "it has to be examined."

I brought my case from the truck which the four policemen were still guarding.

"Open it up!" he demanded, as I returned drenched from the rain.

Rummaging through it he took out a shirt, trousers, underclothes, shaving gear, my little Sony radio, shoes and a couple of books. He picked up my Bible from which I had removed the red cover.

"What is this?" he asked.

"It's the Bible," I explained, pointing out the Book of Genesis.

He seemed disappointed when he didn't find anything.

"You must change the address on your resident permit," he said, handing it back to me. "It still has your address in Lima on it."

"Where do I get that done?" I asked.

"When you are in Cuzco you can go to the PIP (Policias de Investigación del Peru).

"*Muchas gracias, Señor*," we said, as we left.

"What was all that about?" I asked Des, as we drove off. "The *teniente* in Yauri must have been in touch with them."

"I don't think so," replied Des, "it was probably that speech that President Belaúnde gave in Lima last week."

"What was that?"

"He was speaking after the recent spate of terrorist attacks. He said that these terrorists could not possibly be Peruvians. They must be gringos who have come from outside Peru. And he added that he would not be surprised if some gringo priests were involved."

"So we are all under suspicion from now on," I thought.

We passed a large lake on the left.

"Plenty of fish there," remarked Des. "I used to fish a lot when I was in Yanaoca. That lake was formed after the earthquake."

"What earthquake?" I asked.

"About thirty years ago, almost all of Yanaoca was destroyed by an earthquake and many people were killed. The parish priest was interviewing a young lad for the priesthood in his house when the roof caved in. The boy was killed and the parish priest, who was Peruvian, was too frightened to tell the family. So he fled to Cuzco and didn't come back for months."

"The adobe huts must crumble like dust in an earthquake," I said.

"Yes, but they just remake them and build up the houses again. Yanaoca was completely rebuilt in a very short time," added Des.

We drove through Pampamarca with its beautiful church and little else.

"A casual visitor from Mars would be convinced that these people have great faith," I suggested.

"In their own way," replied Des, smiling. "There's a famous well over there in the *pampa*."

"What's it famous for," I asked, "besides water?"

"It's the only fresh water for miles. The *alcalde* of Pampamarca decided that he would do it up and put cement all around it so that it wouldn't get muddy in the rainy season. A short time after the job was done, the well dried up," recalled Des.

"The Indians thought that the *apu* of the well was annoyed with them for interfering with the well. The only way the *apu* can be appeased is by human sacrifice. Who would they choose to be sacrificed? In Inca times

Merchant woman *(centre)* with *campesino (left)* and *misti (right)*

Mothers openly breastfeeding their babies was a common sight

I was amused by how young men wore their *bultos* to attract the girls

Zorenayhua loved to carry her baby brother everywhere

Getting a good view of the dancing
in Oquebamba

My godchild, Geovanna, wearing
traditional Indian costume

I loved to watch the Indians dancing at fiesta time in their colourful costumes

A traditional Indian wedding I performed in Tortora alta

This typical *misti* wedding took place in Apachaco

Women mixing the straw and mud for Mariano to make the adobes

Mamitas sitting patiently with their produce on the way to Chalki

My first view of the lake and village at Langui

During the rainy season I found it more difficult to negotiate the mud tracks

Passing by an isolated graveyard on my way to Santo Tomás

It took me a long time to organise this orderly queue
for baptism at Mamani Huayta

The local band followed me everywhere I went

Babies viewed life from their
mother's back

Gathering for Mass at Huayhuawasi

Life on the *campo* as seen through the eyes of an Indian child

The husband who put down the bicycle and took up the cross for the camera

Crossing the *pura pampa* in my jeep

The procession of St Isidor around Chalki church

it would have been a young boy or girl. They all agreed on Toribio, the village idiot, who was a continual object of fun. One morning he was discovered at the well with his throat cut, his blood seeping slowly into the well. Within a week the water had returned."

By now we were descending the winding road to Combapata, around a series of hairpin bends. Des wrestled with the steering wheel as he pulled it from side to side. Suddenly we went straight for the edge of the cliff, stopping only at the last moment.

"Good God, the steering is gone!" shouted Des, looking out over the edge of the cliff. "We were lucky the brakes held."

"That was a narrow shave!" I breathed, trying to get my heart out of my mouth. We got out and surveyed the situation. The front wheels were only about a foot from the edge of the cliff.

"What do we do now?" I asked, as Des reversed the truck back slowly to the centre of the road. I took the tarpaulin from the back, placed it on the ground and crawled underneath the truck.

"It's the nut on the steering that's gone," I explained. "We must have lost it some time back. The bolt is also missing."

We looked around for something to tie it up. There was nothing to be found. All we had was a piece of rope which we tied around it.

"We will have to go very slowly," suggested Des, "and hope it holds."

We proceeded at a snail's pace.

"There is no priest in Combapata," remarked Des, the sweat streaming down his face, "but we will be alright if we can get to Checacupe. Rosendo might lend us his jeep and we could leave the truck there."

Rosendo was a Spanish Carmelite who was parish priest of Checacupe. It was late in the evening when we eventually reached the village. Rosendo gave us a great welcome and put us up for the night. With all the excitement I had almost forgotten that I had a toothache. The next morning we continued to Cuzco in Rosendo's jeep. We would fix the steering of our own truck on the way back.

In Cuzco we stayed with the Carmelite nuns near the church of San Blas. The church of San Blas is one of the tourist attractions in Cuzco, famous for its pulpit, a carved wooden masterpiece. It was created by an Indian artist and it is said that the skull on the upper part of the pulpit is that of the artist himself (probably held up by the preachers when preaching on death). Miniature figures of the Apostles and of the Virgin

Mary adorn this beautiful masterpiece. The pulpit is not used today but remains a relic of a another era. Opposite the church is the Carmelite convent where the sisters have one of the best known girls' schools in Cuzco.

Even in Cuzco the dentists are not the most modern in the world. I found one off the Plaza de San Francisco. His surgery was archaic. The drill that he used on my tooth made a loud whining noise as if powered by a diesel engine. When he eventually broke through a torrent of blood and pus flowed out. The relief was worth the pain. I had to return each day for a fortnight while he drained the tooth and capped it with a silver crown.

I woke up with a start. The church bell was ringing loudly, but it was still dark. I grabbed my flashlamp and looked at my watch. It was three o'clock in the morning. Sebastian must have gone mad, ringing the bell at this hour of the day. Perhaps there was a fire in the church. I jumped out of bed and rushed outside. Across the Plaza I saw children running to the church in little groups. At the door I met Isabel and Mercedes and a couple of the other catechists.

"What's up?" I asked. "Is there something wrong?"

"*Allillanchu, Papay*," said Mercedes, "No, everything is alright."

"Why is Sebastian ringing the bell at this hour of the morning and where are all the children going?" I asked.

"*Catechismo*," answered Isabel. "We teach the children catechism each morning during Lent." I then remembered it was Ash Wednesday.

"At this hour of the morning?" I asked in surprise.

"We teach the children for forty days from four o'clock to six o'clock each morning," she replied.

There were now hundreds of children gathered in the church, girls with babies on their backs and boys up to sixteen years of age. They were all divided up into different groups, a catechist taking each group. The smaller ones began to sing hymns and recite the 'Our Father' and 'Hail Mary' out loud. The older ones were listening to stories from the Bible. All seemed very eager to learn.

Simple expressions of faith

Each evening of Lent there was rosary and a sermon at seven o'clock. I said the Rosary in Spanish and gave a little talk on each Mystery. The people loved to hear the simple stories about the life of Jesus and Mary. They looked up in awe and listened with rapt attention. Even the old *mamitas* sitting on the floor who didn't understand a word, sat passively without an expression on their faces. Esther was sobbing away as I described the Agony in the Garden.

Des warned me that I had seen nothing until I had experienced Holy Week in Yauri. The whole town takes part, even those who never come to church during the rest of the year. Weeks before, they come to clean the church. The statue of every Saint is taken from its casket and prepared for the processions. There is a different procession each day of Holy Week and a different family is responsible for each procession. Christ on the Cross is taken out and repainted. A new crown of thorns is placed on his head. Every rib on his body is clearly visible. There is blood pouring down his face and side, painted in graphic detail. A new loincloth is put around his waist, with the name of the family who donated it embroidered in bold letters on the side. The solid silver frontispiece of the altar is taken down and polished until it shines. I noticed that all this important work is reserved for the rich people of the town. The poor Indians are left very much in the background. There is no way they could afford the expenses of Holy Week.

The week begins with the re-enactment of Christ's triumphal entry into Jerusalem on Palm Sunday. 'Christ' rides around the Plaza on a donkey with all the people singing and shouting;

"Hosanna to the Son of David,

Blessed is He who comes in the Name of the Lord."

Of course there are no palms, the people wave *pampa* grass and anything else they can find.

The biggest procession of the week takes place on Monday afternoon at four o'clock. It is the procession of Our Lord of the Earthquakes around the town. Christ on the Cross is carried shoulder high by about fifty men with regular stops at intervals along the way where extracts from the Passion are read. Large quantities of flower petals have been brought from Arequipa. Men carry long poles with little baskets attached to the end and shower the petals on the head of 'Christ'. Everyone scrambles to catch a petal as it falls to the ground. They are like gold dust and it is pathetic to see men, women and children fighting with one another for a petal that has touched the head of Our Lord of the Earthquakes. Every family wants the procession to stop outside their house, no doubt in the belief that they will be protected from earthquakes during the coming year. The procession takes four or five hours to complete its journey around the town.

On Tuesday it is the turn of St John the Evangelist and St Veronica to make a tour of the town. Wednesday it is Jesus of Nazareth. The Last Supper is celebrated at four o'clock on Holy Thursday. Pablo, in his new role as major, and all the other town dignitaries take their place around the altar. I wash the feet of twelve people chosen at random from the congregation, six men and six women. Although the washing is meant to be symbolic, some of the feet haven't been washed for years. As I pour the water on one old Indian's foot, he looked down at me and said;

"*Papay*, you could do with a bit of 'Ace' (washing powder)."

Looking down the church during the Mass I could see a group at the back preparing the cross for Good Friday. It was as though they couldn't wait to get to the gory part. Holy Thursday didn't have enough blood and thunder for their liking. The adoration of the Blessed Sacrament continued right through the night. The altar was beautifully decorated with flowers, candles and coloured lights. The church was crowded and the choir sang hymns in Spanish and Quechua.

164

On Good Friday there is the custom of preaching the 'seven last words' or utterances from the Cross. Seven important people from the town are chosen for each 'word'. It is considered a privilege to be chosen, so naturally no Indian is given a chance. The priest doesn't choose the preachers, these are selected by the landowners. One of the people chosen was the leader of the Seven Day Adventists. He arrived with his own choir all dressed in beautiful blue cloaks. As he began to preach loudly with 'fire and brimstone', there was a loud clap of thunder and the hailstones made an eerie noise on the corrugated roof of the church. It was as though the Angel Gabriel had sounded his trumpet for the end of the world.

But the last 'word' was to be the greatest shock of all. Julio Velazques, the *economo* in Yauri, got up to speak. It was he who brought crates of beer to the police the night they tortured and killed the youths after the election rally. He always carried a pistol by his side as he rode around his territory on a motorbike. "To protect me from dogs," he would say, but rumour had it that he wasn't beyond shooting an Indian or two if the need arose. Julio was of pure Spanish descent. He didn't have a drop of Indian blood in him. Of course it was well known that he abused Indian women. Although he was always outwardly polite, he detested the gringo priests and he was working behind the scenes to get rid of them.

"Father, forgive them for they know not what they do," were his chosen 'word'. He began in a quiet solemn tone but the volume rose as he reached the punch line.

"My dear people of Yauri, today we are commemorating the death of Our Lord and Saviour, Jesus Christ. We have come here with deep faith to give him homage and thanks for all he did for us. He has given us life and everything we have in this world. He has given us the sun, moon, and the stars to give us light and warmth and he has also given us land to produce food and animals so that we might live. He has created people differently, some are white and others are black or brown. Some people are more intelligent than others. Some are created to rule and others are created to serve. The important thing is to know your place in this world."

"We have also come here today to ask forgiveness of our Saviour for all our sins. Rich people can commit sins as well as poor people. You remember how it says in the gospel that it was Judas Iscariot who

165

betrayed Jesus for thirty pieces of silver. Well, I want to tell you today that it wasn't Judas who committed the greatest sin. Oh no, it was really Peter who betrayed his master. He denied he knew him three times. And it is the successors of Peter that are betraying Jesus in the world today, from the bishops right down to the priests of the parish."

I looked over at Des and he just raised his eyes to heaven. There and then we resolved that there would be no more bogus preachers on Good Friday. This was the last straw. Next year we would have the Stations of the Cross.

After the Good Friday ceremonies, the figure of Jesus Christ is taken down from the Cross and is carried in a glass casket around the town. The people follow in great distress, crying and sobbing. It is extraordinary how the people treat the statues and images as if they were really human, and they can express all the human emotions as though they were witnessing the death and burial of a loved one.

The figure of Jesus Christ is depicted in a very graphic and cruel way. The crown of thorns is pressed deeply into His forehead with blood streaming down His face. Each rib can be counted as they protrude from His body and the deep wound in His side is oozing blood. The expression on His face is of excruciating agony.

"Why is it all so bloody?" I asked Des, as we returned to the church.

"Life is bloodier here," he answered. "You have to understand how it was when Christianity first came to Peru. There was so much blood and violence and suffering about, that in order to believe that Christ suffered more than they did, they had to see it. Otherwise it would have no meaning for them."

"Did the Incas put people to death?" I asked.

"They certainly did. Normally they were a very peace-loving people but when anyone broke the law, the punishment was severe. They buried people alive, they clubbed them to death, they staked them to the ground and left them to die in the sun, they dropped heavy stones on them from cliffs. Virgins who broke their virginity were strung up by their hair and left to die. They sacrificed young children on the top of high mountains. In Machu Picchu you can still see the place of the tortures."

"What happens now?" I asked, as the casket was brought back into the church.

166

"Wait until you see what happens next," answered Des, with a smile.

The casket was placed on a table in front of the altar. Julio Velazques was directing operations. The figure of Jesus was carefully taken out and placed on another table. Julio approached with a large jar of olive oil and proceeded to pour it over the body, wiping it with wads of cotton wool. Then there was a mad rush by the poor Indians up to the altar, begging Julio to give them a little piece of the cotton wool that had touched the 'body' of Jesus. They returned, wiping their faces with their prized possession. To me it was a very subtle manipulation of sacred things by the *hacendados* to dispense favours to the poor Indians.

"That's the end of Holy Week for the rich," commented Des wryly, as we walked back to the house.

"What do you mean?"

"Once they have crucified and buried Jesus they don't come again. From now on the Indians take over. They celebrate the Resurrection."

And so it was. The Paschal vigil was a beautiful ceremony. The Indians seemed to come into their own when there was anything to do with light. They all gathered outside the church for the lighting of the Paschal fire. Each one lit their candle as we entered the Church singing 'Light of Christ'.

The Paschal candle was carried to the sanctuary where it was placed on a high pedestal. Des sang the 'Exultet' in Quechua to the air of a haunting Indian tune. I baptised six little Indian children with their parents and *padrinos* gathered on the altar. But the most beautiful part was yet to come. Everyone waited in the church for the Mass at sunrise at four o'clock. After the Mass there was a procession of the Blessed Sacrament around the Plaza. Just as we emerged from the church, the sun was rising from behind the distant hills, casting its rays on the tin-roofed huts of the town. The silver monstrance sparkled in the light. Trinidad looked up at me and gave a toothless smile. Christ had risen, indeed, Alleluia! Never had the sequence of the Mass for Easter Sunday carried more meaning for me.

> I saw Christ's glory as He rose!
> The angels there attesting;
> Shroud with grave-clothes resting
> Christ, my hope, has risen.
> He goes before you.

During the month of May the Resurrection would continue to be celebrated in every community during the fiesta of the *Santisima Cruz*. Each community has its cross which is a symbol not of the Crucifixion but of the Resurrection. The Cross is a symbol of life not death. Christ is not present on the cross . . . "He is risen, He is not here." The Cross is draped with the cloths that covered his body and a garland of flowers as a symbol of triumph and joy. Often the cross is carried to the church in Yauri to be blessed and then brought back to be put in a place of honour in the community until the following year. These poor Indians have learned the essential message of the cross which is that death is not the last word of history, life is the last word.

☆　　　☆　　　☆

The local radio station was broadcasting some sombre news. A 'storm' was forecast for later in the afternoon.

"Padre Victor Ramos has been driven out of the Parish of Langui," said the radio announcer with a certain tone of satisfaction in his voice. All the radio stations and newspapers in Peru are controlled by the rich and they are blatantly used as a propaganda machine on their own behalf. The only problem is that the Indians are inclined to believe everything they hear over the radio. The announcement continued;

"He was caught stealing the silver from the church so the people have locked the church and are guarding it night and day. Padre Ramos escaped to Sicuani where it is believed he is being sheltered by the bishop. We are not surprised that he stole from the church because he is from Bolivia where all the robbers come from. He is not one of our own. He is not a Peruvian."

After this they played solemn music as if someone had died.

It was Benigno who told me to listen in. "They are broadcasting it all morning," he said, "It must be true."

I smiled to myself. I knew Padre Ramos well. He *is* a Peruvian, born in Chiclayo to the north. He is a Salesian priest and had ministered in the prelature for many years. I knew there was no way he would steal from the church. Some of the *hacendados* didn't want him working with the Indians. This 'theft' was an age-old tactic used by the landowners to get rid of the priest.

Olga, the nurse from Liechtenstein who had looked after me when I arrived in Sicuani, was working in Langui with Padre Ramos. She escaped with another nun to Sicuani. She had her truck parked in the church grounds in Langui and this was also confiscated. This nearly caused an international incident as the Swiss embassy in Lima made a complaint to the President and asked that the truck be returned immediately.

The bishop and Padre Ramos called a press conference in Sicuani for the radio and newspapers. There are no newspapers in Yauri and there is a very limited distribution in Sicuani and Cuzco. Again people are inclined to believe everything they read in the papers. As the bishop spoke about the honesty and good character of Padre Ramos, some of the people in the audience heckled.

Padre Ramos held up his Peruvian passport and showed them his birth certificate.

"How do we know they are not forged?" asked one radio commentator.

(All official documents can easily be forged in Peru. Even when you go for a driving licence there are people at the door selling forged driving licences. All they have to do is add your name and photograph. It is the same with passports and any other document you might need.)

The bishop suggested that Padre Ramos should visit Langui and talk to the people. When they arrived in the village a large crowd had gathered in the Plaza. The mood was hostile and the police had to restrain the crowd. They had broken into the priest's house and stolen most of his belongings. These were openly displayed to the people. They had also stolen the nun's clothes from next door. Holding up her underclothes to the crowd, they shouted;

"Look at the kind of knickers that nuns wear!" Everybody laughed.

The bishop tried to explain to the mob that they were very lucky to have a priest like Padre Ramos. There was loud jeering at the mention of his name.

"If you don't want Padre Ramos, I have no other priest to give you," the bishop explained.

Some began to shout, "We don't want a priest, we don't want a priest."

The agitators got their way and the parish of Langui was without a priest after that. Although there were Indians in the Plaza who were forced to attend, none of them said anything. It would have been more than their life was worth.

Rumours began to reach Yauri that the next ones to be forced out were the gringo priests.

"They say they will get you when you say Mass in the Plaza for the anniversary of Espinar," warned Benigno.

We informed Tiny of what we had heard and he alerted the authorities. Early on the morning of the Mass a jeep arrived from Sicuani with a group of undercover police from the PIP. Although they were dressed in civilian clothes, the back of the jeep was packed with machine guns and tear gas launchers.

"What do you want us to do?" asked the officer in charge. "The bishop told us you were in danger."

I felt like saying that I didn't want them to do anything but now that they were here I supposed we had better avail of their protection.

"I think you should remain in the background," I replied, "so as not to alarm the people."

"We are here to do a job," he answered. "We have to take all the necessary precautions."

"Perhaps you could man the bridges at the entrance to the town and inspect all the trucks as they arrive," I suggested.

"Certainly," he said, detailing one man in each direction.

"There are only four entrances to the Plaza," I explained, "one at each corner."

The Mass was to be celebrated in the open air on a platform in front of the church door.

"We will also have a man under the altar and if anything happens, you should retire immediately to the church and we will deal with it," the officer declared.

I know how they deal with things, I thought – shoot first and ask questions afterwards!

The Plaza was packed with people for the Mass. No doubt many had heard the rumours and were waiting for something to happen. Little did they realise that they were surrounded by police, armed to the teeth. I had an uneasy feeling all through the Mass, knowing that there was a policeman at my feet under the altar. Little did I realise when I was ordained a priest that I would ever have to say Mass protected by machine guns.

All went peacefully and nothing happened. Back in the parish house I breathed a sigh of relief.

Shortly after this I was due to return home on my first holiday. It was now just two years since I had left Ireland and I was anxious to see my mother again. Des drove me to Cuzco where I would catch the plane for Lima. While we were having a meal together he dropped a bombshell.

"I won't be here when you get back," he said.

"What!" I exclaimed, in disbelief. I knew he hadn't been himself for the past few months but I didn't expect this.

"I'm leaving the priesthood," he continued, "and I hope to get married. I'm not leaving Peru, but I'll be leaving the mountains. I'm going to live in Lima."

When I had recovered from the shock, I wished him well and thanked him for all the invaluable help he had given me since I came to Yauri. It was a sad farewell. Storm clouds were gathering over the Andes and now I would have to weather the storm alone.

9

Guerrilla War in the Andes

There are no drums in Yauri yet the news of my return from Ireland spread like wildfire. 'The padre is back . . . Padre Cristobal has returned.' The first to greet me as I entered the great wooden door was Kimichu. He almost knocked me down with excitement. It was just as well that I had remembered to bring him a bone from Sicuani. The door of my room was locked and I couldn't find the key. Melchor helped me to break open the lock only to find the keys lying on the table inside. Esther came running with a gift of yet more gloves while Trinidad wasn't far behind with her offering of an old hen in a bucket, cooked feathers and all.

"Now we are Christians again, our *Papay* has come back," she exclaimed as she gave me a big hug.

Geovanna arrived with her sister Marisol. Marisol had lost two of her front teeth.

"Look at Marisol!" said Geovanna, as she jumped into my arms, "she is an old grandmother." I felt I had forgotten all my Spanish and found it difficult to speak for a while, but with Geovanna there was never any need for words as she always knew what I was thinking. She was very excited, trying to tell me all the news at once. She had been in charge of the rabbits while I was away and she was quick to tell me that their numbers had increased tenfold in my absence.

"Come and see," she said excitedly, as she took me by the hand to the rabbit hutch. She had given each one a name.

"That's Blackie, Snowy, Long Ears, Hoppy, Puma, Spotty . . . and the little gringo rabbit at the back we call 'Cristobal'," she said, smiling. It was pure white.

"Since the rains stopped it is difficult to get food for them," explained Marisol. "Melchor sowed some alfalfa in the *chacra* but it must be watered every day."

Geovanna and Marisol in their school uniforms

By now many other children had come to say 'Hello'. Benigno put up a net and they began to play volleyball. I couldn't join in as I was still trying to acclimatise to the altitude. My head was light and I began to feel dizzy. Geovanna helped me to unpack my cases. She was delighted with the little presents that the children in Ireland had given me for her. The one thing she had wanted more than anything else was a pair of pink shoes. It was the last thing she said before I left.

"Don't forget my *zapatos rosados*."

I wasn't sure where I could get pink shoes, but when I mentioned it at a Mass while at home in Ireland, a shoe-shop owner who was present that morning told me that he had a pair and as there was no demand for them he would be delighted to donate them to Geovanna.

"*Zapatos rosados!*" she exclaimed, as she took them from the box. The fact that they were about two sizes too big didn't matter at all. In a place where there are no shoes, the size is irrelevant.

They say that the first trip home from the missions is the best and I would certainly agree with that. It is like experiencing the old familiar things for the first time. The simple things that we normally take for granted, like flowers, trees and walking on lush green grass. After the hard barren ground of Yauri it was like walking on air. Going into a supermarket back in Ireland was a culture shock – shelf after shelf of all kinds of food. I was completely disorientated, trying to choose between this and that. It was much easier when everything came out of the big brown pot.

Visiting friends in their lovely luxurious homes felt strange.

"Please excuse the mess, I didn't get around to the hoovering yet. I'm so busy. Can you find a place to sit down?" . . . as I was offered a comfortable chair.

"You must find it strange walking on carpet again?" remarked a friend as I entered the house, imagining that I might not want to walk on carpet after living in such primitive conditions.

"No," I replied, "I really like walking on carpets. I appreciate them much more now."

When you enter an Indian hut there is no fuss. The floor is just the clay earth. Everything is chaos. There are no chairs to sit on and they would never dream of saying, 'Please excuse the mess'. They don't know what 'being tidy' means. Yet they make you feel very welcome.

"Everyone in your country is a millionaire," suggested Geovanna once, when I spoke about Ireland.

My mother was living in a nursing home in Wicklow. Over the last year she had become very forgetful and absent-minded. Late one night she had been discovered walking through the town with her dog. I was afraid that she might not recognise me when I visited, but I need not have worried. As I entered the room she looked up and said with her old familiar smile;

"You got back . . . I knew you would come."

I visited her every day and even though we talked about the same things each time, she seemed very happy and contented. I said Mass in the ward and she could follow it perfectly, making all the right responses. It had become second nature to her. She said the rosary constantly. I hadn't the heart to tell her I was leaving again but she knew much more than I realised. The day before I left she remarked;

"I'm sure you will soon be going back to that strange country with those strange people."

"Soon," I replied.

No community ever forgets its fiesta. If I can't get there on the day, they will wait, they will never forget. So after returning to the mountains, I found myself celebrating the Feast of the Assumption in the middle of October instead of August. Some communities like to bunch a lot of feasts together. One of these is Chaquilla, situated near Negro Mayo at the furthest end of the province. They celebrate the feast of the Exultation of the Holy Cross, Our Lady of All Graces, Our Lady of Sorrows and Our Lady of Mercies as well as the Souls of the Faithful Departed, all on the one day. It took Benigno and me over five hours to get there. It is south of Tocroyoc and Ocururo on the road to Arequipa. The road through the *pampa* had now turned to dust. Luckily the people of Ocururo didn't know I was coming so they hadn't blocked the road in their eagerness to meet me. As I passed through the town I noticed that they hadn't advanced much with the building of the new church since I had visited with Des on the way to Negro Mayo.

"Turn left here," said Benigno as we drove out of the town. "We have to cross that mountain and go through the next valley."

Along the way we passed great herds of llamas and alpacas as well as cattle and sheep.

"This is Nestor Alverez's hacienda," said Benigno. "He lives most of the time in Arequipa, but he also has a house in Yauri. He refused to divide up his hacienda during the reform."

As we descended into the valley I could see steam rising from the river.

"Where's the steam coming from?" I asked Benigno.

"Hot springs," he explained. "There are lots of hot springs around here. We can wash in the hot water."

As we approached the river it was bubbling and there was a strong smell of sulphur from it.

"It never changes, the whole year round. Even when the snow comes the water keeps bubbling," added Benigno.

I stopped the truck and took off my boots and socks. As I put my toe in the river the water was boiling hot.

"We will go down further," advised Benigno, "the water gets cooler further down."

"What happens to the fish?" I asked.

"There are no fish," laughed Benigno, "even the animals don't drink this water."

"I hope we survive," I replied, as we soaked our feet in the warm water.

Waiting for the padre

At last we reached the little mountain chapel of Chaquilla. Hundreds of people had gathered and were scattered around in little groups. I soon realised that each feast had its own devotees. The 'Holy Souls' group couldn't mix with 'Our Lady of all Graces' group. Each had its own *major domo* (leader) and its own particular intention for their Mass.

"Each group wants a separate Mass," explained Benigno, "they don't want the *almas* (souls) mixed up with Our Lady."

The custom in olden times was that the Peruvian priest would say up to ten Masses in succession as long as the people paid. They thought I would do the same.

"Benigno, could you explain to them that Jesus Christ died on the cross on Calvary once. Through his death He saved all mankind. The Mass is the Passion, Death and Resurrection of Jesus Christ. Everyone shares in the one Mass."

"Could you say that again?" he asked with a puzzled look on his face.

176

I tried to explain again. However at the end of all Benigno's translations the crowd came back with the same request.

"But couldn't you say the Masses?"

I didn't blame the people for not understanding the theology of the Mass but there was no way I was going to say ten Masses in succession. Instead I read the gospel references to Our Lady and spoke about the Holy Souls and everyone was happy in the end. Needless to say, there were numerous baptisms afterwards.

"Two of Nestor Alverez's *major domos* were standing at the back during the Mass," remarked Benigno on the way home. "They were the ones wearing big leather boots."

"What were they doing?" I asked.

"Taking notes," he replied.

Hardly a day goes by without news of more guerrilla attacks in the mountains of Peru. Few people took the guerrillas seriously when they began their armed struggle with that first attack on the polling station in Chuschi. However, six months later some residents in Lima were shocked to wake up one morning and see dogs hanging from lampposts and posters praising the Gang of Four in China.

This was only the beginning. Soon the name *Sendero Luminoso* was on everybody's lips. They were called *Senderistas* for short and they were synonymous with terror. Their main activities were centred around a place called Ayacucho, in the mountains on the way from Lima to Cuzco, where they had their origins. Ayacucho in Quechua means 'corner of the dead' and it was soon to live up to its name.

It seemed an unlikely place for a revolution to begin. A town of about 70,000 people high up in the Andes, it had been neglected for centuries by the central government in Lima. Every Peruvian knows where Ayacucho is because it was here that the last great battle for independence took place. The Venezuelan General, Antonio José de Sucre defeated the royalist forces loyal to Spain at the battle of Ayacucho in 1824. Now, over one hundred and fifty years later, while the government was neglecting Ayacucho, the *Sendero Luminoso* were sowing the seeds for another revolution.

It all began in the National University of San Cristobal in Ayacucho.

This university educated the Indians from the surrounding communities and specialised in subjects that would benefit the local community, such as teaching, nursing, and rural engineering. Students spoke Quechua and they did their work experience in isolated communities, where it was hoped they would return after graduation. The university became the cradle for the birth of leftist organisations. They were inspired by Fidel Castro's victory in Cuba and Che Guevara's attempts to start a popular revolution in Bolivia. The greatest impact came from the Sino-Soviet split in 1964. Peru's Communist Party had broken up into several factions: pro-Soviet, pro-Albanian, pro-Chinese. The pro-Chinese faction in Ayacucho was led by a university professor, Abimael Guzman Reynoso.

There were two main events which underlined the power and support that the *Senderistas* had in the Ayacucho area. The first occurred when they took over the city of Ayacucho for a night and attacked the prison, releasing over 300 prisoners, most of them *Senderistas*. Just before midnight four groups of armed men had entered the city. The first group surrounded the headquarters of the Civil Guard, the second surrounded the PIP, the third made for the Republican Guard Headquarters while the main group surrounded and attacked the prison. Their main weapon was dynamite which they stole from the mines. As the main door of the prison was blown open, other guerrillas cut all electricity to the city. When the alarms went off the police rushed out of their various headquarters, only to be met with a hail of bullets. They quickly retreated inside. Another group entered the prison from the rear, using ropes and ladders. Within half an hour the whole operation was over and the prisoners freed. They sang their anthems and raised their red flag. Seven of the freed prisoners were women, among whom was the guerrilla leader, Edith Lagos. They quickly stole all the weapons they could find and vanished into the darkness of the night.

Two policemen lost their lives and eight others were wounded. Among the guerrillas, between attackers and prisoners, ten men died. One hundred and fifty guerrillas took part in the operation. This daring attack on the prison in Ayacucho stirred public opinion all over Peru. One newspaper in Lima reporting on the event commented, "After this, anything is possible". But the newspapers also reported an incident which happened half an hour after the attack and which was to gain the guerrillas much sympathy. A group of uniformed Republican Guards dragged three seriously wounded *Senderistas* from their hospital beds in Ayacucho and shot them in the back.

The second event that surprised the nation occurred when a huge crowd of 15,000 lined the streets of Ayacucho for the funeral procession of Edith Lagos. Shortly after her escape from prison she had been captured and tortured to death. She was just nineteen years old. Through the heavy-handed reaction of the army and the police, and the cruel murder of this young woman, the terrorists were winning the support of the people. The president continued to make statements saying that *Sendero Luminoso* were part of a 'foreign conspiracy' which included Amnesty International, the foreign press and the drug mafia, who were trying to corrupt the 'traditionally peaceful' Peruvian Indian.

Sendero Luminoso made few public statements, but early on in their campaign they did go so far as to describe Belaúnde as 'a fascist dictator whose government was serving the development of bureaucratic capitalism in the country, that is, the capitalism of the great landlords, the great bankers, who under the command of imperialism, especially North American, were oppressing and wounding our people.'

A large contingent of the army was sent to Ayacucho but they soon realised they had an impossible task. As one army general put it; "One doesn't know who they are and where they are, since they have the same characteristics as the people of the sierra. For the police to be successful, they would have to start killing *Senderistas* and non-*Senderistas*. They kill sixty people, and at best there are three *Senderistas*, but of course the police will say that the sixty were all *Senderistas*."

Sendero Luminoso did not confront the army head-on but opted for a tactical retreat into the surrounding communities. The military became more and more frustrated trying to confront an enemy they couldn't identify. Soon the army put into operation the strategy forecast by the army general and hundreds of Indians were killed in raids on remote communities in the mountains. The victims were described in terse military communiques as "*Senderistas* killed in clashes" or as "Indians massacred by *Sendero*". Few prisoners were taken in these 'clashes', the dead were not named, nor were their bodies produced. The army explained this by saying; "We don't have to identify dead *Senderistas*."

The army was being advised by experts from the United States, Israel and Argentina. Peruvian officers were trained in 'non-conventional' warfare in the US and Argentinian police officers were reported to have visited Ayacucho. It is not surprising then that 'disappearances' were daily occurrences as they had been in Argentina under the military junta in that country. Many of those who 'disappeared' were taken from their homes by security forces and most were never seen again. Sometimes their decomposing bodies were discovered on the roadside or in ravines on the outskirts of Ayacucho. As the security forces concentrated on Ayacucho and its surrounding villages, *Sendero Luminoso* stepped up its action in other areas of the country, especially in the capital, Lima.

Their favourite tactic was to blow up electricity pylons and plunge Lima into darkness. They also attacked factories and government buildings. The press, radio and television were hampered by both sides in their reporting of the war. The government and the army fed them a continuous stream of one-sided false information while the guerrillas remained silent and wouldn't talk to anyone. The work of the media was further hindered by the murder of eight journalists in Uchuraccay.

The eight journalists had set out by minibus from Ayacucho for the Indian village of Huaychao more than 12,000 feet up in the Andes. The army had reported that three days earlier this little community had killed seven terrorists with 'courage and virility'. President Belaúnde had joined in the praise of this 'gallant' act of the people. It was said that it was the first time that a community had turned against *Sendero Luminoso*. The journalists wanted to investigate if the killers were indeed the members of the community, and if the victims were *Senderistas*. Later investigations established that three of the 'dead guerrillas' were school children playing truant from school.

After a two-hour bus journey the journalists began an eight-hour walk up the steep mountainside to Huaychao, stopping at Uchuraccay along the way. Although they could communicate in Quechua and carried no weapons, they were violently battered to death with stones and axes. Their mutilated bodies were buried in pairs, naked and face down in shallow graves outside the community boundary. Their corpses were later discovered by a mixed patrol of army and police.

After a national outcry, Belaúnde set up a commission, headed by novelist Mario Vargas Llosa, to investigate the killings. The commission arrived at the "absolute conviction that the killings were the work of the villagers of Uchuraccay." Nobody has ever been tried for the murders. The judicial authorities in charge of the case said that the security forces did not co-operate with the investigation. The investigating judge concluded that for the community to have acted "in such a cruel and horrendous manner it must be thought that it was incited by the police". Many people suspect there was a cover-up. From then on the military forces were able to control information coming from the rural areas around Ayacucho.

Benigno didn't like the police since the day he saw them open fire on the crowd on the day Hugo Blanco was to come to Yauri. He thought the guerrillas were great – "they would put the police in their place." He loved listening to their exploits on the radio.

"Lima is blacked out again!" he would say, as he arrived in the morning. "Now they know what it's like to live in Yauri."

The terrorists hadn't arrived in Yauri yet but people were seeing them everywhere and everyone was under suspicion. Whenever anything was stolen or an accident occurred, it was blamed on *Sendero Luminoso*. They called them *terucas* (Spanish slang for 'terrorists'). The valuable copper mine in Tintaya took on extra protection and a detachment of police was stationed there permanently. No one could get in or out without a pass. At the time they were building giant pylons to bring the electricity to the mine from Machu Picchu.

"The *terucas* will have great fun knocking them down," suggested Benigno as we passed by one day.

I contacted the director of the Tintaya mine who lived in Lima and asked him about the possibility of continuing the pylons to Yauri so that we could all have electricity. I pointed out that the people would be more inclined to protect the pylons if they were getting some benefit from them. (After all, the mining company was stealing all the Indians' copper.) He gave me the predictable answer. He would think about it.

One day the president of the community of Corporaque arrived with a delegation.

"*Papay*, we would like you to come and celebrate a big fiesta in Corporaque. A great honour has been bestowed on us. The new sub-prefect for the whole province of Espinar, Victor Soto, is from our town.

He would like to receive a blessing during the Mass so that he will carry out his duties according to God's will."

"Victor Soto is a big *hacendado*," explained Benigno, as we crossed the bridge at Santo Domingo on our way to Corporaque. "He owns most of the land around the town. He probably bribed the authorities so that he would be made sub-prefect. It gives him more prestige."

"He has two sons who are teachers," continued Benigno. "They say that one of them killed an Indian last year by throwing him off the bridge in Apachaco."

"Is he in jail?" I asked.

"Rich people don't go to jail," he replied, smiling. "He was questioned in the police station for a whole day but no charges were brought against him. Most likely he bribed them."

"What's Victor Soto like?" I enquired, innocently.

"He is a big fat man who is always drunk. He is not very friendly."

"Will he be a good sub-prefect?" I asked, knowing that Benigno wasn't very interested in sub-prefects.

"Sub-prefects don't do any good," he responded.

Corporaque is not very far from Yauri as the crow flies, but it's a long way around by road.

"You can cross the river here," suggested Benigno, "it's much shorter. The bridge farther on is only used in the rainy season. It was built nearly two hundred years ago by a parish priest of Corporaque, Sebastian de la Poliza, a Spaniard. His name is still on the bridge."

We splashed through the river without any difficulty. You could even walk across, the water was so shallow. Up until 1917 when Yauri became capital of the province, all the villages surrounding Corporaque were still run on the *ayllu* system. This system of working as a community had been inherited from the time of the Incas and beyond. Some of these communities had come to this region as early as the thirteenth century when the Incas conquered the Aymaras and held on to their ancient customs and traditions. There was no such thing as private property; no buying or selling of land. All work was done in common and work was exchanged, not paid for. Then came the Spaniards who took vast areas of the best land and formed them into haciendas. The Indians worked as slaves on these haciendas for little more than their keep. Taxes had to be paid to the hacienda owner and to the state. These taxes were collected by a continuation of the old Inca system of *curacas*, which the Spanish called *caciques*. Later the Indians called them *mistis*.

The Church too had vast tracts of land. The State gave a portion of land to each parish for the support of the Church and the clergy. These became known as the 'haciendas of the church' and very often the parish priest had the biggest hacienda in the area. These haciendas got bigger and bigger as the church was given more land by wealthy Spanish families. Rather than let the land fall back into Indian hands it was willed to the church.

At one stage in the eighteenth century the parish priest of Corporaque owned all the surrounding land. He was a Spaniard called Vincente de la Puente. He was despised by the Indians for not only being a Spaniard but also a *hacendado*. When they could take it no longer they rose up against him. They attacked Corporaque by force. They first took the church tower to prevent the ringing of the bell. Then they advanced on the priest's house. In all such conflicts the women were the most hostile. An empty coffin was carried from the church to the parochial house where it was placed in front of the door. Crosses were placed in the Plaza. The people sang solemn songs. The hate that was generated towards the parish priest was intense. When he would not come out, two of the women entered the house and dragged him out. They tried to choke him with his priestly robes. The people beat him incessantly as they marched him to the prison. There they left him for dead, bathed in his own blood, his face beaten to pulp. It was said that he looked like a 'swollen monster'. The same fate befell his son. As they danced they sang an old Inca war song;

> We will drink chicha from the skull of the traitor,
> We will wear his teeth as a necklace,
> We will make flutes of his bones,
> And from his skin, a drum.
> Afterwards we'll dance.

The Indians had won the day but when the news eventually reached the bishop in Cuzco he excommunicated the whole town. The people of Corporaque still talk about their turbulent history.

So it was with a certain amount of fear and trepidation that I drove into the town. I made my way through a narrow street into the Plaza. The same church bell was pealing out its solemn tones, but at least now it was ringing out in peace, calling the people to celebrate. Already a large crowd had gathered in front of the church. On my right was the parochial house, a grim reminder of bygone days. There stood the door through which the women had dragged the unfortunate parish priest. Today the parochial house was locked up and empty. The last pastor to live there was the Peruvian priest, Julio César Mendoza, who was now serving in Velille with his family. He too had to leave in a hurry.

The church at Corporaque

The Plaza is dominated by a magnificent church, built by Sebastian de la Poliza, the same Spanish priest who built the bridge. All the money was donated by the greatest *hacendado* of his day and the last *curaca* of the region, Eugenio Sinanyuca. He co-operated with the parish priest in building the church. He was also the last Indian *curaca* in Peru. He was an Indian nobleman, but he despised his Indian origin. He was a captain in the colonial army and took the Spanish side during the Indian rebellion of 1780 led by Tupac Amaru II. It was because of this and his immense personal fortune that he remained as *curaca* for over thirty years. He imported mules from Argentina and carried on a thriving business bringing dried meat and coca to Cuzco. Just before his death he had renewed his herd of sixty-two mules. He also built a *beaterio* like the one in Yauri where Indian women came to live religious lives. This was to be his memorial. There are still *beatas* in Corporaque to this day.

As I reached the great door of the church one of the *beatas* was on her way in – a plump lady dressed in a long brown habit tied around her waist with a cord. On her head she wore a wide-rimmed sun hat. Just before she entered the church she squatted down on her hunkers and went to the toilet. Looking up she greeted me from that position!

Although the church was very dark inside I could see that the altar was adorned with silver and gold and there were some beautiful oil paintings on the walls. I was attracted to a magnificent painting of Our lady of Mount Carmel when out of the corner of my eye I saw a most extraordinary picture. It was Our Lady of the Milk and it depicted Our Lady with bare breasts! With her hands she was squeezing the milk from one of her breasts into the mouth of a young man at her feet. I had never seen anything like it before. I couldn't believe my eyes.

The extraordinary painting of Our Lady of the Milk

As I prepared to begin the Mass for the fiesta, I noticed that Victor Soto had not yet arrived. Just as I was about to start the Mass the president of the community came up and asked me if I would greet the sub-prefect at the door. As I reached the door of the church three men on horses came riding up. In the centre was Victor Soto mounted on a beautiful white horse. He was dressed in full military uniform from the Spanish colonial days, with a long sword in a silver scabbard by his side. One each side of him were his sons, also in uniform and riding dark chestnut horses. The Spanish viceroy could not have arrived with more pomp and ceremony. Victor dismounted awkwardly, extracting his foot from the stirrup with great difficulty. He almost tumbled over. It could have been a scene from Gilbert and Sullivan, but Victor and his sons were not acting and they certainly weren't singing. This was all very serious. The Indians had to be made aware of his authority and dignity. I sprinkled him with holy water as we entered the church. Three high chairs with kneelers were placed in front of the altar. Victor and his sons remained solemn and silent throughout the Mass. Afterwards he rode around the Plaza many times to the applause of all present, his silver sword sparkling in the sunlight. He had made his point. Benigno looked at me and smiled.

As I crossed the bridge at Santo Domingo on the way home, some men were standing in the centre of the road. At first glance they looked menacing.

"*Papay*, we have carried our mother from Pichigua. Will you come and see her?" asked one of them.

"Where is she?"

"Just over there beside the river," he replied.

I followed them along the bank of the river. There on a sandy patch was an old woman in a blanket. Beside her were two poles. With these they had made a stretcher and carried her across the mountains. I knelt down beside her and she looked up at me.

"*Papay*," she said feebly, "*hamunki* (you have come)."

I asked her sons to wait a little further downriver while I heard her confession. Then I anointed her. She grasped me with her two hands and said;

"*Gracias, Papay.*" She was perfectly happy and peaceful. I recalled another woman of long ago:

"Now, you can dismiss your servant in peace, O Lord, because my eyes have seen my salvation."

One of her sons took two eggs from his *bulto* and handed them to me. Although it pains me to take food from these poor people, they would be very offended if I refused.

"*Gracias*," I said, "where were you taking your mother?"

"To the church," he replied, "she wanted to see the priest. When we reached the bridge we heard you were in Corporaque. We knew you would have to pass this way. We waited here by the river."

As I drove away in my truck I glanced back. In the distance I could see them carrying her home across the mountains . . . to die.

☆   ☆   ☆

The rains haven't come yet and the ground is hard and dry. The slightest breeze raises a great dust storm. Everyone is talking about the *sequía* (drought). In an area where so much depends on the seasonal rain, it is disastrous when it doesn't come. I called a meeting of all the presidents of the communities in the parish centre. The reports were grim.

"In Tocroyoc nobody has sown any potatoes," complained Sergio. "In six months' time there will be nothing to eat."

"And there will be no seed for next year," added José from Apachaco.

"Maybe the rain will come next month," I suggested.

"No, when it hasn't come by December it won't come at all."

A *campesino's* 'kitchen' in the corner of a corral

It always amazed me how expert they were at forecasting the weather. Normally it's not too difficult. The sun is shining or it's raining. But they know exactly when it's going to rain. How often have I looked up into a clear blue sky and remarked;

"It will be a beautiful day today," only to be told, "it will be raining by late afternoon," and sure enough it was.

"Soon the rivers will run dry," said Felipe from Mullacahua, "and our water supply depends on the river."

"What about the sheep?" said Tomás from Urinsaya. "They will not survive without water. Many of them have died already in our community."

"The llamas and alpacas don't need water so much," added Miguel from Condoroma, "They eat the roots of the *ichu* and survive much longer than we can."

In Inca times provision was always made for the drought. They built great storehouses at intervals across the mountains and during the years of plenty these were filled with surplus food. No one ever went hungry when the rains didn't come. The Spanish could feed their army for months on the food they found in these storehouses. Now the Indians asked the church to help them. They knew the government would do nothing.

All the priests of the prelature met with Tiny in Sicuani to plan their strategy. The international aid organisation, Caritas, was willing to send a shipload of food for the Sicuani region under one condition: the food must be distributed through the parishes and not through government agencies. They had learned from sad experience that when the food was distributed by government agencies most of it disappeared or ended up on the black market. Tins of cooking oil and sacks of flour all marked 'Donated by the US. Not for resale', were openly on sale in the markets and shops in Cuzco.

Soon giant Volvo trucks arrived in Yauri with sacks of flour and tins of vegetable oil. These were distributed from the parish centre. The president of each community came with his committee and a list of all the families in his community. Llamas, alpacas and mules were loaded up and the distribution began. I loaded my truck and set out daily for distant communities. This was an emergency. It was a matter of life and death. The old and the young were the ones who suffered most. But

I soon realised that even the poor don't like receiving something for nothing. They want to preserve what little dignity they have left.

I started to think about how the Indians could help themselves and began to look for some projects in which they could use their various skills. I started a co-operative in the parish centre for buying and selling Indian products. One of the first things I noticed when I came to Yauri was the extraordinary skill which the Indians have in producing lovely coloured fabrics. They are experts at spinning and weaving. From recent excavations it has been learned that every method of textile weaving and decoration was known to the ancient Peruvians. Their weaving of finer fabrics has never been equalled from the point of view of skill. Along the coast they used cotton, but in the mountains there was an ample supply of the finest material in the wool from the llama and alpaca, not to mention the vicuña. For the non-expert it is impossible to distinguish between the fine wool of the alpaca and that of the vicuña. The wool of the llama is much coarser and is generally used for making blankets and the trousers that the Indian men wear. Linen and silk were unknown in Peru.

Although the men weave most of their own ponchos and clothes, the women do most of the spinning. They never seem to stop. A typical sight is a woman busily spinning as she runs along with a baby on her back. They use a drop spindle called a *ppuska* (*rueca* in Spanish), a stick with a piece of wood at the end of it to give it weight. Sometimes the children just put a potato at the end of a stick. With this they can spin the finest wool. Although I know nothing about spinning I was always amazed at their expertise. They showed me how they spin clockwise for a single ply and in the opposite direction for a double ply. They are also experts at dyeing the wool. The vegetable dyes come from the jungle and are sold in the market. They spread them out on the ground in tins in all the colours of the rainbow. They use their own urine to set the dye.

But the most ingenious of all is how they can produce the most beautiful patterns and designs out of their heads. Nothing is written down. For people who could neither read nor write, I found this astonishing. Whenever they made me a *chullo*, they always asked would I like my name woven into it.

"Write it down!" they would say. I wrote C R I S T O B A L. They just took one look at it and reproduced it perfectly.

(Top) Homespun shawls *(Middle)* Spinning wool *(Bottom)* Weaving on the loom

Knitting was unknown in ancient Peru but today the women are expert knitters. They usually knit a jumper a week for the co-operative. They never wash the wool before they knit it.

"It makes it too difficult to handle," they said.

So whenever I wore a new jumper, Kimichu took a particular interest in me, barking all the time. I suppose he thought I was an alpaca.

Another project I started was the setting up of a forge in the parish centre where the men could learn how to make things from metal. They were soon producing their own primitive implements for working in the fields. They also became experts at fixing their own bicycles. It soon became obvious to me that these people were not lacking in intelligence or physical skills. All they needed was a little help in putting their talents to good use.

Many of the young people were becoming idle in their communities with no work in the *chacras*. Some were talking of leaving to find work in Arequipa and Lima. I wondered what I could do to help. I decided to rebuild the high wall around the parish house. It was about three feet thick and twelve feet high. Made of adobes, it was over a hundred years old and was beginning to disintegrate. This would provide work for the next six months. Forty boys and girls came for a week at a time and stayed in the parish centre. The girls began making the adobes while the boys knocked down the wall and prepared the foundations. At the end of the week I gave them food and money for their families. Each community came in turn and they were reluctant to leave at the end of the week. In the evenings the boys played football while the girls joined the other girls of Yauri in a game of volleyball. All was going very well until one day there was a catastrophe.

"Padre Cristobal, come quickly," shouted Benigno as he ran towards me.

"What's the matter?" I asked, wondering what all the fuss was about.

"They have all gone," he replied, "they just ran away."

"What are you talking about?" I asked, "who ran away?"

"All the young people working on the wall," he said, "they are afraid."

"Afraid of what? What happened?"

"They dug up a corpse," he explained in a low voice, as if afraid to say it out loud. "Come and see."

I followed him down to where the boys had been digging.

191

"Over there," he said, pointing. "I'll stay here."

I walked over and looked into the foundation. There was a large earthenware pot partially uncovered, with a hole in the side of it. I took up the pick that had been hurriedly discarded and carefully picked the clay from around the pot. The clay pot which had been damaged by the blow fell apart to reveal a skull and some bones. There was also an earthenware bowl and a little statue covered in clay.

I cleaned the statue to discover it was made of silver. There were also some *chuños* and two husks of maize. This was obviously a very old burial ground. It was an ancient Inca custom to bury children and young people in a natal position in clay urns. I took the bones, together with the other objects up to my room for safe-keeping and radioed Tiny in Sicuani to tell him of my find. I suggested that he get in touch with the museum in Cuzco and ask them to send someone out. In the meantime no-one would come near my room.

"Where are you going to sleep tonight?" asked Benigno.

"In my room, of course, where else?"

"With the spirits?" he asked in disbelief.

Early next morning a jeep arrived from Cuzco with two archaeologists. I imagine they came quickly because they heard I was a gringo. They imagine gringos want to steal all their Inca treasures. I showed them what I had found and brought them to the spot. As they walked along they began to pick up little pieces of pottery.

"Very interesting," they remarked.

They dug all around the place where I had found the urn but discovered little else, apart from a few broken pieces of pottery. They spent two days digging and then declared that I could continue with my wall.

"The objects will be exhibited in the museum in Cuzco," they declared, "the skull and bones you can rebury."

About a month later they returned to tell me that this had been an ancient staging post for llama trains going to Bolivia, dating back long before the time of the Incas. I buried the skull and bones near where they were found and sprinkled the whole area with holy water. The spirits were appeased and work on the wall continued.

☆   ☆   ☆

It never ceases to amaze me the fear that people have of the dead. They seem to fear the spirits of the dead much more than the living. For months now Roxana and her eight-year-old daughter Isabel had been coming to the eleven o'clock Mass every Sunday. Roxana was a teacher out in the community of Oquebamba on the way to Santo Tomás. There were two Oquebambas in the parish, the other was on the way to Sicuani. Isabel was a beautiful little girl and she always ran up to the altar to give me a big hug at the kiss of peace. Every Sunday Roxana came to the sacristy with Isabel before the Mass and asked me to remember the souls of Oquebamba during the ceremony. November is the month of the Holy Souls but for Roxana it was the whole year around. I wondered where she got such devotion to the Holy Souls. One day when I went to celebrate a fiesta in Oquebamba I found out.

One evening when Isabel was just two years old, she went missing. Roxana searched for her everywhere. No one had seen her. The whole community joined in the search, but as darkness fell she still hadn't been found and was given up for dead. There was no way she could survive the freezing cold of the mountains. Next morning a young boy was leading his llamas out to pasture when he thought he heard a cry coming from the graveyard. In the distance he could see Isabel sitting by a grave. She was alive! The whole community was overjoyed, especially Roxana. One would imagine that she would want to thank the Holy Souls for looking after Isabel during the night, but Roxana was filled with a terrible fear that the souls had possessed Isabel and that they would do her harm. Hence the need for a remembrance at Mass every Sunday that the souls would not cast a spell on her daughter.

10

Under House Arrest

The church in Yauri is always locked and is only opened for Mass, baptisms and marriages. The priest never keeps the key. The church's treasures are recorded in an *inventario* and have to be guarded at all times by the *economo*. A person is selected by the people of the town for this position and is appointed by the bishop. The *economo* is usually chosen to serve for a period of three years but Julio Velazques has been in the position for the past ten years. (It was Julio who had denounced the priests during the Good Friday ceremonies.) Sebastian is the assistant *economo* and as well as sleeping in the church every night in case of robbery, he also keeps possession of the large and cumbersome keys.

Julio Velazques is by far the most influential *hacendado* in the whole province of Espinar. He owns three haciendas with large herds of llamas, alpacas and sheep, as well as herds of cattle in the lower valleys. Hundreds of Indian families live and work on his haciendas and are totally dependant on him. A few are happy with their lot, content that they have enough to eat and a mud hut to live in, but most despise him. He has a big house on each hacienda and another in Arequipa but he usually stays with his mother in his house behind the church in Yauri. Although he is almost forty years of age, he hasn't officially married, but recently he has been living with his godchild, Natividad, with whom he has had a child. Apart from the prestige and power that his wealth gives him, he also considers himself very religious.

"*Estoy muy Catholico*! (I am a very good Catholic!)" he would say. He goes on pilgrimage each year to the shrine of El Señor de Huanca just outside Cuzco run by the Mercedarian Fathers. They are frequent visitors to his haciendas where they say Mass. They usually return home to Cuzco with a truckload of sheep or cattle as an offering to El Señor de Huanca. Julio is *padrino* to almost all the children born on his haciendas. He would consider it an insult not to be asked. Like many *hacendados*

Julio resisted the agrarian reform of President Velasco and distributed very little of his land among the Indians, in defiance of the law.

It is difficult for law and order to penetrate into the Andes. There were many land 'occupations' which were ruthlessly put down with the help of the police and many Indians were killed. What little land Julio did lose he is now in the process of recovering through the courts. Whoever pays the biggest bribe wins the case. Most of the judges and lawyers are from the hacienda class. The bishop has set up an office in Sicuani where all poor Indians can receive free legal aid and advice.

Although Julio was always very friendly, he obviously felt threatened by the presence of the 'gringo priest'. There were many rumours in the town that he was plotting to get rid of me.

"*Buenos días, Padre Cristobal*," he said one day, greeting me with a big hug. He had a strange habit of never actually looking at me eye to eye. He was wearing his usual '*hacendado* attire' – great leather boots with spurs, a belt around his waist with a pistol hanging by his side and a wide-rimmed cowboy hat on his head.

"*Buenos días, Julio*," I replied, looking straight at him.

"I have a letter for my good friend, the bishop," he said, handing me an envelope, "perhaps you will be going to Sicuani soon."

"Not for a while," I replied. "Is it urgent?"

"Not really, it's a letter of resignation from the position of *economo*," he answered, playing with Kimichu. "I have been *economo* now for ten years and it's time to give someone else an opportunity."

"Oh you don't have to send your resignation to the bishop," I explained. "I can accept your resignation as parish priest. The town proposes three names for the new *economo* and I will forward them to the bishop. From these three names he will choose a new *economo*."

"We'll have to call a meeting of the whole town," he said.

"The whole Christian community," I pointed out. "It won't involve the Mormons or Adventists. Perhaps in about a month's time to give the people time to think about it," I suggested.

"Very good," he agreed and he turned to leave.

"Before you go, Julio, I'd like to say something to you."

"Certainly, Padre."

"It's a delicate matter, but you realise that you are giving scandal by living with Natividad and having a child."

"What do you mean?"

"Well, you are not married, and Natividad is your godchild. You would need a dispensation to marry her."

"What about the Indians?" he responded indignantly, "they usually have lots of children before they are married."

"Yes, that is their custom of *sirvanacuy*, but you are not an Indian."

"Thank God for that!" he exclaimed, almost choking with the thought, "I have enough trouble with them on my hacienda. They are dirty and lazy, it's impossible to get them to work."

"And not so very long ago they owned all this land," I added.

"Maybe they did, but look at the mess they made of it. My ancestors fought hard for this land."

"Julio, history can teach us a lot. Do you mind if I tell you something?" I asked.

"Not at all. I'm sure you are going to tell me anyway."

"I come from a little country in Europe called Ireland and not so very long ago there were many landlords in my country who owned all the land. The poor Irish peasants owned nothing and when the potato crop failed, many died of hunger. Today the landlord system in Ireland has gone and the land is owned by the people."

"That will never happen here," he replied in a defiant tone of voice, "at least not in my lifetime."

"In the meantime," I suggested, "don't forget to have your child baptised."

"Ana Luz was baptised a month ago," he replied with pride in his voice, "in my chapel in the hacienda. Father Macario came all the way from Cuzco to perform the ceremony and we celebrated with a big fiesta."

"Where did he register Ana Luz?" I asked.

"I don't know. The important thing is that the child is baptised."

"Perhaps you could ask him for the details and I will register her here."

"Very good!" he replied, and as he bade me farewell he added, "and I'll call that meeting in about a month's time."

At last my new jeep had arrived! I had to go to Lima to collect it. I got a lift to Cuzco with Loisa who made the round trip every week with a truckload of Cusquena beer, returning on Sunday afternoon with the empties. He had been coming to Yauri for the past twenty-seven years and knew every inch of the road. As we left Yauri he recounted the many accidents that had occurred during his lifetime. He drove along at a snail's pace and the one hundred-mile journey took over twelve hours!

Early next morning I took the first flight from Cuzco to Lima. As the plane accelerated down the runway for take off, it suddenly came to a screeching halt. The pilot had noticed another plane about to land. It missed us by what seemed like inches to spare. We taxied back up the runway and began again. Our plane was full of tourists returning from a whistle-stop tour of the Inca ruins.

"What did you think of Machu Picchu?" asked the American lady sitting beside me on the plane. 'Here we go again', I thought to myself.

"I haven't been there yet," I replied. "I hope to go soon."

"You mean, you plan to come back to Cuzco?" she asked, in amazement.

"Yes," I replied, "I live here."

"You live in Cuzco? How nice, it's a beautiful city. Arnold and I visited all the ruins. Of course we are almost ruins ourselves! It was a really wonderful trip. We wouldn't have missed it for the world. We didn't climb all those steps, you know, up the 'Sexy Woman'. Most of the younger ones did though. They enjoyed the 'Sexy Woman', but for me Machu Picchu was the best of all. You are so lucky to live here."

I had a feeling this was going to be a long journey. This woman loved to talk, and did so in great bursts.

"How long have you lived here?" she eventually asked.

"Almost four years now," I replied. "I work with the Indians."

"How lovely. We saw some Indians from the train on our way to Machu Picchu. They were working in the fields. One was leading two oxen while another walked behind with a wooden plough. The women were carrying their babies on their backs. I loved their multicoloured clothes. It's all so primitive. Tell me, why do they wear those little bowler hats?"

"Nobody knows," I replied, "they don't even know themselves. It's just a custom."

"It's certainly not to keep the sun off their heads," she said, "they are much too small. Arnold got sunburned when we went to the Indian market in Pisac. I told him to wear his hat but he never takes any notice. They wanted to sell him one of their little hats, but he couldn't find one big enough. Arnold has a big head. We bought a beautiful alpaca rug. It was very cheap; fifty dollars and we didn't even have to bargain."

"You could have got it much cheaper than that," I suggested, "they expect you to bargain. They normally ask twice what they hope to get."

"You couldn't buy a rug like that in Minnesota," she explained, "all my friends are really going to be jealous. The only misfortune we had was that Arnold had his camera stolen. You won't believe it, but it was taken from around his neck. One minute it was there and the next it was gone. He didn't feel a thing. He wasn't worried about the camera, but he was very disappointed that he lost all the photos of Machu Picchu."

I was happy to see that the 'Fasten your seatbelt' light had come on. We were about to land in Lima.

"Arnold won't sit beside me," she explained, "he says I talk too much."

As I stepped from the plane I was overcome by a gush of warm sultry air. I took off my warm mountain jacket as it was going to be a very hot day. It's extraordinary how an hour's plane journey can change not only the season, but a whole culture. I pushed my way through the throng of taxi-drivers at the exit and walked the short distance to the gate where I got a taxi to Miraflores at a bargain fare. I felt I had enough energy to run a marathon. Now I know why athletes train at high altitudes. I always looked forward to a break in Lima; back to civilisation again! My clothes were sticking to me by the time I reached the Carmelite house. A great welcome, a shower, summer clothes and no cooking . . . I was in heaven!

I spent the next week going through all the *tramites* (red tape) that was necessary to import a jeep. As the Church doesn't have to pay import tax there is a mountain of paper work. You must have a letter from your superior, then you go to the cathedral to have it stamped by the cardinal, then to the Ministry of Justice. All the papers are examined in minute detail. You must also present the documents of the vehicle with precise details of chassis and engine numbers.

Alas! An error is discovered by an official at the Ministry. There is an 'eight' missing. The engine number ends with two 'eights' instead of three. Consternation! I must begin again. I must write to Japan and get the original engine number, but this could take months. I have just come down from Yauri. (Of course he has never heard of the place.)

"I have to have my jeep to drive back," I pleaded. All to no avail.

"You can return to your parish," he suggested, as if it was just around the corner, "and come back when the papers are in order. There is an 'eight' missing. We have to find it."

As I was leaving the building I noticed that the Minister's offices were on the second floor. I decided to have a go. I took the lift to the second floor. There were two policemen with machine guns guarding the entrance. I showed them my Church pass. (The Church is held in very high esteem in Peru and a Church pass, although of no legal status, will get you anywhere.) They saluted me and let me in. I went first to the secretary's office, where I explained my problem. Would it be possible to have a word with the Minister?

"The Minister is a very busy man but I'll see what I can do. Wait a moment!"

The next thing I knew I was being ushered into a spacious office. The Minister was seated behind an enormous desk at the other end of the room.

"*Buenos días, Señor,*" I said, greeting him with a formal handshake (he wasn't an Indian).

"*Buenos días, Padre,*" he replied, "take a seat. What can I do for you?"

I told him of my difficulties with the importation forms.

"There's an 'eight' missing," I explained, "and I need my jeep as soon as possible for my work in Yauri. They won't release my jeep without the other 'eight'."

"But where did the 'eight' go?" he asked, "how is it missing?" (This was becoming a farce.)

"I don't know, but they won't release my jeep without it," I replied. "Could you ask your secretary to type in the missing 'eight'?" I asked hesitantly.

"Oh, that would be impossible!" he answered, "you cannot interfere with official documents."

"But you are the Minister," I pleaded, "if you gave the order, it could be done. It's only an extra eight." He smiled.

"If I wanted my baptismal certificate changed, would you do it?"

"Of course I would," I replied, "if it was only a question of a mistake. I rectify them all the time in Yauri."

He called his secretary and asked him to type in another 'eight'.

"Now I know where to go if I want my baptismal certificate changed," he smiled. "We appreciate the wonderful work you are doing with the poor in our country," he added as he bade me farewell.

I collected my jeep from the *depósito* (warehouse) at the port of Callao. It had been there for months and various things had been stolen, including the spare wheel. I had to pass through about five inspections on the way out and at each one I had to bribe the inspector, otherwise he would have taken hours to inspect the vehicle. Once I gave him the money he just stamped the form without looking at it. Now I was ready for the long journey back to Yauri.

Early the next morning, while I was still asleep, there was an urgent phone call to Miraflores from Ireland.

"Your mother died during the night." . . . There was no easy way of saying it.

Although I was preparing myself for this moment, it came as a terrible shock in the end. Being so far away made it worse. I wished I had been with her when she died, but she died in her sleep. So even if I had been at home, I probably wouldn't have been present. I must go home for the funeral. I had always promised her that. But there was a problem. My *salida* (white paper) was out of date and I couldn't leave the country without it. More red tape was looming before me, but there is a way around everything. Lucho, a retired airforce colonel who lived in the parish, had a friend at the airport and he could get me on the plane without passing through emigration. I was driven straight to the steps of the plane and arrived in Ireland within twenty-four hours.

However my main problem arose when I returned to Peru. It is just as difficult to get back into the country without your *salida* as it is to leave.

"How did you leave Peru without your papers being in order?" asked the passport officer on my return.

"It was an emergency," I explained, "I had to leave quickly."

"You must always be prepared for an emergency," he replied sternly.

"Report to immigration tomorrow at eleven," he said, holding on to my passport. I thought I would never see it again.

The next day when I returned to immigration I was put sitting at a desk and told to copy what was written on the chart.

"You must not exit the country without your papers in order." I had been a naughty boy!

When at last I set out on the perilous journey back to the mountains in the new jeep, I was accompanied by Guilliermo, a Colombian Carmelite brother. It was four o'clock in the morning and we were just about to leave Lima. As I made my way across the street with my bags to collect the jeep, a police car came from nowhere and screeched to a halt. Four policemen jumped out and surrounded me with machine guns. This was a spot check. A gringo carrying bags at this hour of the morning looked very suspicious. They must be full of dynamite and ammunition. I quickly raised my hands in the air and tried to explain who I was. (Every gringo was presumed to be a terrorist since President Belaúnde was convinced that Peruvians couldn't be involved in terrorism – he was completely out of touch with reality.) I showed them my identity card and they seemed very disappointed that they didn't discover any guns or explosives in my bags. They were mainly full of goodies and essential provisions for survival in Yauri. The police were always surprised and could never understand why a gringo was living and working with the poor Indians in the mountains.

The first part of the journey followed the coast southwards with the Pacific ocean on the right. Once you leave the outskirts of Lima you travel for hours through sandy desert. The Pan-American highway is just a narrow strip of roadway with barely room for two cars to pass. It is in a state of disrepair and great skill is needed to avoid the potholes. It is also 'bandit country'. Sometimes the bandits conceal themselves in the trucks in Lima and disgorge the load as the truck speeds through the desert. The unfortunate driver arrives in Arequipa with an empty truck.

I was warned to fill up with gasoline in the oasis town of Ica, about one hundred and fifty miles south of Lima, because the next station was more than three hundred miles away in Camana. Just south of Ica the road passes through one of the world's great archaeological mysteries, the Nazca Lines, drawn on the rock-strewn *pampa* of San José. The Nazca culture flourished about 200 BC. It produced a very fine form of textile art embroidered on shawls. The Nazca ceramics were also very finely decorated with colourful pictures depicting daily life, including stylised animals, plants and human figures. But Nazca is known most of all for its 'lines'. These gigantic outlines of animals and birds were drawn on the ground by removing the brownish stone from the Nazca plain and exposing the light earth underneath. These designs range from straight lines, which stretch for over five miles, to outlines of human and animal shapes. The origin and meaning of these shapes have stirred people's imaginations for centuries. Many theories have been put forward, one of which attributes the work to extra-terrestrial intervention! Another theory is that they were part of an immense astronomical calendar, noting the rainy season in the highlands and the seasonal changes in the region's climate. However, most recent research suggests that they were constructed as supplications to the rain gods during forty years of devastating drought. One of the best ways of seeing the lines is from the air, in one of the many overflights from the nearby Nazca airstrip. However this is not recommended for anyone suffering from airsickness as the area experiences a lot of air turbulence and the small aircraft can give you quite a bumpy flight.

We decided to stick to the road and continued on our way. We stopped briefly at Camana to visit a Maltese Carmelite who was working there. Then we turned inland and began the long steep climb to Arequipa, the second city of Peru. Arequipa is over seven thousand feet above sea level and is known as 'the white city' because of the white volcanic rock from which most of the city is built. It never rains in Arequipa and the climate is mild and cool the whole year round. As a result many wealthy families like to retire to Arequipa.

It was late in the evening by the time we arrived. The long and winding road had seemed never-ending. We were lucky to be able to stay with another Maltese Carmelite who runs a parish there. The following day we visited the famous Dominican convent of Santa Catalina just off the Plaza de Armas. It is a veritable miniature walled town, founded in 1579. Once inside, the nuns never left this five-acre convent. It even had its own cemetery. In its heyday there were over four hundred residents – nuns, slaves and servants. It reflected the society of its time. One had to pay to join the convent and the nuns were separated according to their dowry. The more luxurious cells were reserved for those from aristocratic families and these nuns had their own servants or slaves. Their food was prepared in the tiny kitchens attached to each cell. Today just twenty nuns live in one part of the convent and the rest is opened up as a tourist attraction.

Unfortunately further sightseeing of Arequipa would have to wait for another time – we had to be on our way. The next stage of the journey was a nightmare. We climbed higher and higher into the Andes, up past the Misti volcano which towers over the city of Arequipa. On the left is the Nevado Ampato, another 20,700 foot high volcano, where recently they discovered the mummy of an Inca maiden, sacrificed to the Gods of the mountain over five hundred years ago. The road had long since turned into a mountain track. Luckily the jeep had four-wheel drive.

Suddenly we found ourselves driving through a snowstorm! The track had disappeared under a blanket of snow. I was beginning to suffer the first effects of altitude sickness and Guilliermo was wishing he had stayed in Lima.

We had left the main road from Arequipa to Puno and began to head north. Towards evening we reached Condoroma on the outskirts of the parish, but we were a still a long way from Yauri. We stopped in Condoroma where we had a hot cup of *mate de coca*. My head was throbbing. Now we had to negotiate the hairpin bends of the notorious *Escalera Diablo*. It seemed a very long time since I first encountered them with Des. It had begun to rain and even the viscatchas had retired for the night. The headlights of the jeep illuminated the dark mountainside as I heaved on the steering wheel and tried to negotiate the sharp bends. They seemed to be never-ending. As I rounded a bend the road was suddenly blocked. A recent landslide obscured most of the mountain track. I got out to see if there was a way past. It was difficult to walk as the mud and stones began to give way underneath my feet. In four-wheel drive I could just about make it. Guilliermo got out to guide me as I gradually made my way across the rubble. But the real nightmare was still to come . . . In the distance I could see the flickering lights of Tocroyoc – just ten more minutes and we would be safe for the night. It was then that it happened. The jeep slowly began to sink in the mud until it was almost up to the bonnet.

"*Estamos plantado*! (We are stuck!)" shouted Guilliermo. He had wonderful powers of observation!

I had to climb out through the window of the jeep to have a look, but the night was pitch black and I could hardly see a thing.

"*Arena movediza*! (Quicksand!)" exclaimed Guilliermo, just to cheer me up.

We abandoned the jeep and set out to walk to Tocroyoc. Frans and Regina were delighted to see us and their hospitality was much appreciated. Early next morning when we walked back to the abandoned jeep we could clearly see how we had veered into a sea of mud in the dark. Luckily there was an electric winch on the front of the jeep. Normally you would simply unwind the steel rope and attach it to a nearby tree, turn on the motor and out it would come. But where there are no trees it is not that simple. I always carried an iron bar for such an emergency. I hammered the bar into the ground, attached the rope and we were soon on our way again.

As we approached the bridge on the far side of Tocroyoc I could see the central span of the bridge was missing – a truck had broken it the previous day. I wondered what would have happened if I had tried to drive across the bridge the night before. We slowly made our way through the river instead. Perhaps mud and quicksand have their place in God's plan after all!

The first time I used my new jeep was to visit the community of Mullacahua where Pablo, our new mayor, was president. Guilliermo had left for Sicuani from where he would travel to Checacupe to work with Rosendo. Mullacahua is across the river from the mine in Tintaya. It doesn't celebrate any particular feast but every Monday the whole community meets from ten o'clock in the morning until three in the afternoon for prayer and reflection. Men, women and children come together to pray, sing hymns and study the bible. Pedro, the catechist, leads them in prayer. He is the most important member of the community. He teaches the children their prayers, prepares the parents for baptism and marriage and is the person to whom everyone goes for spiritual advice. Every community has its own catechist. All the catechists come to the parish centre in Yauri for three days each month for instruction and study of the bible. Where there is no priest, the work of the catechist is invaluable.

Pedro was waiting on the main road to guide me across the River Salado. We would cross where the local people usually cross on foot.

Although the river was wide it wasn't very deep, except in the middle where it was fast-flowing. Benigno sat on the bonnet of the jeep to test the depth with a stick. Kimichu had made his own way across and was waiting on the far side. The important thing is to keep going at all costs and not let the engine stop. The four-wheel drive made all the difference. I don't think we would ever have made it in the old Dodge truck. Once on the other side we sped through the *pampa* to a little chapel in the distance.

The local band playing a happy tune

All the people of Mullacahua came out to greet us. The little band played a happy tune as we marched from the jeep to the chapel, Benigno walking proudly beside me carrying the Mass kit. The *alferado* asked me to say a Mass of Thanksgiving for all the community. As I began the Mass there was a man at the front who was very drunk. He kept singing out of tune and interrupting me by asking me questions. Everyone was shouting at him to shut up, but the more they shouted the more noise he made. Eventually four men came up and carried him away. Afterwards Pablo came to apologise for his behaviour.

"He will be dealt with very severely at the next community meeting," he said.

The young people had erected a makeshift volleyball net and were enjoying a game of volleyball. To their astonishment Kimichu joined in, jumping high into the air to head the ball over the net. They imagined that I had taught him to play. Meanwhile I was partaking of the 'big brown pot'. As I lifted the spoon to my mouth I found a large eye looking up at me. It was the eye of a pig. I'm sure his long ears were lurking somewhere in the background. Never before had I eaten soup that looked back at me. I shut my eyes and hoped for the best. Apart from the taste, which is hard to describe, it was like eating grapes.

On the way home my new jeep got stuck in the middle of the River Salado. The engine stopped and wouldn't restart. Benigno ran back to the community to get help. I just sat and waited. As I looked up towards the hill I saw the whole community running towards the river. It was like a scene from the Bible, except this time the waters didn't part. Everyone waded into the water, waist deep and surrounded the jeep. At a given signal they just lifted the jeep out of the water. There was a loud cheer as the engine started and I was on my way again.

Just as I arrived back in Yauri there was a group of women in the middle of the road, frantically waving for me to stop.

"*Papay*, come quickly, Maria is dying," they shouted.

I followed them down a narrow street to a mud hut at the far end of the town. I could never have been prepared for what I was about to witness. As I entered the little door on my hands and knees I could hardly believe what I saw. There was a woman of about twenty-seven years of age lying on a blanket on the clay floor, in the process of giving birth. Her legs were raised in the air as two women held her by the arms. The hut was dark and there was none of the necessities that I would have associated with childbirth – no towels, no water, no soap . . . nothing. The baby was lying sideways in the womb and the unfortunate woman had been in labour since early morning. With all the pushing and pulling, the baby's little hand was already protruding from the mother's body. Her two young children were looking on in amazement. Her husband was outside in the patio tending to some animals. I realised that if she didn't get medical help immediately she would die.

"We took her to the *curandero* (medicine man) this morning but there was nothing he could do," explained one of the women.

I knew the nearest hospital was in Sicuani, but that was a good seven hours away, driving through the night. As it was a matter of life or death it was worth a try. I rushed back to the parish house and grabbed an old mattress and some blankets and threw them in the back of the jeep. When I returned and told her husband I was taking his wife to the hospital he replied;

"It's only a waste of time. She's going to die anyway."

We wrapped Maria in a blanket and lifted her gently into the back of the jeep. Her husband was reluctant to come with me.

"If she dies along the way, we'll come back immediately," he said, "it's no use going on for nothing."

We began the terrible journey to Sicuani. As the jeep bounced up and down on the dirt road the poor woman cried out in pain. After a while she began to sing in a high-pitched voice to try and take her mind off the pain. I too was going through agony. Now and then she would stop crying and each time I was sure she was dead.

When there was a prolonged silence I stopped the jeep, only to find that she had lapsed into unconsciousness. I kept going and the journey seemed to take forever. It was almost daybreak by the time I reached the hospital. Then I had to try to find the lady doctor. One of the nurses showed me where she lived. She came immediately and performed the operation. Maria's life was saved but the baby was already dead.

The next day when I visited her in the hospital she was sitting up in bed. She put her arms around me and gave me a hug.

"*Gracias, Papay* for saving my life. Please, can you give my baby a blessing?"

She pulled a cardboard box from under the bed. I opened the box to be confronted by a terrible sight. There was just a little head and the arms and legs. The body had been hacked to pieces during the operation. I blessed the mother and her child.

Some weeks later I met her husband on the street in Yauri.

"How is Maria?" I asked.

"Ah, *Papay*, she's good for nothing. You should have let her die when you were at it. We should never have gone to Sicuani."

At last the trouble which has been simmering for months has erupted. I am confined to my room, the church has been closed and padlocked and I have been given fifteen days to leave Yauri. The atmosphere in the town is very tense. It all began very innocently when it was announced over the radio that Julio Velazques had resigned as *economo* of the church and that a meeting would be held on Friday at two o'clock to choose three new candidates. Sebastian began ringing the bell at midday. Apart from the solitary sound of the bell, an air of silence descended over the town. It was the calm before the storm. Benigno sensed there might be trouble.

"*Papay*, I have a feeling something is going to happen. I saw the *hacendados* meeting down the town. They are planning something. The sub-prefect, Victor Soto, was with them."

"What can they do?" I asked, "we are only going to change the *economo*."

"I don't trust Sebastian," he said after a long silence. "He is very annoyed since you moved him from the office. Now he has no way of making money from the Indians."

"How did he make money from the Indians?" I asked.

"He used to charge them extra for the baptismal certificates. The longer it took him to find them the more he charged."

The solemn tones of the bell rang out again.

Gradually people began drifting towards the church – even groups of merchants, who normally don't come to church except for the processions of Holy Week. The people of the town considered that anything to do with the church was their affair. They began to take up their positions in order of importance. First in line were the *hacendados*, who owned the big haciendas around Yauri. They were elegantly dressed with their wide-rimmed cowboy hats and high leather boots with spurs. They usually carried a pistol in their belts. Next came the merchants with their white hats. Some were *mestizos* but the majority were of Indian origin, although they didn't like to be reminded of that. Then there were a few poor Indians from the surrounding communities but they weren't considered very important.

Just before the meeting Nestor Alverez, who owned the big hacienda near Ocururo, came into the sacristy.

"*Buenas tardes*, *Padre*, I want to tell you something as your friend."

This approach surprised me because this *hacendado* had never spoken to me before. He continued;

"I want to warn you that they are out to get you at this meeting. We all know why you came here and what you are doing out in the communities. You go out in your jeep every day to stir up the Indians and preach Communism."

"That's news to me," I responded, "how do you know what I do out in the communities?" (Nestor Alverez only ever came to church during Holy Week so he would not have been aware that as the parish priest I went out to the communities to say Mass for the fiestas as well as baptise and marry the Indians. He automatically presumed that I had other sinister motives.)

"My men have told me," he replied. "They have been following you around for months. However I have come to help you. Maybe we can come to an arrangement before the meeting. If you decide to leave Yauri quietly I would be willing to help you financially."

"I really don't know what you are talking about," I said, "and I will leave Yauri when my superiors decide."

"There would be no problem if you co-operated with the people but you have taken the side of the Indians," he said, raising his voice.

"I am here to preach the Gospel to everyone," I explained, "especially those who are most in need. Jesus Christ came to bring the good news to the poor."

"I can fix it with the others," he promised, "if you agree to co-operate."

"There is nothing to fix," I answered. "Now, we have a meeting to choose candidates for a new *economo*."

"We will see!" he exclaimed as he stormed out of the sacristy.

Sebastian had placed a table and some chairs outside the door of the church. He had taken out the benches from the church also. I was wearing my Carmelite habit which I did for all religious events in the church. As I came to the door I could see a large crowd of people had gathered around. All the authorities were seated on the front bench. Victor Soto sat in the middle. He was in a jovial mood and obviously quite drunk. The *teniente* sat beside him. Other police stood at the edge of the crowd. Many children had come to watch the spectacle. It was like a day out at the Colosseum in Rome. I began the meeting with a prayer. Everyone joined in. Then I continued;

"First of all I would like to welcome the authorities to this important meeting, especially the sub-prefect, the mayor and the police. We, the Christian people of Yauri, have gathered here today to select three candidates for the position of *economo* of our church. I would like to thank the outgoing *economo*, Julio Velazques, for his service to the church during the last ten years. I would also like to thank Sebastian Choqque Huanco, the assistant *economo*, for guarding the treasures of the church during the past number of years. My first duty here today is to ask Julio if he wishes to resign."

With that Julio stood up and read out the letter he had written to the bishop. When he was finished everyone applauded.

As I was about to continue, Sebastian began to speak in Quechua. He was holding up a letter. Isabel, one of the *beatas*, who was sitting near me, translated, as my knowledge of Quechua was still limited.

"People of Yauri, I have something important to tell you. This is a letter which I received some time ago from the bishop in Sicuani. He is ordering Julio and myself to resign from the position of *economo* and assistant *economo* in the church of Yauri." (Of course this letter was a complete fabrication.)

With that some people at the back began to shout.

"Gringos out, gringos out!"

Everyone stood up and joined in, waving their hands in the air. Victor Soto, who could hardly stand up, began to speak.

"People of Yauri, remain calm. As sub-prefect I am the highest authority in this town. I have been appointed by the government. I represent the President himself, Fernando Belaúnde Terry. I speak with his authority." Then turning to me he shouted;

"With what authority do you speak?"

I couldn't believe what I was hearing. What was I to say?

"I speak as your parish priest," I answered, "appointed by the Church, with the authority of God."

"You are a gringo," he shouted, "you are not one of us."

"God doesn't make any distinction between people," I replied calmly. "We are all equal in the sight of God. There is no difference between black and white, brown or yellow."

"Gringos out, gringos out!" they shouted again.

I knew there was no use trying to continue, so I got up to leave.

"The meeting is closed!" I said and walked away.

With that, some of the merchant women picked up stones and threw them at me. The anger in their faces was terrifying. I began to run. Luckily the stones just struck my habit. Meanwhile the police stood idly by . . . watching. When I was safely in the patio I locked the door. I could hear the noise of the stones as they bounced off the wood. Kimichu came into my room to console me. All I needed now was to be shipwrecked a few times and I would be following in the footsteps of St Paul.

The meeting continued for a further three hours without me. Afterwards Benigno recounted all that had taken place. Victor Soto had taken charge.

"People of Yauri, I am one of you. As your sub-prefect I will guarantee your rights. I am a good Catholic. My witness is Our Lord of the Earthquakes here behind me. He will testify to all I have to say. We don't need that cursed gringo to tell us what to do. Many years ago I got rid of a priest from Corporaque (Julio César Mendoza). Today I will do the same in Yauri. You are my people. (At this point he stumbled and had to be supported by two *hacendados*.) I hate gringos . . . they come to our country to deceive our people." He suddenly realised that no one was taking notes of the meeting.

"We need a secretary to record everything that is said."

Hernan Herrera, the director of education in Yauri, volunteered.

"You are no good," retorted Victor, "you can't even write."

Eventually one of the women teachers came forward and began to write.

"What are we going to do with the gringo priest?" continued the sub-prefect. Sebastian stood up to speak.

"I have been sacristan in this church for the past sixteen years. I sleep in the church every night when I should be at home with my wife and family. I help with all the rites, customs and ceremonies in the church. I was very happy working for the former parish priest, Padre Angel Ojeda. He always treated me well and let me do everything I wanted. But since the gringo came, he won't let me do anything. I am finding it hard to make ends meet."

"How much does the gringo pay you?" someone shouted.

"Hardly anything at all. I used to be able to make some money in the office but he has put Maria in the office now."

Someone suggested that they make a collection for Sebastian. They collected 41,000 soles ($20). He accepted it with grateful thanks.

Next it was Socorro Choqque, one of the merchants, who wanted to speak.

"I'd like to know what that gringo is doing, going out to the communities every day and sometimes he doesn't come back until late at night. You can be sure he is up to no good."

One of the Indians tried to speak but he was shouted down. Pablo also tried to speak, but the people rebuked him;

"You are a friend of the gringo. If it wasn't for him you would not be mayor today."

Nestor Alverez stood up to speak.

"People of Yauri, as the Pope said; 'Cobbler attend to your shoes.' We all know that this gringo is mixed up with politics. We must get rid of him. We all know he is up to no good. I am a good Catholic and I say he should go. We should close the church until he goes." (At that moment, a jeep with a Polish kayaking expedition entered the Plaza and headed for the parish house.) Alverez continued;

"There is the proof of what I'm saying. Look at how those gringos head straight for the gringo priest. Soon we will be completely overrun by gringos. Not only must we close the church but the parish house as well. We all know what goes on in there. The Indians can come and go whenever they please. They are always having meetings in the parish centre and are being deceived by that gringo."

A faint voice was heard from the back of the crowd. It was Trinidad!

"People of Yauri, you don't know what you are saying, you don't know what you are doing. *Papay* Cristobal is our friend. He has made a great sacrifice in coming to our country. He has left family and friends to come and live with us and this is the way we repay him. He left a beautiful country to live in this barren place. He has come to help us, to baptise our children and to say Mass for our souls . . . " She didn't get any further, she was shouted down.

The sub-prefect spoke again.

"I say we give him sixty days to get out. We have to try and be human and act with a little understanding."

"No, no, that's too long!" shouted the merchants.

"Twenty-four hours," shouted one.

"One hour!" shouted another.

At last they settled on fifteen days. At this point the bishop's jeep drove into the Plaza. Tiny was on his way to Santo Tomás with another Peruvian priest, Padre Leonidas. This was a pure coincidence and they knew nothing of what was going on. Of course the people thought that I had contacted Tiny by radio and asked him to rescue me. Before I knew and could warn him, Tiny innocently went over to the crowd to say 'Hello'. To his astonishment he was met with a storm of abuse.

"You are another gringo," shouted the sub-prefect, "I am the only authority here."

With that, he called on one of the police to arrest the bishop and put him in jail. The bishop tried to talk to the crowd but they continued to shout him down. As it was impossible to reason with the mob, he too walked away. Some of the people jeered as he left. The sub-prefect locked the church and took away the key.

Indians reading the interdict notice on the church door in Yauri

The next day the bishop put the church under an interdict. A notice was posted on the door of the church. It read;

> To the authorities and people in general of Yauri
> Owing to the drunken behaviour of a small group of people in the church of Yauri on Friday, 8 July, and their total disrespect for their bishop and parish priest, it is forbidden under 'suspension a Divinis' to celebrate the Mass or Sacraments in this church, until this affair is satisfactorily resolved.

Tiny advised me not to move outside the house for the next couple of weeks until everything had died down.

"These people are ruthless and will stop at nothing," he warned.

He continued on his way to Santo Tomás with Padre Leonidas. On his return he would go to Lima and see the Minister of the Interior who is responsible for appointing the sub-prefect. He would denounce Victor Soto for having overstepped his authority in closing the church and taking the key. In Peru there is a distinct separation of Church and State.

Geovanna came running into my room. I was delighted to see her. I didn't know how much she had seen or heard.

"I had to crawl underneath the door to the patio," she said, "because it was locked."

"Kimichu made that hole under the door for you," I said, "he is a good dog."

"He is not good when he jumps up on me," she complained, "he nearly knocked me over."

"He is only playing with you," I explained, "he likes playing with Geovanna."

"I can't play today. Papa told me that I have diarrhoea and that I am not well." (She didn't have to tell me, I could smell her a mile away!)

"How did you get that?" I asked.

"Papa says I ate too much *cebiche* (a typical Peruvian dish of raw marinated fish) yesterday."

There was a loud banging at the door. I ignored it for a while but it got louder and louder. Eventually I opened the door. It was Hipolito, the local solicitor.

"*Buenas tardes, Padre*, I have an official letter for you from the sub-prefect," he explained as he held up an envelope.

"What's it about?" I asked, "I'm sure it's not good news."

"You have fifteen days to leave Yauri," he said, looking away in embarrassment.

"Oh I don't like letters like that," I replied. "The sub-prefect has no authority to expel me from Yauri."

"I'm only doing my duty, *Padre*," he protested.

"I know that, Hipolito," I responded, "it's not your fault, but you can bring the letter back to the sub-prefect and tell him that Padre Cristobal is parish priest of Yauri and he is not going anywhere."

11

The Lost City of the Incas

Melchor stood by the back door all day. People were coming to console me and to pledge their support. The local radio broadcast continuously that I had been expelled from the province and that soon a Peruvian priest would come and everything would return to normal. Pablo came to see me.

"It's not so much the church being closed," the mayor complained bitterly, "but what they did to you, and you having been so good to us."

"Don't worry, Pablo," I replied, "I won't be leaving."

"But you haven't heard the latest," he exclaimed. "Victor Soto has denounced you to the Minister of the Interior. He is accusing you of being a *commandante* in *Sendero Luminoso*. He says you are organising armed groups out in the communities. If the Minister believes that, you will be out of the country within a week."

"That man will stop at nothing," I said, "he is a lunatic, but a very clever one. There is method in his madness."

"The communities are signing petitions of support for you," Pablo assured me, holding up pages filled with fingerprints which appeared as hundreds of ink blots.

"I don't know what good that will do!" I responded doubtfully, "who will take any notice of fingerprints?"

"I'm going to Lima to present them to the Minister," he exclaimed proudly. "Everyone wants me to go."

"That might be dangerous," I suggested, "they will surely try to prevent you from going there."

"When the sub-prefect heard that we were gathering petitions, he sent a notice to all the communities warning them that owing to the state of emergency in the country, all assemblies of more than five people are unlawful. Anyone attending such an assembly will be put in jail."

"He's only trying to frighten you," I suggested, "he couldn't put everyone in jail." With that, Benigno came rushing in.

"Sebastian is going around the town with a petition for your immediate expulsion from the parish."

"Are many people signing it?" I asked.

"Only the merchant women who threw the stones."

"Of course Sebastian is out of work now," I said, "he won't be happy with that."

"He still has to sleep in the church every night. He goes in the back way," Benigno added.

"It was just like Holy Week again," said Trinidad coming in and putting her arms around me to give me a hug.

"Holy Week!" I said puzzled.

"Yes," she replied, "we had Herod, Pilate and the Roman mob, and even the soldiers were there and they did nothing."

"I heard that you spoke up for me, until you were shouted down. You were like Veronica," I reminded her.

"Judas Iscariot only got thirty pieces of silver, but our Judas got 41,000 soles," she remarked.

"You were lucky to get away with your life," I said. "You had great courage to speak."

"You were in more danger than I was," she replied, "I was very frightened when the women starting throwing stones."

"Luckily they missed," I added jokingly.

There was a constant stream of people coming to the church to look at the notice on the door. Only a few of them could read it. They were heartbroken. Everything revolves around the church. What would they do? Where would they have their children baptised? Where could they be married? Above all, how could they visit their friends, the Saints, and pray at their shrines.

The presidents of all the communities held a meeting at the parish centre and presented me with a request. Would it be possible to say Mass in the parish centre or in the patio? They would let the people know and everyone would come. As the celebration of Mass was exempt from the law of unlawful assembly, there was nothing that the sub-prefect could do.

Although there was no bell, people came from all directions. The old women sat around the patio chewing their coca leaves and waiting for the Mass. With each Sunday the crowds got bigger as word spread. The children were baptised and marriages were celebrated. This was a wonderful time to live through, although it was frightening at times. It was a great opportunity to take the side of the poor and oppressed. Their only hope was the Church. This was one battle I just had to see through.

Early one morning Esther came running in.

"They have put the mayor in jail," she sobbed.

"What for?" I asked.

"False charges," she replied, "they say he stole money from the council. One of the *hacendados* denounced him."

"They will stop at nothing," I thought, "they don't want him to go to Lima."

"They say that you are next to go to jail," she said.

"Will you come to visit me?" I asked with a smile.

"Every day," she replied.

☆   ☆   ☆

As usual on Sunday I went to the market with my basket to do my shopping. The Indians had spread all their produce out on the ground in front of them. There was a wonderful variety of fruit – oranges, bananas, papaya, grapes, chirimoya, avocado, plums, cherries and pineapple. All the fruits were in their natural fresh state, grown without the use of

Market day – the Indians lay out their produce on the ground

preservative sprays. Although they looked quite dirty, with a little wash they became wholesome and appetising, retaining their original taste and colour. It always struck me as quite odd that up here in the mountains where nothing grows, people could produce such perfect fruit. (This fruit, in fact, was tropical fruit brought by trucks from the jungles of the Amazon.)

On my way back from the market I happened to meet Nestor Alverez. He just stared at me for a moment. He was dumbfounded. He was sure I had left.

"*Buenos días, Nestor,*" I said as I passed by.

As I reached the house a young policeman came up to me. I was expecting to be arrested at any moment.

"*Buenos días, Padre,*" he said.

"*Buenos días, Señor,*" I replied.

"My name is Felix," he said, "I would like to get married."

"But the church is locked," I explained. "You will have to wait until it opens again. Of course you could get the keys from Victor Soto, the sub-prefect."

"I have just come here from Lima and I don't agree with the church being locked. I am sure the sub-prefect would not open the church for me. Could I not get married in your patio?"

"When do you want to get married?"

"As soon as possible. My girlfriend has come to visit me from Lima and I would like to marry her before she goes back."

"Have you got your papers in order?"

"What papers do I need?"

"You need a recent baptismal certificate, showing that you were baptised and that you weren't married before."

"My girlfriend has her papers with her. I'll send a radio message to Lima and ask my mother to send mine on."

A few days later he arrived with a piece of paper.

"My certificate came," he explained, handing me a badly typed piece of paper which read;

"Felix Martinez Pizarro, baptised on the 5th day of June, 1960, in the Church of Our Lady of Fatima, Barranco, Lima. Signed: Juan José Cruz."

"Where did you get this?" I asked.

"My mother sent it from Lima," he replied, without a moment's hesitation.

"It doesn't say anything about the *padrino*," I said.

"The priest must have forgotten to put it in."

"You forgot to put it in," I suggested. "This is a forgery. You typed it yourself."

"How could you think such a thing, Padre, my mother sent it from Lima."

"The wedding is off," I said, "I have to be sure that you are baptised before I can marry you, otherwise it's not a sacrament."

"Alright, Padre, I'll ask my mother to send a telegram."

"Who wrote the other one?"

"My friend in the police station typed it out for me," he admitted.

"He really wasn't doing you a favour," I replied.

The telegram arrived from Sicuani just hours before the wedding was due to take place. All the police assembled in the patio. They had arrived from all the surrounding towns. Even the superintendent had come from Cuzco. They were all dressed in their police uniforms. I asked them to leave their weapons in the corner during the ceremony and they duly obliged.

Afterwards they celebrated with crates of beer. The following day I discovered that all my tools (hammer, pliers, chisel, etc) were gone. They had stolen everything. I decided against reporting that particular theft to the police!

Meanwhile the bishop had gone to Lima to visit the Minister of the Interior, Lucho Percovich. On arriving he telephoned the Minister's office to make an appointment. The Minister who lived near Miraflores rang back and invited Tiny to supper. He had three sons in our college in Lima and he knew the Carmelites well.

"This is unbelievable!" he exclaimed, showing the bishop the letter of denunciation from Victor Soto, 'A *commandante* in *Sendero Luminoso*'. That's a very serious charge but he offers no proof whatsoever. Who is this sub-prefect anyway?"

"Victor Soto is a large landowner from Corporaque. He has a powerful group behind him," explained Tiny.

"How can they propose someone like that to be sub-prefect?" he sighed, "I have to rely on the advice I'm given. It's not easy to get good people to be sub-prefect in these remote towns in the mountains. But Padre Cristobal is a Carmelite and a good priest. He came to our country to work with the poor. Not many Peruvian priests want to do that, and this is the thanks he gets.

"I arrived at the end of the meeting. Victor Soto was quite drunk, as were a lot of the group," Tiny explained.

"But closing the church and taking away the keys, he wasn't too drunk for that. He has no authority to interfere in church affairs," said the Minister angrily.

"It's a custom that goes back a long way," replied the bishop. "These landowners had a lot of power and they find it hard to relinquish it."

"But he can't close the church, he has gone too far this time. I will replace him immediately. The difficulty is to find someone to take his place. Do you know of anyone who would be suitable?"

"Not really," replied the bishop, "but I'd rather not be involved in political appointments. It's the poor Indians who suffer. Their church is closed."

"I will appoint a new sub-prefect immediately and the church will be re-opened as soon as possible," the Minister concluded.

It was dull and overcast as I set out early one morning for Condoroma. If this were Ireland I would say 'We will have rain before long', but a cloudy sky doesn't mean rain in the Andes. There was a heavy overnight frost and the little droplets on the *ichu* sparkled like diamonds in the morning light. It was bitterly cold, even the llamas and alpacas in their long woolly coats were feeling the cold. The little barefoot shepherd girl who was leading them out to pasture waved as we drove quickly past. Benigno wound down the window and shouted a greeting in Quechua. A cold blast of air filled the jeep. Kimichu availed of the opportunity to bark loudly through the open window. Sequndo, the president of Condoroma, wrapped in a red poncho with a *chullo* pulled down around his ears, sat impassively in the back of the jeep.

"I saw Victor Soto in the town yesterday," remarked Benigno.

"What was he doing?" I asked.

"Drunk, as usual. I shouted after him that Padre Cristobal was asking for him," he said with an air of mischief in his voice.

"What did he say?"

"He just looked at me and growled '*Siquita muchay*'."

Sequndo burst out laughing in the back of the jeep.

"What does '*Siquita muchay*' mean?"

"It's a very bad word!" he said laughing, "I can't translate it into Spanish."

"Does it not exist in Spanish?"

"Yes, it does. I'd say it exists in all languages, but I don't want to translate it, it's a bad word. People only say it when they are angry or drunk." He laughed again.

"Do you think that Victor Soto knew what it meant?"

"He certainly did . . . he would say anything against you."

As we reached Mullacahua, Ignacio, the new president of the community, was standing by the side of the road with his *bulto*. He held up his hand to stop us.

"*Allillanchu, Papay,*" he shouted, as the jeep came to a halt.

"*Allillanmi,*" I replied.

"Can I come with you to Condoroma?" he asked, "I want to buy some sheep in the market." He jumped in beside Sequndo.

We turned right towards Tintaya to avail of the mine road to Condoroma.

"*Papay*, do you remember the drunken man who interrupted your Mass when you came to our community?" asked Ignacio.

"Oh yes," I recalled, "the one who was singing out of tune."

"He was doing much more than that. We had a meeting shortly afterwards and he was castigated for his conduct."

"What happened? What penance did he get?"

"He was ordered to rethatch the church."

"Did he do it?"

"Yes, he did, otherwise he couldn't have remained in the community. He was very apologetic, he knew he had drunk too much *chicha*. He completed the work in a week. Now we have a lovely new roof on our church."

We had just passed the Tintaya mine and were speeding along on a comparatively decent road when there was a rumbling noise at the back of the jeep. It was as though we had bumped into pothole or hit a rock. I had to pull tightly on the steering wheel to keep the jeep in a straight line.

"There's a wheel passing us out!" shouted Benigno in alarm as a wheel sped past us. I slammed on the brakes. I just managed to stop the jeep before it toppled over. Ignacio and Sequndo were thrown headlong on top of Kimichu. Benigno put up his hands to save himself from hitting the windscreen. There was silence for a moment. Nobody panicked.

"Look where the wheel is now!" said Benigno, pointing to the wheel floating in the centre of a small lake on the side of the road.

We all got out to see what had happened. The jeep was tilting to one side, the back hub resting on the ground where it had been dragged along. Two of the bolts were wrenched off, and one was bent. All the nuts were missing.

"The nuts came off!" exclaimed Benigno.

"Nuts don't just come off," I said, "someone must have loosened them."

"I'll try and get the wheel," said Benigno, taking off his rubber sandals.

"The water is freezing," he yelled, as he rushed in.

"It's too deep," I shouted, as the water reached his knees, "don't go in. We'll have to throw stones and try to float it to one side. In the meantime I'll take off the spare wheel and see what I can do."

I jacked up the jeep and gently put the spare wheel on the remaining bolts. Sequndo, Ignacio and Benigno began throwing stones at the wheel in the lake. I took some nuts from the other wheels and eventually I got the spare wheel on but I couldn't tighten the nuts very much. By now the floating wheel had reached the other side of the lake and Benigno was able to retrieve it. As the wheel was barely on the axle, it was too dangerous to continue. I made my way slowly back to Yauri with Benigno and Kimichu. Ignacio and Sequndo continued on foot to Condoroma.

It was dark by the time I arrived home. I had time to reflect and thank God that none of us had been killed or injured. It was obvious that the nuts on the wheel had been tampered with. What will these people think of next? As I got into bed that night I felt something soft and slimy touch against my leg. I quickly jumped out thinking it was a snake, only to discover a giant green frog looking up at me. A *zapo* (frog) is a symbol of evil and bad luck among the people of the mountains. They have a terrible fear of frogs. No doubt someone had been well rewarded to place it in my bed while I was out. I was just relieved it wasn't a snake.

The national radio from Lima announced the good news. Victor Soto had been removed from his post and a new sub-prefect appointed for the province of Espinar. By now the situation in Yauri had become a national issue and the media in Lima were reporting on the events. The local radio in Yauri remained silent. The feeling of joy and relief among the Indians was unbelievable. They came in droves to congratulate me and to give me a big hug. This was the first time that the *hacendados* had been defeated.

"Now we can live in peace," cried Esther, wiping the tears from her eyes and presenting me with a new pair of gloves. Trinidad brought two guinea pigs.

"*Papay Cristobal*," she said, "now you can stay in Yauri forever. You have wonderful powers, first the *teniente* and now the sub-prefect."

I hadn't the heart to tell her that I would soon be leaving. I had been in Yauri almost five years.

A new *economo* was appointed and the church was open again. A delegation from the town came to see me. It was led by Julio Velazques.

"We have to talk to you, Padre," he began, looking shyly at the ground.

"Come and sit down," I said as I showed them into the kitchen.

"First of all we would like to assure you that we had nothing to do with closing the church. It was Victor Soto and his friends who organised the whole thing."

"That is all over now," I replied, "and I don't hold anything against anyone. The church is open and everyone is happy."

"That's what we would like to talk to you about," responded Julio, "we would like to ask you a great favour."

"What is it?" I asked with surprise. This group wasn't in the habit of asking favours.

"Will you keep Sebastian on as sacristan in the church?" they asked.

"Certainly not!" I responded, without a moment's hesitation. "He is the one that is responsible for what has happened. He has betrayed the Church, the priest and the people of Yauri. He must go. I have appointed a new sacristan, Alejandro Mamani Champi."

"But Sebastian has been sacristan for years. He has a family. How is he going to support them?"

"He should have thought of that before he caused the trouble. He has his shop, and I will give him some money to help him with his business. I don't hold anything against him but he cannot stay."

"You are a hard man, Padre," concluded Julio, "when your mind is made up there is no changing it."

The church bells are pealing out around Cuzco as the sun breaks over the surrounding mountains. People are making their way to the many churches to begin their day with early morning Mass. The tourists too are on the move, but not to church. Few tourists come to Cuzco to pray, yet they are on a kind of spiritual pilgrimage. This morning I am joining the throng on my way to Machu Picchu, the 'Lost City of the Incas'. The train leaves at 6.25 am from the station behind the market.

I arrived before six o' clock but the gates were still closed. Hundreds of tourists from all over the world were waiting outside. Most were on a three-day package tour, Lima – Cuzco – Lima. Back-packers were sitting idly on their haversacks, catching up on some lost sleep. Life for them moved at a very leisurely pace. The older people looked pale and forlorn as they stood around in little groups. Most were suffering the effects of altitude sickness and were anxious to get a move on.

"Wouldn't you think they would open the gates and let us in?" complained an elderly lady in a loud voice. She was obviously more used to the order and discipline of life in the United States.

"Perhaps they weren't expecting us," suggested a small man standing beside her, trying to cheer her up.

"The stench is terrible," complained another lady, ankle-deep in cabbage leaves, banana skins, orange peel and other rubbish left over from the market. She was busily spraying perfume behind her ears and on her face.

"We'll be lucky if we don't catch some disease," remarked her companion.

"I've already caught one," said another man in a mournful tone of voice. "I've had diarrhoea since I arrived yesterday. I hope there's a toilet on the train."

He made no effort to conceal a roll of toilet paper which he carried at the ready.

Some German tourists stood stoically in silence, glancing at their watches now and then. Eventually the iron gates opened with a loud clash of metal and there was a sudden surge forward. Everyone was carried along with the crowd.

"Masie, hold on to your handbag," shouted a voice from behind.

"For dear life," came the reply.

The train to Machu Picchu is known as the 'Gringo train' and there is a special inflated rate for tourists, the best part of $100, but at least you have a comfortable seat. As Cuzco nestles in a deep valley surrounded by high mountains, it is a miracle of engineering that the train can get out of the city at all. Naturally it can't go vertically up the mountain so we begin a series of forward and reverse zig-zag movements, climbing a little each time. It can be very disconcerting to suddenly find the train going backwards, not realising that we are actually climbing.

"Bob, I think we're going backwards," a fat lady complained to her husband as the train went into reverse.

"Must have forgotten something!" came the reply.

The huts of the poor Indians line the track, so near that you could almost put out your hand and touch them. The train moved slowly just feet from their front door or more often through their back yards. Children jumped on and off the train at will in what appeared to be a very dangerous game.

Higher and higher we climbed. Looking back there was a beautiful panoramic view of the city of Cuzco with its red-tiled roofs shining in the morning sun. A huge cross towered over the city from its lofty perch by the ruins of Sacsayhuaman.

"The Incas built Cuzco in the shape of a puma," remarked a French lady to her friend, as she pointed out the various parts of its body.

We crossed over the mountain and began our rapid descent into the Sacred Valley of the Incas. This river valley was once the breadbasket of Cuzco, the Royal garden of the Incas and even today supplies most of its fruit and food. The train sped past fields of wheat and maize.

"Look at the Indians!" someone shouted and everyone ran to the window to get a picture.

A young Mexican boy sitting beside me introduced himself as Carlos.

"You speak Spanish very well," he added.

"Yes," I replied, "I have been here for some years now."

"My father has a travel agency in Mexico City and he sent me on a tour of South America to learn the business."

"Where have you been so far?" I asked.

"I began in Colombia, then I flew to Quito in Ecuador and from there to Lima and yesterday I arrived in Cuzco. The highlight of my trip is the visit to Machu Picchu. I am really looking forward to it."

Two girls who were sitting opposite joined in the conversation.

"I am Maria and my friend is Ana. We are from Switzerland and we have taken a year off work in Zurich to visit South America."

They both spoke Spanish fluently.

"We went to night school for one year," explained Ana.

"Last week we visited the Galapagos Islands off Ecuador. It was very expensive but very interesting. We saw the giant turtles and the iguanas that so surprised Darwin when he visited there in the *Beagle*. It was there that he formulated his theory of the 'Origin of the Species'."

"Are you convinced that we all descended from monkeys then?" asked Carlos.

"Probably," she responded with a smile, as some tourists in the next seat were busily eating peanuts.

"You certainly didn't come to Peru to visit the mountains," I suggested, "Switzerland has beautiful mountains."

"But we have no Machu Picchu!" responded Maria. "It has always been my dream to visit Machu Picchu since I first read about the Incas as a child. There is a wonderful sense of mystery about this place."

"I am looking for the 'soul' of the Incas," explained Ana, "and I think I might find it in Machu Picchu."

"That's the River Vilcanota," said Maria, looking at a map, as we crossed over a bridge. "From here it runs north to Machu Picchu where it becomes the Urubamba and then continues to where it joins a tributary of the Amazon."

The train had come to a stop at Ollantaytambo, the last outpost at the end of the Sacred Valley. Rising above us were the giant terraces leading up to the Inca fortress which not even the Spanish had been able to capture. On the top were the ruins of the temple walls and the watch towers which warned the Incas of Spanish attacks. We were immediately besieged by hundreds of Indians selling their wares. Women held up ponchos, alpaca jumpers, hats and little Indian dolls. Youngsters boarded the train with crates of Inca Cola, Chiclets and bars of Inca chocolate. Others had little plastic bags of coca leaves, especially made up for the tourists.

☆　　☆　　☆

When Pizarro and his small group of soldiers had entered and captured Cuzco in 1533, the Inca Empire was in disarray. To prevent the Inca military chieftains and disaffected *curacas* from organising themselves against the Spanish after Atahualpa's execution, Pizarro selected a young Inca nobleman named Manco and placed him on the throne of his ancestors. The new Inca, known as 'Manco II' was very pleased with this great honour, but soon learned that he was merely a puppet who had to take orders from the Spanish. His ambitious spirit led him to revolt against the small band of Spanish soldiers, less than two hundred in number. But the bows and arrows, spears, clubs and slings of Manco's troops were no match for the Spanish blunderbusses. The Spanish could also depend on large numbers of dissatisfied Indians who had no feeling of loyalty to the new Inca.

In 1536 Manco's troops were eventually defeated and fled with him past Ollantaytambo down the Urubamba valley. They carried with them the large golden image of the Sun from the Temple in Cuzco. Manco II also brought his three sons and the mummies of the dead Incas as well as large herds of llamas and alpacas. All along the way the last of the remaining Incas set up fortresses and temples built on the natural precipices of the mountains until they finally settled in the great city of Vilcapampa or Machu Picchu as we know it today.

The Spanish made many attempts to penetrate the Urubamba valley with no success. In 1570 two Augustinian missionaries, Marcos and Diego, came over the mountain and up the valley. With great religious zeal they destroyed and burned all the pagan shrines to the Sun that they found in their path. They also built many churches and placed huge crosses in the places where the pagan shrines had been. They baptised many Indians and even reached Vilcapampa which they called the University of Idolatry, where lived the 'teachers, enchanters and lords of abomination'.

Friar Diego, who was renowned for his powers of healing, attended the sick bed of Titu Cusi, son of Manco, who had succeeded him as Inca. But this was to be his undoing. The Inca had an attack of double pneumonia and died. The Inca's wives charged Diego with his death and the friar was put to death with great cruelty. Friar Marcos, on hearing of his friend's death, tried to return up the valley but was drowned crossing the river.

So in 1571 it was the turn of Tupac Amaru, Manco's third son to become Inca. His reign was to be short-lived. The new viceroy, Don Francisco de Toledo, determined to root out and kill the last Inca, sent an ambassador to Vilcapampa to invite The Inca to talks in Cuzco. Tupac Amaru's warriors waylaid the ambassador in the mountains and killed him. News of the death of the ambassador and the martyrdom of the two Augustinian friars reached the viceroy at the same time. This was the last straw and the viceroy sent a small band of well-trained troops to capture The Inca. Tupac Amaru was snatched by surprise and taken to Cuzco along with his wife and children where the viceroy put on the grand spectacle of a mock trial. The Spaniards used great brutality when torturing Inca chiefs. Tupac Amaru's wife was mangled to death before his eyes. He was beheaded and his head placed on a pole in the Plaza in Cuzco.

The Urubamba valley fell silent and the great city of the Incas was lost for almost three hundred and fifty years until it was rediscovered by Hiram Bingham on 24 July 1911.

The train was now slowly making its way through the Urubamba valley and the scenery was breathtaking. The train followed the contours of the River Vilcanota as it wound its way through the narrow canyon. The sheer sides of the mountains rose perpendicular to the sky and almost blocked out the sun. The air had become warm and sultry and the dense undergrowth on either side told us that we had entered the jungle. High up we could see the ruins of a fortress or an old Inca shrine. The crosses had long since disappeared.

"Look at that cave high up on the rock!" remarked the lady sitting behind us.

"Did the ancient Incas live in caves?" she asked.

"I don't think so, Emily," answered her husband, "I never read anything about that. Of course if you go back far enough they probably did. We all lived in caves at one time."

"They buried their dead in caves," said a friend opposite. "I read that when they found Machu Picchu they discovered lots of bones in the caves underneath the mountain."

"This would be a beautiful journey even if it led nowhere," remarked Maria, looking up from the book she was reading.

"I hope I have the energy to enjoy it," said Carlos, his teeth a bright green from chewing coca leaves. "I didn't get a wink of sleep last night."

"We all stayed in the hostel off the Plaza de Armas," explained Ana, "and there were people coming and going all night."

"That's why we are going to stay at the hot springs near Machu Picchu," added Maria, "to relax for a day in the warm water. Tomorrow we hope to go to the top."

"Unfortunately I have to return to Cuzco this evening," said Carlos, "my plane leaves for Lima in the morning."

The man with the toilet roll made his way past us for about the fifth time. Suddenly there was a loud screech of brakes as the train gradually came to a halt.

"Is this Machu Picchu?" asked the lady behind.

"Doesn't look like it," replied someone else, "nobody seems to be getting off."

One of the Swiss girls put her head out the window and asked an Indian where we were.

"*Aguas Calientes* (Hot Springs)," he replied. With that, Ana and Maria grabbed their haversacks and jumped off the train. From the side of the track they waved a quick goodbye.

The next stop was Machu Picchu and everyone piled out and on to minibuses to make the short journey up the snake-like track called 'Bingham Way'. This was the same route that Hiram Bingham had taken with his Indian guide on that memorable day in 1911. Hacking his way through the undergrowth, undeterred by the presence of poisonous snakes, he eventually reached the top. Although it was almost completely covered by trees and scrub, the ruins that he observed peeping through, immediately told him that he had found the 'lost city' of Vilcapampa. He asked an Indian who was living on the site what this place was called.

"Machu Picchu," came the reply, and that is how it has been known ever since. Machu Picchu is the name of the mountain and it just means 'old peak' in Quechua. Opposite there is a smaller mountain called Huayna Picchu or 'young peak'. In between, covering an area of five square kilometres, lie the ruins of the 'Lost City of the Incas'. It is an awe-inspiring sight, no less so today than when Hiram Bingham first saw it. It is surely one of the great wonders of the world. I climbed up the stone steps to the highest point and sat down on a rock and observed the scene.

My visit to the wondrous Machu Picchu

Machu Picchu is indeed a spiritual experience. How could anyone build such a place on top of a barren mountain? Its origins and history were never written down and archaeologists and scientists are still trying to discover its hidden secrets. Over seventy per cent of the ruins have been restored using the original stones which were still in place and it is possible to distinguish different sectors of the city. There is the agricultural sector with its system of terraces covering a large section of the mountain. The rich clay used in these terraces had to be carried on people's backs from the valley below. There is the sector of the nobles and the Military Tower, under which is the Royal Mausoleum hewn out of the granite rock. The city is served by a system of aqueducts, an extraordinary work of human ingenuity to be able to carry and distribute water at such heights. The water still flows to this day. There is the palace of The Inca, the sacred Plaza, the Temple, the famous Three Windows and at the highest point the *Intihuatana* (Sun dial). The Sun dial is hewn out of one huge granite rock. *Intihuatana* in Quechua means 'the place where the Sun is linked to the earth'.

Machu Picchu is above all a very personal experience. It means different things to different people and no words can describe its grandeur – you have to see it for yourself. I didn't need an organised tour of its various parts. I just sat there and contemplated its beauty. Some llamas and alpacas grazed lazily among the ruins. As I reflected on the indomitable human spirit of a people that could create such a work of art against a background of such natural beauty, I thought here indeed was the true soul of the Incas.

My contemplation was suddenly disturbed.

"That must have been the kitchen, Nigel," suggested a lady entering one of the ruins.

"I wonder what they used for fuel?" asked another.

"I wouldn't like to have to walk up all those steps every day," observed an old man as he sat on one of the steps.

Then a group of schoolgirls from Lima appeared just below me. They were giggling and laughing together. They had spotted a young German tourist, six feet tall with blonde hair and blue eyes. (I should mention that all Peruvian girls have long black hair and dark eyes. Their ideal boy is any gringo but especially one with blonde hair and blue eyes.) They all descended on the poor innocent German. Each one wanted their photo taken with him. Not a word was spoken. The German boy was shy and embarrassed, but they didn't want to let him go. He wanted to get away. He had come to see Machu Picchu – the experience of a lifetime.

12
Return to the Mountains

A llama train in Combapata

Combapata could be described as a 'one-horse' town, if it had a horse! It is situated on the Sicuani–Cuzco road between Tinta and Checacupe. It nestles in a beautiful valley where two rivers meet, the River Vilcanota and the River Salcca. One of the four great Inca roads leading out from Cuzco, the *Collasuyo*, passes through Combapata on its way south to Lake Titicaca. The *Antisuyo* is the great road that goes eastwards. *Antisuyo* means 'the land of the *Anti*' or 'place where the Sun is born'. It is thought that this is the origin of the word 'Andes', the range of mountains that formed the backbone of the Inca Empire.

The Inca would have stopped at Combapata on his journeys south. There would have been an important *tambo* beside the river. Today a giant iron bridge crosses the River Salcca just outside Combapata and alongside it are the remains of three other bridges dating back to the old rope bridges of Inca times. Just up the road beyond Tinta are the famous

232

ruins of Raqchi where the Virgins of the Sun came to stay at certain times of the year. Combapata was a very important historical site in the time of the Incas. The name 'Combapata' is made up of two Aymara words meaning 'the place of defeat'. It was here between the two rivers that the Incas gained their decisive victory over the Aymaras and stopped their advance on Cuzco. The surrounding mountains still retain their Aymara names.

When the Spaniards conquered Cuzco and went in search of their El Dorado, they soon discovered that the mountains around Combapata contained vast deposits of gold, copper and zinc. Today the remains of the old Spanish mines can be seen everywhere. The conquistadors brought with them their priests and missionaries who built beautiful churches with their new-found wealth. The church in Combapata is one of the earliest churches built by the Spanish in Peru. First a giant cross was placed over the place of Inca worship and afterwards a church was built on the spot. In this way it was hoped that all semblance of idolatry was obliterated. The church was built in the old colonial style and has recently been declared a national monument by the Peruvian Institute of National Culture.

☆   ☆   ☆

"*Allillanchu, Papay,*" said Lorenzo, the *economo*, as he opened the giant doors of the church on that first Sunday morning.

"You are very welcome to our church in Combapata. We very seldom have Mass here."

"*Allillanmi, Lorenzo,*" I replied, "there's a large crowd of people in the Plaza for the market. Will they all come to church?"

"When they hear the bell some will come. They don't know we have a new priest yet. There should be a lot of baptisms afterwards. We haven't had baptisms for a long time."

"Is the baptismal register in the sacristy?" I asked.

"No, it is kept in Sicuani. Padre Leonidas just wrote the names on a piece of paper, and what he did with them after that no one knows. He didn't come to Combapata very often."

We made our way up the darkened church to the sacristy. Our footsteps made a strange eerie sound on the stone floor of the empty church. I had brought the vestments and chalice I would need for the

Mass. On either side there were adobe altars dedicated to various saints. On one was placed a replica of St Isidor with his wooden plough and pair of oxen. He was dressed as an Indian. There were a few dilapidated benches near the high altar. On the walls were beautiful oil paintings with scenes from the Bible. Some were beginning to fray at the edges. At the back of the church there was a high balcony for the choir with an intricately carved banister in front.

"That's the famous shrine to 'La Virgen del Rosario'," explained Lorenzo, proudly pointing to a beautiful glass shrine in which was placed a statue of Our Lady of the Rosary.

"We celebrate her fiesta on 7 October every year. The fiesta lasts three days and people come from all over Peru."

The statue was dressed in the finest robes with a silver crown on her head. Her cloak was a dark blue, embroidered at the edges with gold and diamonds. In one hand she held the child Jesus, dressed in a white sailor's suit with a Peruvian naval officer's cap!

"Was Jesus in the navy?" I asked jokingly.

"He was often in a boat," he replied seriously, "and the Apostles always caught fish when He was with them."

In her other hand Our Lady held a pair of pearl rosary beads. The whole shrine stood out like a bright jewel in an oasis of misery.

"What's that?" I asked, pointing to a cartwheel attached to the side of the sanctuary, with little bells all around it.

"They are the bells," he replied solemnly. "They are very old. They say the Spaniards brought them to Combapata. We use them during Holy Week but there is a knack to ringing them."

The high altar was backed by a magnificent wood carving which stretched from floor to ceiling. In the centre was Christ on the cross surrounded by various saints placed in niches carved out of the wood. I recognised St John the Evangelist and St Toribio.

"I have been *economo* for over twenty years, but I have very little to do," explained Lorenzo as he unlocked the padlock on the sacristy door. "I think I'll retire soon."

"Don't tell me we're going to have another election for *economo*," I thought to myself. That would be too much.

"I sleep in the sacristy every night to guard the treasures," he added.

"Has anything been stolen?" I asked tentatively.

234

"Not yet," he replied with a note of relief in his voice. "We have been very lucky, but last year the *economo* in San Pablo was murdered and all the treasures of the church were stolen."

"Do you have a gun?"

"No, but my dog sleeps with me. Now you will have to excuse me, *Papay*, I have to go and ring the bell, otherwise there will be no one at the Mass."

He slowly ascended a narrow stone staircase which led from the back of the church to the bell tower. The sacristy was in utter chaos. Just inside the door some boards were placed on adobes with a poncho thrown on top. This was where Lorenzo slept with his dog. There was a crate of empty beer bottles beside his bed. Things were strewn all over the room. A glass casket with a broken panel lay in the middle of the floor. There were statues of different shapes and sizes, all in various stages of undress. There was a strong smell of musty clothes. Ancient wooden trunks were placed one on top of the other, each securely fastened with an old Spanish lock. They looked as if they had just been unloaded from some Spanish galleon. Old oil paintings were stacked haphazardly side by side, the precious works of art being slowly eaten away by church mice. The vestment bench was covered with an inch of dust. As I pulled out the drawers there were Latin missals and old maniples together with half-used candles. Everything was in a state of decay and there was a huge hole in the ceiling where the plaster had fallen down.

The solemn tones of the bell rang out and the whole place began to vibrate. I decided to vest in the sanctuary.

"Where are the cruets for the wine and water?" I asked Lorenzo.

"We haven't got any," he replied casually, "Padre Leonidas always took the wine from the bottle."

I was to be the first resident priest in Combapata in living memory. When I decided to return to Peru, having served as parish priest in Knocklyon in Dublin for three years, Tiny asked me where I would like to go.

"Wherever the need is greatest," I explained, "somewhere that needs building up."

Although my heart was in Yauri I didn't particularly want to go back. It would be like beginning again. I had built it up during my five years there and now an American priest was carrying on the work.

"Combapata is just the place," the bishop suggested, "it has been neglected for years and you will have to begin from scratch. There isn't even a parish house there."

The parish stretches for miles out into the surrounding mountains with most of the communities along the fertile valley of the River Vilcanota. The climate here is not as harsh as that of Yauri. Maize and wheat are grown, together with all kinds of vegetables. Even the eucalyptus trees, imported from Australia long ago, do well here. Although we are still surrounded by mountains, Combapata is about a thousand feet lower down than Yauri.

I lived in very primitive conditions in a hut beside the church while the new parish house was being built. My toilet was again a hole in the ground and I longed for the sound of flushing water. I was lucky to get a 'handy man' named Pedro who came from Sicuani and was an expert at building huts. He even knew a little about plumbing and electricity.

Adobes from an ancient burial ground

We began with the adobes. As we dug the foundations we discovered we were in the middle of an ancient burial ground. It has always been the custom to bury the dead near the church. People believe that the nearer they are buried to the church the nearer they will be to God forever. Skull after skull of all shapes and sizes were dug up. Many were clearly of little babies. These skulls were very well preserved with all their teeth in perfect condition. The Quechua word for 'sweet' is *miski*, but in general the Indians don't like sweet things. Consequently they don't normally suffer from tooth decay. Each morning we noticed that all the skulls we had dug up the day before had vanished. As is the usual practice the Indians were coming during the night and taking them away to put in their houses to ward off other evil spirits.

Each day Pedro gave me a list of materials and I later made the long journey to Cuzco or Sicuani in my jeep. Italy is financing the construction of a new road from Cuzco to Puno. Very soon now the journey will be much less hazardous.

When I arrived back in Peru from Ireland I had to drive by jeep from Lima along the coastal route to Arequipa and from there via Yauri to Combapata. It was strange seeing my old parish again, remembering all that had happened. I had some very happy memories and a few sad ones. The Plaza de Armas was quiet and almost deserted as I made my way to see Geovanna. It was a very emotional meeting. I wanted to surprise her, as she didn't know I was coming. I tried to slip in by the back door unnoticed but the dog began barking. Marisol ran out to see who it was. She looked at me for a moment.

"Padre," she shouted and ran to put her arms around me. Geovanna appeared at the door and stopped dead in her tracks. She just stared in silence. She couldn't move. She was barefoot, dressed in her grey school uniform as if she had just returned from school. Her long black hair was uncombed and dishevelled. We looked at each other for a moment which seemed like eternity. I put out my hands and she came running towards me. She jumped into my arms and hugged me, the tears streaming down her cheeks.

"Geovanna!" I said.

"I knew you would come back," she cried, "I told Marisol. Last night I dreamed that you would come back again."

She held on to me tightly. She didn't want to let me go.

"Wait until you see the rabbits!" she exclaimed, by now laughing and jumping with delight. (I had given her all my rabbits when I left.)

"I gave one to Trinidad every month as you told me. The mammy rabbits had plenty of babies."

Now she just wanted to talk and talk.

"I can write my name," she boasted, "and I am learning all about the Incas in school."

"What class are you in?"

"I went into fourth class this year. I want to ask you a favour but I will wait until tomorrow."

"Can you still count up to ten in English?" I asked.

"One, two, buckle my shoe," she began, holding up her fingers.

"Three, four, open the door. Five, six, I'm in a fix. Seven, eight, I'm going to be late. Nine, ten, I don't know when."

This was a rhyme I had taught her when she was about three years old and she never forgot it.

"Tell me about the little piggy that went to the market," she said, laughing.

"Let's go on a picnic to Santo Domingo tomorrow and we can catch fish in the river, just like before," I suggested. This was where we always went for a day out.

"And I can drive the jeep," she added, "I'm sure my feet can reach the pedals now." She loved to steer the jeep through the *pampa* while sitting on my knee.

As I turned around Trinidad had just entered the patio. She put her arms around me and gave me a big hug.

"*Papay*, it is wonderful that you have come back. I thought I might die and not see you again. You know you have to say the Mass for my funeral."

"That won't be for a long time," I replied. "You knew I wouldn't forget you."

"I never forgot you," she said, "you have to forgive me, *Papay*, but I haven't got a chicken for you this time. (The one in the bucket, cooked, feathers and all!) I don't have money to buy gifts at the moment. Maybe the next time." Her excuse was a gem of an understatement as Trinidad never had any money. I smiled to myself thinking of the chicken and thanked God for small mercies.

Aurelia arrived. She was obviously pregnant.

"I'm expecting a baby tomorrow," she explained. "If it's a boy I will call it after you. Even if it's a girl I can still call it after you."

Her mother would help her deliver the baby on a blanket on the clay floor of her hut. She was just fifteen years of age. Maria, the parish secretary, was still working in the office. She had now become an expert on the typewriter that I had bought her shortly before I left.

"Where's Benigno?" I asked.

"He's probably in the *chacra* but he'll come quickly when he hears you are back."

The political and economic situation in Peru deteriorated drastically during the three years I was away. The country is going through the worst economic crisis in its history and that is really saying something. Inflation has now reached over 3000%. They say that people in restaurants in Lima are paying for their meal at the beginning because by the end it will have doubled in price. And as always it is the poor, the elderly and the children who suffer most. People are queuing six or seven hours each day for bread and milk. In a country so rich in natural resources there is a shortage of sugar, flour, rice and tinned milk. They

"It is always the poor who suffer"

say that even potatoes are being imported. Ships are waiting in the harbours to be paid before they unload their cargoes. More and more the poor are losing their dignity as human beings. Even little children are peddling on the streets. They will sell as little as one match and one cigarette at a time. The only redress that the people have against the government is to go on strike, but strikes rarely achieve anything and are usually put down with brute force by the police. At the moment the mines, banks, schools, transport, hospitals and universities are all affected by strikes.

One of the methods that the strikers use is to block the roads with huge boulders and stones. Even in the mountains you can suddenly come around a bend to be confronted by stones all over the road. There is no one to be seen and slowly you must remove the stones to make a way through. The country is in chaos. This has been the aim of the terrorists and they thrive on such confusion. They blow up the electricity pylons around Lima and plunge the city into darkness for days on end. They have also contaminated the water by destroying the filtering system.

The terrorist campaign is also gathering pace in the mountains. Almost every town and community has been infiltrated by terrorists. They find willing recruits among the young people who have nothing to do. Their main targets are the police and government agents but often women and children are killed as 'collaborators'. The name *Senderista* has become synonymous with one man, their leader, Abimael Guzman Reynoso, known by his *nom de guerre*, Camarada Gonzalo. He has become a kind of Scarlet Pimpernel, appearing everywhere, yet the police find it impossible to catch him. He is a master of disguise.

Abimael Guzman was born in 1934 in the southern coastal town of Mollendo, the offspring of an unmarried woman's liaison with a married man. At the age of fourteen he was sent to the Catholic High School in Arequipa. He was very intelligent and studious, always receiving top marks for good conduct. "He was a model boy, a priest's dream, a mother's pride and joy," recalls a former classmate. At the University of St Augustine, in Arequipa, Guzman studied philosophy and law simultaneously, earning degrees in both. His thesis in philosophy was 'About Kant's Theory of Space", and in law 'The Democratic Bourgeois State'. He was also interested in classical music and literature, especially James Joyce and Ernest Hemingway.

By 1968 Guzman and his followers had gained control of the University of Ayacucho. Guzman, who had spent some time in China, eventually became the director of personnel, and brought his political influence to bear on the University's 'hiring and firing' policies. It was said that even the night watchman was a *Senderista*. Guzman decided to begin action in 1980 in the belief that the ideal conditions for revolution existed and that the road to Communism in Peru was through a 'prolonged popular war.' From Mao and the Chinese Long March, *Sendero Luminoso* derived the strategy of a 'prolonged popular war' to surround the cities from the countryside. Its goal was to create a 'Republic of the New Democracy', a peasant workers' republic to be headed by President Gonzalo.

In choosing Ayacucho and the central southern sierra as the site for the 'prolonged popular war', Guzman showed shrewd judgement. Ayacucho and its surrounding areas form the poorest and most neglected parts of Peru. This part of the country has always been known as La Mancha India (The Indian Stain). The majority of its inhabitants are Indians, scratching out a living in some 500 communities scattered over the bleak Andean mountainside and its remote valleys. The area had been ignored by governments in Lima for centuries and state investment in the region was non-existent. Most of the people had neither water nor electricity.

The basis for the revolution had been laid at the University. For many years now, the courses had been taught by professors who were *Senderistas*. When the graduating students returned to their communities as teachers, they sowed *Senderista* ideology. As one student wrote, "*Sendero* didn't send out cadres – it sent teachers." They were sent back where they came from, teaching Marxism with the *Sendero* line. Just as Lenin had used the workers and Chairman Mao the peasants, so *Sendero* used the University for its own ends.

Their main weapons are dynamite and fear. Their main targets are the 'corporate State' and 'imperialist technology' in all their manifestations – public works projects, electricity pylons, agricultural research stations, and agricultural co-operatives. They have also carried out selective assassinations of village mayors and officials, rural traders, large landowners and rustlers.

Just a short time ago they attacked an aid project in Santo Tomás. A group of French volunteers were working on a project in the nearby mountains. The terrorists entered the area and captured two of the French group along with some Indians and accused them of being imperial agents. They brought them before the people in the Plaza for a 'popular trial'. The final verdict was left to the mob.

"Are they innocent or guilty?" they asked. When the people shouted 'guilty', they were brutally tortured and killed. Once more the women took a more active part and were much more brutal in these tortures than the men. The 'accused' were given a Communist death sentence: hammers and sickles. They beat them with the hammers and cut their throats with the sickles. Afterwards they desecrated the bodies by ordering the people to urinate on them.

They have also targeted the tourist industry. The Mayor of Jersey City in New Jersey and his wife visited the Mayor of Cuzco with a view to twinning the two cities. The highlight of their tour was to be their visit to Machu Picchu. The terrorists sabotaged the train in the Urubamba Valley and it plunged down a ravine, killing both mayors' wives instantly. The international publicity of this event has since reduced the volume of tourists considerably. A young Dutch couple set out to walk the Inca Way over the mountains to Machu Picchu and disappeared. Their bodies were later discovered in a shallow grave.

More recently the terrorists have declared war on the Catholic Church, threatening to kill all foreign priests and nuns unless they leave the country. In the beginning they avoided attacking the Church, claiming that it was on their side but recent events have shown that they have changed their strategy. A short time ago they captured two Polish Franciscan priests and a nun and took them to the mountains to be judged. The nun managed to escape but the two priests were killed. Their only crime was that they were working with the poor. Recently they shot an Italian priest as he got out of his truck having just said Mass in a poor community.

One night in May a column of about sixty members of *Sendero Luminoso*, some no more than teenagers, and many in their pre-teens, entered the village of Huasihuasi. They had a list of people who had been 'sentenced to death'. They gathered everyone in the Plaza and lined up the people on the list before them. One of these was an Australian nun, Sister Irene McCormack. All the 'accused' were put lying face down and the charges were read out. Sister McCormack who distributed food from Caritas to the poor, was accused of being a 'Yankee Imperialist'. The people protested that she was not American but Australian. One of the terrorists shouted;

"Does anyone want to volunteer to take her place?"

There was a long silence. No one uttered a word. She was the first to be killed. Her only crime was that she ran soup kitchens for the poor. She first began with one soup kitchen for seventy children and ten elderly people but with the deteriorating economic situation she had expanded her work to twenty-five soup kitchens.

Tiny called a meeting of all the priests and nuns of the prelature. We discussed the situation and everyone was given the option of going or staying. We were aware of the dangers. All foreign priests were under 'sentence of death'. We all decided to stay.

The building of my house in Combapata advanced very quickly. Within a few months I was able to move in. There is wonderful satisfaction in being able to design and build your own house. It's not a very complicated architectural design. It consists of a kitchen and a sitting room with a little alcove off it for my bed. Tiny gave me a large wooden bed that belonged to the former bishop and was too big for his own room. I was able to build the alcove around it. At the front of the

My house in Combapata under contruction

house there is a meeting room, an office and an extra bedroom. The most important part of the house is the toilet and the shower. I had gone to both Sicuani and Cuzco to buy all my kitchen utensils and I was reminded of the journey I made from Yauri with Des. There is one great difference between Yauri and Combapata and that is the presence of electricity. I have an electric cooker and electric light. This is paradise. No more cooking with *bosta*.

Finland had generously donated the electrical equipment to Combapata. A ship arrived in Lima with transformers, cable, sockets, bulbs, switches etc. From there the equipment was transported by truck to Combapata. They even sent the electricians to install it. The electricity comes from Machu Picchu. So far only the town has electricity, but gradually it is hoped to extend it to the communities. The only thing that Finland forgot to supply was meters, so up to now everyone has free electricity. That will certainly be rectified very soon.

The first thing I wanted to set up in the parish was an office where the Indians could come and arrange for baptisms, marriages and masses. I also needed a group of catechists to teach the people in the communities and prepare them for the sacraments. I was lucky to get a young girl called Nemesia as parish secretary. She is an Indian and an orphan. Her parents are not dead but they have abandoned her. About eighteen years old she is very intelligent, having just finished school this year. At least I don't have to teach her how to read and write! I got a baptismal register in Sicuani and she has already begun to enter the names and index them. She also prepares the families for baptism. She speaks Quechua fluently and is very good with the Indians.

During the building of my house I took the opportunity to do an intensive Quechua course in Cuzco. Back in the seventeenth century the Church always encouraged the speaking of Quechua and no one could be appointed parish priest to the Indians unless they could preach in Quechua. Like all American Indian languages, it functions on completely different grammatical principles from that of European languages. This makes it extremely difficult to learn. Although Quechua has a very complex grammar system it has one redeeming quality – it conforms to rules. It has words for everything. For instance there are three different verbs 'to lift'. It depends on how high you are lifting something – as far as the knee, the chest or above your head. This would have corresponded to the 'lift' necessary to put *bosta* on the fire, a *bulto* on the llama, or thatch on the roof.

One of the difficulties with Quechua is understanding all the different accents and dialects from the various regions of the mountains. This is where Nemesia is invaluable. I am able to say Mass, to baptise and perform the marriage ceremony in Quechua. All the Indian women go to confession in Quechua and sometimes they 'get away with murder'. I couldn't understand for a long time what *chaymanta* meant. It was repeated many times during confession. One day on a visit to Sicuani I asked Padre Leonidas what kind of sin was *chaymanta*. He laughed and explained that it wasn't a sin at all. It was a connecting word that meant 'and next'. Many Quechua words have been adopted into English, mainly the words for certain plants and animals such as puma, llama, alpaca, condor, chinchilla, coca, quinine etc.

The parish house in Combapata is beside the police station and faces on to the Plaza. There isn't the same tension with the police as there was in Yauri but apart from bidding them the time of day, I don't get over-friendly with them. One never knows when I might have to denounce them for some injustice or other. The sergeant, a fat chubby man, a typical South American policeman, always jokes that he must keep friends with the Padre in case I'll excommunicate him. I really think he believes it because this was always the threat during colonial times when the Church wielded great power.

Being beside the police station has its disadvantages as it is usually the first place to be attacked by terrorists and I was in the line of fire. I put a large wooden cross on the wall outside my house so that the terrorists wouldn't mistake me for the police. I would hate to be killed, mistaken for a policeman, or worst still as an 'Irish Imperialist'!

Many police stations in the mountains have been abandoned because of fear of the terrorists, much to the delight of the local people. As the police spend most of their time playing cards, following cockfights or abusing the Indians, the people feel that they could get on very well without them. It is true that in these remote areas life can be more peaceful without them. The local communities have their own vigilante groups which are much more effective than the police. The communities also administer their own justice which means that lawyers and judges could also be dispensed with. The police are often drunk and the usual bribe when one is caught for some slight misdemeanour is a crate of beer. If you cannot pay you are thrown in the calaboose of which there are a number in every police station. Torture is a normal part of police training in order to obtain confessions. Sometimes at night I can hear the roars and screams of some unfortunate victim who is being tortured.

A short time ago a young Indian was brought in, accused of stealing a *chakitaklla*. The story emerged later that they began to torture him by holding his head under water and then prodding him with electric wires. He died of electrocution. His body was hastily buried in an unmarked grave and the next day the real culprit was found.

Tiny has set up a committee in Sicuani to investigate abuses of human rights. All their investigations are published and the abusers named. The police are extremely worried. When I asked the sergeant if he had caught the culprit for a recent robbery he replied;

"If it wasn't for this issue of 'human rights' I'd have solved it long ago."

The police have no transport and they are always looking for a lift in my jeep. I soon realised that this would make me a prime target for *Sendero* so I had to come up with a plan. There were two things that were forbidden in my jeep. The first was that you couldn't smoke. This applied mainly to the other priests. The Indians never smoke. The second was that you couldn't carry firearms. This took care of the police as they all wore a pistol. Of course when the police put up their hand you had to stop.

"*Buenos días, Padre*. Can you give me a lift to Cuzco?"

"Certainly, no problem. There is just one difficulty. You will have to leave your pistol behind. As a priest and follower of Jesus Christ, the Prince of Peace, I don't carry firearms. I don't believe in violence."

"But where can I leave my pistol? I must wear it at all times."

"Oh, I'm very sorry, maybe some other time!"

I have to suppress a smile as I drive away.

Shortly after a terrorist attack nearby, the police brought a machine gun into my office and put it on the table.

"You will need that for your protection," they said.

"No thanks," I replied, "we don't use firearms."

A machine gun would be of little use against the terrorists. They always had much more powerful weapons than the police.

Today I am on my way to the community of Huantura with Nemesia to celebrate the feast of the Assumption. The communities in Combapata are not as far away from the town as those in Yauri and they can usually be reached by jeep in a couple of hours. If I have to travel by horse it can take all day. As we crossed the new suspension bridge over the River Salcca we could see below us an Indian fishing from a little island in the middle of the river.

"Are there much fish here?" I asked Nemesia.

"There is plenty of trout," she replied, "Combapata is famous for its trout. It is very tasty when it is roasted on *bosta* but you have to be careful that the fish are not from the River Vilcanota."

"Why is that?"

"The Vilcanota is completely contaminated from the hospital in Sicuani. They throw all the waste directly into the river."

"All fish look the same to me," I said, "how can you tell the difference?"

"A woman in Combapata once found a syringe inside a fish from the Vilcanota."

"Maybe it was on drugs," I suggested, jokingly.

No reaction. An Indian's sense of humour is much different from mine.

"Did you ever go to the hospital in Sicuani?" I asked.

"That would be the last place I'd go if I was sick. They say that if you are alright going in, you will certainly be sick coming out."

As we drove up the valley we saw some children on their way to school. They were taking a shortcut through the river. The water was up to their thighs as they waded across.

"That looks very dangerous," I remarked.

"They are used to it," Nemesia explained, "they come from Culcuire at the other end of the valley. If they don't cross through the river they have to come all the way around by the bridge. They can't cross in the rainy season, but of course some try. Every year two or three children are drowned in the river. Sometimes their bodies are carried all the way to Cuzco."

"In the time of the Incas," I suggested, "they would have built another rope bridge."

"I wish the Incas were here now," she sighed.

"How do the children dry themselves?" I asked.

"They don't," she replied, "they just let the sun dry them."

"But their legs will get chapped and sore," I suggested.

"They have a secret remedy," she responded, smiling.

"Can you tell me the secret?"

"They urinate on their hands and rub it into their legs," she explained, as if it was the most natural thing in the world. "This prevents them getting chapped."

"Go on," I retorted incredulously, "you're pulling my leg."

"Pulling your leg?" she repeated.

"Joking," I explained.

"It's true!" she said, "look at that boy who has just come out of the water."

Sure enough, he was urinating on his hands and rubbing his legs. Of course urinating in public is second nature to them. They are not embarrassed. The other children proceeded to do the same.

"The Indians use urine for everything," she continued. "It heals wounds, it soothes your feet after a long walk and mothers give it to their children to cure some illnesses."

"I would have thought it would kill them," I said, trying to imagine how you could possibly give urine to a child.

"And the Indian women wash their hair in it," she added, "it's a wonderful shampoo."

Cleaning the hair and searching for fleas

"Shampoo!" I repeated, surprised.

"Yes," she said, "they save their urine and leave it in the sun for five or six days and then they shampoo their hair with it."

"What about the smell?" I asked.

"The smell disappears after about five minutes, and it leaves your hair clean and shiny."

"I often wondered how the Indian women got their hair lovely and shiny," I commented.

"It also kills all the fleas and lice," she added.

What a conversation to have on the way to celebrate the feast of the Assumption. But then Indians are not accustomed to the niceties of life, they are more in tune with the reality.

By now we had turned on to a twisting track running up the side of the mountain and were in sight of Huantura. A boy in the bell tower spotted us coming and began ringing the bell. The band was waiting for us a short distance from the church. The drums began to beat and the tin whistles struck up a merry *huayno* (traditional Andean) tune. Some of the band were a little unsteady on their feet. Obviously they had begun to celebrate a little early with the *chicha*. A group of dancers dressed in animal skins formed a guard of honour as I entered the chapel. One of the group was dressed as the Devil with a mask over his face and a long forked tail behind him.

The people were dressed in their multicoloured costumes as they gathered around the door of the chapel for Mass. I greeted them in Quechua and Nemesia proceeded to explain the meaning of the Mass and the fiesta. A large statue of Our Lady of the Assumption stood on a pedestal beside the door. The *alferado* took pride of place before the altar with his wife and children. He was holding a banner on which was embroidered the date and the feast, with his name underneath. This is a very important day for Cirilio as he was responsible for the celebration of the feast, its organisation and expense. He had volunteered for this honour the last time the feast was celebrated and perhaps he would never have the privilege again in his lifetime.

Nemesia started a hymn in Quechua and the Mass began. There is something special about saying Mass in the open air, high up in the Andes and surrounded by nature. The poor Indians took part with a sense of awe and reverence, not understanding much of what was happening, certainly not knowing any of the responses. But what was lacking in intellectual understanding was made up for by physical presence and attitude.

Afterwards the statue of Our Lady was carried in procession around the four corners of the village, stopping at each corner for a blessing. As the procession returned to the chapel the president of the community addressed the crowd;

Nemesia leading the procession

"I would like to thank Padre Cristobal for coming to our community today. It is indeed a great honour and privilege for us all. We are happy to have a priest with us again. I would also like to thank Cirilio for being *alferado*, and for the way he has organised this feast. Our Lady will give him many blessings. Now we need an *alferado* for the next feast. Who would like to volunteer?"

A great silence . . .

"How about you, Marco? You haven't prepared a feast yet."

"Not this time," protested Marco, "some of my animals have been sick and I wouldn't be able to take it on."

"Climaco, how about you?"

"The children are not well and I have a lot of responsibilities."

One after the other they declined the offer, not so much because of the honour but because of the expense involved. Eventually a young man

250

called Abdon, who was standing beside Cirilio, decided to accept and everyone clapped.

"Now we can continue with the celebration!" shouted the president.

What he really meant was that now we could begin eating and drinking. We proceeded to Cirilio's hut where a poncho had been placed on a stone in the patio, behind a little home-made table. I took my seat in the place of honour and everyone sat around in a circle. Nemesia sat on one side of me and Cirilio asked the local teacher to sit on the other side. It was important to find someone who could talk to the padre. The women were busy in the 'kitchen' except there was no kitchen. All the cooking was done outside. There was a fire in the corner made of *bosta* with one large brown pot cooking on it. From this pot the concoction was ladled out on to tin plates. I was first to be served.

I had learned from experience not to examine the contents too closely. On one occasion when I discovered 'peas' in my soup I couldn't understand where the Indians had got them. On closer examination I realised that they were sheep droppings they had forgotten to clean out.

"How is your wife?" asked the teacher as I was about to start my soup. (I wasn't surprised. This was something I had learned to expect. Everyone asks about the wife. In the beginning I used to try and explain, but they never listen to explanations. At the end they would usually say;

"But she's keeping well?"

The easiest way out of a problem in Peru is to agree.)

"She's fine," I replied, "I left her at home." Nemesia giggled. I gave her a nudge to keep quiet.

The band began to play. That soon stopped the conversation. I couldn't hear a thing. They have an idea that the louder they play, the better the music. I put my hands to my ears to indicate it was too loud, but they thought I couldn't hear it so they played louder!

Next came the main course. It was roast guinea pig carried solemnly to the table. I know now how Henry VIII must have felt at a medieval banquet. Of course he didn't have guinea pig.

I had seen it being prepared earlier. Every Indian family keeps guinea pigs. Over twenty million guinea pigs are eaten annually in Peru. They breed frequently and have litters of up to thirteen at a time. They shed their milk teeth in the womb and are able to eat within a day of being born. They live and sleep with the Indians in their huts and they love the warmth of the fire. They come in various colours but are usually light brown, sometimes with a white streak.

I always think it dreadful that such beautiful little creatures are running around one minute and the next are being roasted on the fire. The woman just bends down and picks out the fattest little guinea pig. With one twist of her hand she kills it. She then cuts it open and cleans it out, at the same time skinning it. It is then roasted on the fire, cooked whole, with a stick through it to keep it stretched. Some hot stones are placed inside it to make sure it is completely cooked. Although it looks revolting, it is quite tasty and when you are hungry you can't be too choosy. A roast guinea pig was the gift that the Indians offered to The Inca when he visited their village. They always offer the best to their guests.

13
A Visit to the Medicine Man

Geovanna made her way quickly along Hatun Rumiyoc Street in Cuzco towards the church of San Blas. She didn't even notice the stone of the twelve angles, one of the great tourist attractions of the city. A miracle of engineering, this great stone is part of the old Inca wall which still forms part of this street. It is one of the oldest streets in Cuzco and has remained untouched since Inca times. Even the many earthquakes that Cuzco experiences have failed to move this structure.

Geovanna had other things on her mind. Dressed in her brown track suit and runners she carried her school bag over her shoulder. It is early morning and she is on her way to the Carmelite convent at San Blas. The name of her school is written in bold letters on her tracksuit 'Las Carmelitas, Cuzco'. On the front is the Carmelite crest with the motto clearly visible. It is written in Latin, *'Zelo Zelatus Sum Pro Domino Deo Exercituum'* (With Zeal I am Zealous for the Lord God of Hosts).

As she begins to climb the steep stone steps, her friends Angelica and Ines join her. They too are nervous and excited. They immediately begin to discuss tactics; the angles of the shots, the blocking, the marking. Today's match is the highlight of the season. La Merced is the strongest team in the championship. Their girls are taller and have the advantage at smashing and blocking. These are the skills needed in volleyball. The Carmelites, although smaller, are more skilful and have greater stamina. Geovanna is the captain of the team. Her altitude training on the high *pampa* of Yauri has prepared her well. She runs up the stone steps with the greatest of ease. They pass some tourists who have stopped to rest on their way to see the wooden pulpit in the church of San Blas. The effort is too great for some and they give up. As the girls turn the corner into the Plaza in front of the church, the bell sounds for the beginning of class. They run to reach the door before it closes. Otherwise they will have to wait outside until after assembly and face the wrath of the head nun for arriving late.

This was the great favour that Geovanna wanted to ask me when I returned from Ireland. It was while we were fishing in Santo Domingo that she brought up the subject. Putting her arms around me she said;

"Could you get me into a school in Cuzco? I don't like the school in Yauri since Marisol left."

"It won't be easy," I said, "you know there is a waiting list for every school in Cuzco."

"But you can work miracles," she insisted.

"I could ask the Carmelite nuns, they might do me a favour. Where would you stay?"

"I could stay with Melba," she replied excitedly.

Melba is Geovanna's eldest sister. She works in a hospital in Cuzco. Melba had looked after Geovanna since her mother died and Geovanna grew up to love Melba as her real mother. She always referred to her as 'Mama'. Melba lived in a small ramshackle house on Avenida Tullumayo under which flowed one of the ancient rivers of Cuzco. This river forms the 'tail of the puma' as you looked down on the city. It was just a short distance from the Plaza de Armas, and the nearest school was the Carmelite convent.

Geovanna had been attending the local school in Yauri, situated behind the parish house, for some years now. I will never forget the first day I brought her to school. Emmanuel had come to ask me if I could bring her as he was busy in his shop. She looked lovely, dressed in her grey uniform and black shoes. In her bag was some roast maize and bread, together with an orange. The school was an adobe structure consisting of three classrooms with benches and desks. It was painted a bright green as are all schools in the mountains. She was reluctant to go in. Eventually I left her with one of the teachers and returned to the parish house. Geovanna was there before me!

"I wanted to see the rabbits," she explained, "and I wanted to say 'Hello' to Kimichu. Anyway I don't like school." She didn't go back until the following year.

Geovanna loved the Carmelite convent in Cuzco. Marisol was already going to another school in Cuzco called San Antonio Abad. They often came to stay in Combapata at weekends and whenever I went to Cuzco we visited the many sights together.

Geovanna at Sacsayhuaman

"Let's go to the *rodedero*," she would say, as we made our way up to Sacsayhuaman.

The *rodedero* was a huge slide which was formed out of the rock and had been used since Inca times. We also explored the many tunnels which exist all around the ruins. They say that one tunnel connects the fortress with the temple of the Sun but we never found it. Further up the mountain we visited the Tampu-Machay ruins (or the Inca baths, as they are known). Water still flows from the centre of the mountain along stone aqueducts. Geovanna liked to paddle in the crystal clear water and wet her hair to cool off from the extreme heat of the sun. These baths were sacred in Inca times and this was where The Inca came to bathe. Cleanliness was very important for The Inca. (Unfortunately this is one aspect of Inca life that has not been passed on to the Indians of today.) The importance of these baths is evident by the presence of military posts and observation decks to guard them. The view from the top of the baths is breathtaking. On one occasion as I looked back on the city with its surrounding snow-covered mountains, I remarked;

"Geovanna, isn't that a wonderful sight?"

She looked around for a moment and casually replied;

"Yea, but do you know where the most beautiful place in the world is?"

"Where is that?" I asked.

"Yauri," she responded without a moment's hesitation.

Good God, I thought, there are many things one could say about Yauri but being beautiful is not one of them. But I knew what she meant. Yauri was where she was born, where she grew up and where her roots were. It was where she got all her familiar smells and Yauri abounds in smells.

How often had I found my mind wandering back to The Copse, a little spot in Wicklow between Glendalough and Rathdrum where the road meanders up and down like a switch-back railway. To me it will always be home. It is where I was born and grew up, surrounded by forests and with the Avonmore River flowing gently through the valley below. How often have I climbed the hill beside the house and looked out over the Wicklow hills and thought,

"This is the most beautiful place in the world."

In my mind's eye I can see it still. There is something of the salmon in each one of us, we want to go back to our origins.

Geovanna's mother was buried in the cemetery in Cuzco and we often went there to pray. The cemetery has become so overcrowded that they have to bury people in tiers. Her mother was up on the third floor. Her name was written on a little glass door for which there was a key. Fresh flowers could be placed inside in a vase. The tombs are only leased for fifteen years, after which time the remaining bones are given to the family and the tomb is given to someone else. We just gazed up for a while and said a silent prayer.

"When you pray do you talk to God in Spanish or Quechua or English?" she asked one day while we were standing there.

"I certainly don't pray in Quechua," I said, "mostly I pray in English."

"But Mama doesn't know any English," she said, "she won't know what you are saying."

"But God understands," I said, "and I'm sure your Mama is with God."

"And Our Blessed Lady," she added. "You know I pray to Mama sometimes. I ask her to watch over me and when I'm sad I just talk to her. Do you think she hears me?"

"I'm sure she does," I replied.

"I think she sent you to be my *padrino*," she said with a smile.

256

One day Marisol was very excited when I arrived in Cuzco and she couldn't wait to tell me the news.

"I met a woman in the market yesterday," she said, "who saw Mama on the train last week."

"But she couldn't have seen your mother!" I explained, "you know your mother died in the train crash. Don't we go to her grave to visit her."

"But maybe she didn't die. Maybe she lost her memory and doesn't know her way home. She could be wandering around, not knowing where she is."

"And who is buried in the cemetery?"

"It could be someone else, maybe they buried the wrong person."

"Marisol, you know your mother was killed in the train crash. Your Papa went to Arequipa and identified her. He saw her."

"But how could the woman in the market see her?" she wondered.

The woman was mistaken," I explained, "she just thought it was your mother."

Geovanna never knew her mother, but her death affected Marisol very deeply. No one ever wants to believe a loved one is dead unless they see them. Marisol never saw the body of her mother. She was four years old at the time.

"Look what I found!" shouted Geovanna, as she returned from school one day, holding up a fifty dollar bill.

"Where did you find it?" I asked.

"In the Plaza," she answered, "I was just walking along and there it was on the ground. I was very lucky."

"Some tourist must have lost it," I said, "you will have to leave it at the police station."

"What!" she exclaimed.

"But it doesn't belong to you, Geovanna."

"Why should I give it to the police? It certainly doesn't belong to them."

"Whoever lost it will report it to the police and they will be able to return it to its rightful owner," I explained.

"But the police will keep it," she insisted.

I suddenly remembered that I was in Peru, and Geovanna was right. The police would most certainly keep it. I wondered what we should do.

"I'm sure the person who lost it would not mind some poor person finding it," I suggested.

"That's me," added Geovanna.

"Alright, you can keep it and buy some school books with it."

"And maybe an ice cream with my friends," she added with a smile.

I was reminded of the first time I came to Cuzco with Geovanna. She was only about four years old and for her it was an overwhelming experience. She marvelled at everything.

"The streets don't get muddy in the rain like they do in Yauri," she exclaimed. She loved to just stare into shop windows, especially shoe shops. At one point I thought I had lost her. When I looked around she wasn't there. I quickly retraced my steps and eventually I found her sitting down on the side of the footpath.

"What happened, Geovanna?" I asked.

"You think that I have big long legs like you," she replied. "Well I have only little legs and I couldn't keep up with you. I got tired, so I sat down."

Geovanna loved to go to the restaurant. There were tablecloths, knives and forks and wonderful things to eat. She never wanted to see the menu. There were too many things she never heard of.

"I just want chicken," she said. Always chicken, roast chicken, " . . . and chips," she would add almost as an afterthought. Of course she couldn't finish her large portion. She had enough to last her for a week. And it usually did. Never was a 'doggy bag' put to such good use. Needless to say the 'doggy' didn't see much of it. When I paid the bill she wanted to take the tablecloth and cutlery home as well!

"You paid for it, didn't you," she claimed.

On one occasion she asked me if we could take her maths teacher out to dinner.

"Is she a good friend of yours?" I asked. "Do you get on well at maths?"

"That's the trouble," she replied, "she's not very friendly and I don't do well at maths. I don't think she likes me."

"Why would you want to take her out to dinner then?" I asked.

"So that she would give me extra marks in the exam," she explained. "I think I'm going to fail maths."

"Oh Geovanna, how could you think of such a thing. I'm sure she would never be dishonest."

"All the other girls take her out," she complained, "that's why she doesn't like me."

(By the way the 'Carmelitas' beat the girls from La Merced and won the volleyball championship. Geovanna got the winning score. Her tactics worked.)

☆   ☆   ☆

I couldn't believe my eyes. There they were, decorating the seats of the church with white toilet paper.

"What's going on, Lorenzo?" I asked in astonishment as I came in to say Mass. "Why are they putting toilet paper on the seats?"

"Toilet paper!" he exclaimed, with a surprised look on his face. "That's not toilet paper. The people around here don't use paper when they go to the toilet. They usually use a round stone from the river or some *ichu*. Normally they don't use anything at all."

"But why are they putting it on the seats?" I asked. I didn't particularly want an explanation of their toilet habits just before Mass. Anyway I was quite familiar with them at this stage.

"Is it some kind of custom?"

"It's not a very old custom, I don't think it goes back to the time of the Incas."

"I'm sure it doesn't," I said, "You can't blame the Incas for that."

"It's for the wedding," he explained, "the *padrino* is from Arequipa and he said they do it in Arequipa all the time. Sometimes the girl even wears a white dress."

Then I remembered the wedding. Alipio and Juliana from Orascocha were getting married today. They came in the week before to ask me what they would need for the wedding. I explained they would need baptismal certificates and witnesses, the custom here was two witnesses for the man and two for the woman.

"What about the *padrino*?" they asked. Like a baptism it is the *padrino* who looks after most of the church expenses. He also helps with any difficulties that might arise afterwards in the marriage.

"The *padrino* is one of the witnesses," I explained. "The most important thing you need is your baptismal certificate. Where were you baptised?"

"I was baptised here," said Alipio, "and Juliana was baptised in Tinta."

"Juliana will have to go to Tinta for her certificate but I can look up yours here," I said. "What is your full name and what year were you baptised?"

"Alipio Mamani Quispe," he replied, "and I don't know what year I was born. My mother said I was born after the *Santisima Cruz*."

"That narrows it down to May or June," I said. "How many years have you been living together?"

(The Indians practise the custom of *sirvanacuy* which means that they live together for many years and have children before they get married in the church. They usually come together in their late teens and don't get married until their late thirties or forties. The reason for this is mainly economical. A marriage ceremony in the community lasts three days and everyone joins in the celebration. Music and dancing continues day and night. No expense is spared in food or drink. A young couple could not afford this so the marriage is postponed.)

"I have two children living," said Alipio, "and four under the ground."

I made a quick calculation and came to the conclusion that he must be in his mid-thirties. He looked about sixty. I looked up the index which Nemesia had prepared.

Mamani Huillca
Mamani Condori
Mamani Champi
Mamani Ccama
Mamani Huaracha
Mamani Cuyo.

"There is no Mamani Quispe in the book," I said, "are you sure you were baptised?"

"Daniel Phoccohuanca Mendoza is my *padrino*," he said, "he lives in Arequipa. My mother always said I was baptised. Anyway I wouldn't have a *padrino* if I wasn't baptised."

"You are not in the book," I said, "but of course that doesn't mean that you weren't baptised. The priest just didn't register it."

"What can we do now?" he asked, anxiously.

"Don't worry," I said, "I'll fix it up. Were your parents present at your baptism?"

"Yes," he replied, "but they are both dead."

"Your *padrino* can witness to it when he comes, or if not, I can baptise you conditionally. The important thing is that we are sure you were baptised, otherwise your marriage would not be a sacrament. Come in next Saturday before the wedding to sign the papers and have the necessary preparation."

They duly arrived on the Saturday afternoon. Daniel, the *padrino*, was with them dressed as a *misti* in a bright grey suit and tie. Alipio had a new poncho, while Juliana had layers of skirts, a beautiful *llicla* over her shoulders and a little bowler hat embroidered with coloured tassels. She went over to the corner of the room and proceeded to take off her two outer skirts, to reveal a beautifully embroidered dark skirt which had been prepared especially for her wedding. In all, women wear about five layers of skirts. The inside one is used for wiping the nose and other parts of the body.

Their children were with them, a boy about ten years old and a girl about eight years old. Juliana brought her certificate from Tinta, and Daniel witnessed to Alipio's baptism by swearing on the Bible. There is a form of about two pages with detailed questions to be answered before it is signed by the couple and witnesses. The questions have to be translated into Quechua for Juliana. They answered 'Yes' to everything without a moment's hesitation. Most of the questions they don't even understand. Alipio signed with an illegible scrawl while Juliana dipped her finger in the ink pad and left her prints on the place where it said 'signature'.

I used to feel terrible when the women signed with their fingerprints, thinking how embarrassed they must be at not being able to write. But now I know they are not embarrassed at all. They don't know they are supposed to be able to write. The same with the children. I used to think they must feel embarrassed having children out of wedlock, but again they are not embarrassed at all. They don't know they are supposed to be married before they have children.

I give them a little talk on the meaning of the sacrament of marriage. Nemesia translates into Quechua. An important part of the talk has to be about violence in marriage. It is an accepted custom in the Andes that husbands beat their wives. It is a way of proving that the man is 'macho'. On one occasion when I was walking down a side street in Arequipa,

I saw an Indian beating his wife. She was on the ground and he was really thumping her. I went over to try and stop him. The wife jumped up and turned on me.

"Mind your own business," she said, "he is my husband and he has a right to hit me."

Women seem to accept the fact that they can be beaten by their husbands. This usually happens when he comes home drunk from the market. The men even boast about it in the Plaza.

"I'm going home now to choke the old sow."

And Nemesia told me that the next day the husband takes delight in having beaten his wife. When he sees the marks on her body he doesn't have any remorse. He says mockingly;

"You squealed like a pig when I was beating you last night."

Of course when I told Alipio that he must never beat his wife he was indignant at the very thought.

"I would never do such a thing, *Papay*."

We then had a little rehearsal of the marriage.

"You stand here, Alipio," I said, pointing to the spot.

"And you are on this side, Juliana."

"The witnesses stand on either side. The *padrino* carries the tray with the ring and the silver coins."

"I don't have a ring," said Alipio

"Don't worry," I answered, "we'll use mine." I wore a special gold and silver Carmelite ring for such occasions. It was made from silver from one of the mines in Yauri and gold found in the River Salado.

"You hold each other's hands while you are repeating the marriage vows," I explained.

(Indians don't normally show signs of affection. They never kiss – this is a gringo custom. At the fiestas the boys wear a little *bulto* around their backsides to make themselves attractive to the girls. They also show themselves off by dancing. The girls observe from a distance. The old custom was that the girls didn't dance with boys until they were married. One never sees an Indian boy and girl holding hands. They have no hang-ups about sex. They never take off their clothes when they sleep together in their mud huts. The man takes off his poncho and makes a pillow of it while the woman takes off the outer skirt and makes a pillow of that. Breasts don't have anything to do with sex. They are purely functional. Sometimes the women wear bras but not for covering their breasts. There are two big holes in them to facilitate feeding their babies. (There is a story told of the visiting bishop who wasn't familiar with Indian customs. He was shocked when he noticed the women openly displaying their breasts during Mass as they fed their babies. He made a frantic gesture to them to cover their breasts. They duly obliged by pulling up their skirts over their breasts only to reveal that they weren't wearing any underclothes. That's one way to learn Indian customs fast!)

Alipio and Juliana held hands very awkwardly, their eyes looking down.

"Alipio, do you take Juliana as your lawful wife?"

Alipio continues to look down in embarrassment.

"Alipio, would you look at Juliana. She is your wife. You are supposed to be friends. Are you not good friends?" I asked.

"No," he answered, but I think he didn't understand the question.

"Now you exchange rings," I explained. He held out the wrong hand.

"The other hand," I said. Of course they would never know which finger the ring was supposed to go on, so I devised a foolproof system.

"You must make the sign of the cross on her hand. You begin with the thumb," I explained, "and say *'Dios Yayac'*, then the next finger, *'Dios Churic'*, then the next, *'Dios Espiritu Santoc'*, and then *'Suntimpi'*. When you get to the *'Suntimpi'*, you put the ring on that finger."

I was always very careful to remove my ring quickly from their fingers, otherwise I would never see it again. Then it was time to exchange the silver pieces. These were the old Peruvian coins and were made of pure silver. They are very valuable and are widely used at weddings. Alipio put the coins into the hands of Juliana and then she put them into his.

"This means that you exchange all your worldly goods," I explained, "all your llamas, alpacas, vicuñas, *cuys*, viscatchas and sheep."

At last a little smile comes over their faces. They have very little to exchange except themselves. When they came to confession before their wedding, I discovered that they had never been to confession or Communion before. This really wasn't surprising. How could they when there was no resident priest. So I prepared them for their First Confession, their First Communion, their marriage, and after the Mass the two children were baptised. That really deserved a fiesta. It even deserved a roll of toilet paper!

☆　　☆　　☆

The new tractor

The road from Cuzco is long and tiring when you are driving a tractor. It took me hours to reach Combapata. In the trailer I had a plough and a harrow. The threshing machine would come later. Word of my arrival spread quickly around the nearby communities.

"Padre Cristobal has returned and he has brought a tractor and trailer."

Let me explain how all this came about. I had been in Combapata for two years and I was due to take a holiday. Just before I returned to Ireland I had been out in the community of Huatucani. The rains had come and they were preparing the land for the potatoes. They were using a primitive wooden plough pulled by two oxen. One man guided the oxen from the front while another walked behind with the plough. This method of ploughing goes back to the first century and beyond. It barely seemed to scratch the surface. Some women and children cleared away the loose stones while others sorted the potatoes for sowing. The whole community was involved.

A little group went along with sacks of *bosta* that they had collected from the dung-heaps outside their huts. The corrals beside the houses produce large amounts of *bosta*. Lastly another group followed with sticks and made holes in the ground into which they popped the little potatoes. The first time I saw Indians sowing potatoes using this method I was quick to point out to them that this was the wrong way to sow potatoes.

Ploughing the *chacra*

"You make drills," I explained, "then you put in the manure, and after that the potatoes."

Then it suddenly dawned on me how stupid I was. Potatoes originated in Peru so why shouldn't they know how to sow them. Archaeologists have discovered that agriculture first appeared in Peru about 7000 BC. The potato was widely used as a food source long before Inca times. There are many different varieties and they are cultivated up to 14,000 feet above sea level. The Spaniards didn't appreciate their value and it was Francis Drake who finally brought them to Europe in 1579, when they were sown in England. But they didn't become popular in England at this time. From here they went to Germany and it was Frederick William of Prussia in 1651 who realised what a great source of food they were. Later in the reign of Louis XV they arrived in France and from there to the whole world.

The rise in population in Europe at this time is attributed to the introduction of the potato. Prior to this the main crop was grain which was easily and adversely affected by bad weather – wind, hail and rain. Potatoes were a cheap alternative, rich in vitamins and they produced twice the calories with half the work in half the time. In Ireland the people came to depend so completely on the potato crop that when the potatoes failed in the Great Famine of 1845 – 47 over one million people died and two million had to emigrate.

It was during one of these visits to Huatucani that the subject of the tractor was brought up. I had just celebrated the fiesta of the *Santisima Cruz*. We had all gathered in the patio outside Faustino's hut. We sat around in a circle and discussed the problems of the community. Times were hard.

"Two of my children died during the last year," said Faustino. "What future have we when our children are dying? If only we had a little medicine."

"We spend most of our time in the *chacras* cultivating the hard earth with very little to show for it," complained Hernan.

"The River Salcca flows through our community," added José, "yet we have to depend on the rain for the crops. Last year when the rain didn't come, the potatoes were only fit for *chuños*."

"If only we could build canals to divert the water," suggested Genaro. "The Incas were able to transport water thousands of miles, even to the top of Machu Picchu. We are using the same implements as in Inca times with less results."

Then Faustino stood up.

"*Papay*, you are soon going back to your country to visit your family and friends. Could you tell them about the conditions in the community of Huatucani? Ask them to help us. They are all millionaires. They have plenty of money. Maybe they would be able to send us a tractor. We are tired of using our *chakitakllas* and wooden ploughs. A tractor could plough our *chacras* much more quickly and easily and we could grow better crops. Our president in Lima is always promising us help but it never comes."

Everybody clapped as he sat down.

"I will ask my friends in Ireland to help you," I assured them. "I can't promise you anything, but I will do my best."

I got my opportunity when I was invited onto the Andy O'Mahony radio programme back in Ireland. I spoke about life in the Andes and I made an appeal for a tractor. The response was overwhelming. The idea of a tractor seemed to catch people's imagination, especially the farming community who couldn't understand how anyone could still be using wooden ploughs. I had many offers from farmers inviting me to visit their farms and promising that they would teach me all about the operation of a tractor. One farmer suggested that I would be able to enter for the National Ploughing Championship on my return to Ireland! But I also had many letters from old-age pensioners and the poor with their small contributions. Many wrote long and interesting letters about their fascination with the Indians of Peru. Many also suggested that I should write a book about my experiences. I never thought I would. The end result was that I had enough money to buy a tractor back in Peru.

The new tractor in action

Now that Combapata had a tractor there was only one problem. I was the only one who could drive it. Those first few weeks back in Peru were very difficult. I spent from early morning until late at night out in the *chacras* of the communities. I soon realised that driving the tractor in the *chacras* was not like driving on the road. This was virgin territory. It had never been ploughed by tractor before. I had to be extra careful about stones and rocks. I hopped up and down like a jack-in-the-box and by the end of the day I could hardly stand up. It was very tiring as I also had all my regular parish work to do. The Indians would come out to the *chacras* to arrange for baptisms and marriages. Then one day a young lad named Juan from Ccolccatuna came to ask me if he could learn to be a tractor driver.

"Do you know anything about tractors?" I asked.

"I saw one in Cuzco once," he replied.

So we had to start at the beginning. He really knew nothing, but I was amazed how quickly he learned. It was an advantage that there wasn't much to crash into, except the river which we narrowly missed on a number of occasions. After about a week he was ready to go solo and from then on he improved every day. His nickname was 'El Zorro' (the fox) and I soon realised that it suited him. He was extremely clever and wise, but he never went to school.

The tractor was kept each night in the patio at my house. Juan was soon in our midst everyday and he and Nemesia gradually got to know each other very well. I never saw them showing any signs of affection, but one day when Juan had already gone out with the tractor, Nemesia told me she had something to tell me which came as a surprise.

"Juan asked me to marry him, and I said 'Yes'."

"That's wonderful news, Nemesia. Juan is a very good boy. Does that mean you are going to live together in *sirvanacuy*?"

"No," she replied, "we want to get married in the Church first. I am a catechist and I prepare the people for their wedding. The least I might do is show them good example."

"Is Juan agreeable?" I asked.

"Yes, that's what he wants too. We hope to get married by Christmas."

I was in the process of building a new parish hall so I suggested that we build on some extra rooms and they could live there. They were delighted with the idea.

They were both happily married the following Christmas. I sent them to Arequipa for a week on their honeymoon even though they didn't know what a honeymoon was. Shortly before this Lorenzo had resigned as *economo* and Juan was appointed in his place. So now I had a secretary, an *economo* and a tractor driver all in the family. Things were beginning to look up.

I was suddenly awakened by loud banging at the door. Pulling back the curtain a little I could see it was still dark. I looked at my watch. It was three o'clock in the morning. The banging continued. Indians don't normally go out at night, so this must be something serious. I dressed quickly and went to the door. We had been warned not to open the door at night because of terrorists. I shouted out;

"Who's there?"

"Santo Ccanahuire from Acomayo," came the reply.

I unbolted the door and opened it a little.

"*Allillanchu, Papay,*" said a middle-aged man. His poncho was wet and there was sweat pouring down his face. Although he was sweating he was shivering with the cold. It was obvious that he had travelled through the night. Acomayo is a good day's walk away across the mountains. It is in the diocese of Cuzco, but many families come to Combapata to have their children baptised.

"I came to ask you a great favour, *Papay,*" he said, handing me a plastic bottle. "Could you give me some holy water? I need it urgently."

I was very aware of the importance of holy water in the life of the Indian. They use it for everything – to bless the crops, to heal the sick, to ward off evil spirits, to sprinkle on newborn babies, to pour on the graves of the dead and much more besides. They also believe that the more you use, the more effective it is. So I wasn't really surprised that he wanted holy water but I was curious to know why he wanted it at three o'clock in the morning.

"Why do you need holy water so urgently?" I asked.

"My brother is very sick and I brought him to the *curandero*. He gave me a long list of things I must get to make the magic potion to cure my brother. The first on the list is holy water. I must get holy water from three different parishes. Combapata is my first stop. Next I will go to Tinta and then Checacupe."

I worked out that it would take him about three days to get the holy water from the three parishes and after that he had to get the other things on the list. In the meantime his brother would probably be dead.

"I'm afraid I would not be able to give you holy water to be used in a magical rite," I explained.

His face dropped. He was dumbstruck. He knew he shouldn't have told me what he wanted it for. He changed his story immediately.

"No, *Papay*, that's not really what I want it for. I need it for my sick animals."

"That's not true," I suggested, "I'm afraid I can't give you holy water for magical purposes." He continued to plead but to no avail.

As he went away he was very annoyed and he turned around and shouted, "*Siquita muchay*". There was that phrase again. I wondered what it meant.

A short time later another Indian came knocking at the door. He too wanted holy water, but he handed me the same plastic bottle. Santo was not going to give up easily!

Curanderos abound here in the mountains where there are no doctors. Many do achieve amazing results and the herbs they use do have curative properties. When people are dying and in pain they will look for relief anywhere they can find it. The Indians believe that all sickness is the result of unnatural causes. As with all pre-scientific peoples, they believe that no misfortune, accident, or illness just happens. It is always the result of something, or someone else, usually some superior force. Disease and death are caused by the ill-will of someone else. It could be the anger of the Gods or some evil spirit found in the wind or the water. Often it can be the spirit of a dead relative or friend. That's why the souls are feared so much. So an illness which has a supernatural cause has to be treated in a magical or religious way. Even the cures of healing herbs are presumed to be magical. The medicine man is not just a doctor with a knowledge of medicine, he is said to have supernatural powers. He often gets these powers in a vision or dream, or perhaps by curing some serious illness by accident. Of course faith healers are known in every country. In Ireland curative powers are often attributed to the seventh son of a seventh son.

Curanderos are experts in psychology. They use the power of suggestion while giving the patient hallucinatory substances. These are derived mainly from cactus plants found in the Amazon jungle. They are also found in mushrooms. The Indians believe that illness is caused by an evil spirit putting some foreign body inside you, such as a stone. So when the *curandero* sucks at the point of the pain, he has to pretend to extract a stone and show it to the patient. The *curandero* usually diagnoses the illness by 'magic'. Then they make out a list of things the family must do, such as bringing holy water from three different parishes. (I don't know how they would recognise holy water, much less that it came from three different parishes.)

Very often they use a live guinea pig when diagnosing an illness. The guinea pig is the sacred animal of the Incas and as such it is believed to have magical powers. They rub the unfortunate little animal over the stomach of the sick person – a form of X-ray. Then the guinea pig is dissected and the 'illness' that is 'discovered' in the guinea pig is

270

regarded as corresponding to the illness of the person. The patient is then operated on and the illness cured.

Sometimes the *curandero* decides that one of your ancestors is annoyed with you so you must go to their grave and place food and drink on it to appease them. You may even be told to go and wash in the river, preferably at the junction of two rivers. Every plant is thought to have some magical power for good or for evil. Animal and mineral substances are also used, such as fresh meat, animal fat, blood, urine, mercury, sulphur and arsenic.

I had unknowingly paid a visit to a *curandero* once myself. It was shortly after my arrival in Yauri. At the eleven o'clock Mass I could hardly talk because of a sore throat. Afterwards a young man came into the sacristy. He was dressed as a *misti*, in a suit, and he carried an umbrella which was most unusual in Yauri. He also had a peculiar walk which I didn't notice at the time. He spoke in a high-pitched voice.

"*Buenos días, Padre,*" he began, "I'm Felix. I have a business in the town. I notice you have a very bad throat. It's the atmosphere here, you know. It really plays havoc with the vocal chords, especially for a gringo. I know a man who could cure you immediately."

"Is he a doctor?" I asked hesitantly.

"Much better," he replied. "If you would come with me I will show you where he lives. It is not very far away, just at the edge of the town."

We walked together down the middle of the road and it was then that I noticed his walk. I got some peculiar glances from passers-by. They looked at me and then at him and passed on without saying a word. Eventually we came to a mud hut. I bent down to enter the little door and was greeted by a most unusual sight. The hut was filled with all kinds of objects. There were little bundles of dried plants and herbs hanging from the roof, together with all kinds of dried animal skins. There were half-filled earthenware jars everywhere. An old man was sitting in the corner, motionless. I didn't notice him when I entered the hut because of all the junk.

"Uri, this is Padre Cristobal," explained Felix, "he has a sore throat."

The old man looked at me and slowly bowed. I bowed back.

"Sit down," he said. I looked around for a chair and then sat on the ground with my legs crossed. The old man proceeded to mix some herbs in a jar. He then mixed it with some liquid.

"Drink," he said, as he handed me the jar of liquid. I didn't dare ask him what it was. I closed my eyes and drank it. It tasted terrible. I handed him back the jar. He didn't say anything. He didn't even ask for any payment.

"*Gracias, Señor,*" I said, as I left the hut, hoping that I wouldn't drop dead on the way home.

The next day I met Trinidad.

"I saw you walking through the town with Felix yesterday after Mass," she remarked.

"Yes, he was taking me to the medicine man to be cured."

"He could do with being cured himself," she suggested, "you know he's a *marecon.*"

I had learned a new word, and my throat was cured.

14
Beggars in Paradise

Life in the *campo*

It has been a long day in Combapata. As in Yauri, Sunday is market day. I was awakened at daybreak by the sound of the Indians arriving from all directions with their animals; llamas, alpacas, sheep, cattle, pigs, hens, ducks, and donkeys, all laden down with all kinds of produce. Giant Volvo lorries arrive from the jungle with various varieties of tropical fruit. It has taken them three days to get here from Porto Maldonado northeast of Combapata near the Bolivian border. They will start their return journey this evening, to be back again next Sunday. Makeshift stalls spring up all over the Plaza, each one vying with the other to attract customers. A magical incantation is said over the goods to drive away evil spirits and bring good luck in their sales. No prices are displayed. You must haggle for everything, pretending to walk away a few times before eventually ending up paying half the original asking price. Beautiful multicoloured blankets, together with ponchos, *chullos* and *lliclas* hang idly on the stalls and blow gently in the breeze. The fruit and vegetable sellers sit on the ground with their produce spread out in little heaps in front of them. If you buy they always throw in one extra for good luck.

In spite of the huge number of people a strange silence pervades the whole place. No one shouts or cries out. Everything has its own particular place, the textiles, the fruit, the vegetables, the meat, the hens and the ducks. Down on the banks of the River Vilcanota is the animal market. Buyers come from all over Peru to buy cattle in Combapata. They are then transported by train to Arequipa and from there by truck to Lima. Many die on the way. Huge wads of notes change hands. Hardly a Sunday goes by without cattle dealers and Indians coming to the parish office to swear on the Bible. Tough-looking men with long hair argue over some misunderstanding about money.

"I sold him three heifers for one thousand five hundred soles and when I counted it there was only one thousand four hundred."

"I gave you all the money. I remember distinctly putting it into your hands."

There is very little room for manoeuvre. One says one thing and the other denies it. One would need the wisdom of Solomon.

"We want to swear on the Holy Bible," they insisted. It's the only thing that they both agree on. I have long since learned that this solves nothing.

"What are you going to swear?" I asked one.

"I'm going to swear I gave him all the money."

"And what are you going to swear?" I say to the other.

"I'm going to swear that he left me one hundred soles short."

"What difference will swearing on the Bible make then," I ask, trying to think logically.

"At least I'll know he's telling the truth," said one.

"Well, now you know," I said, "so there is no need to swear on the Bible."

They looked puzzled but went away happy. The most important thing in these situations is that no one loses face. The fact that the other tried to deceive is much worse than the loss of money.

I had just returned from the market with my basket of food for the week when Nemesia informed me that there was a family to see me. As they spoke only Quechua she would help me with the translation.

"I am Justo Qquelcca Condori," said the husband as I entered the office. He proceeded to give me a hug.

"This is my wife, Rufina, and my daughter, Nieves."

I greeted each in turn. Nieves looked terrified as I came near her and didn't put her arms around me. You can tell a lot from how an Indian is dressed, such as where they come from and how well off they are. The colour of a man's poncho often tells you what community he comes from: Justo was dressed in woollen trousers and a red poncho and *chullo*. He had some hairs growing on his face and one of his front teeth was missing. (This is usually the result of a fight or an accident as their teeth don't normally decay.) Rufina had the usual layers of skirts, with a colourful *llicla* around her shoulders and a flat hat on her head, embroidered at the rim. Nieves was dressed in a similar fashion. All their clothes were homespun. This family was obviously from a very primitive community.

"*Maypi tiyanki?* (Where do you live?)" I asked.

"Parupata," he replied.

"Parupata is one of the highest communities in the parish," said Nemesia. "It is high up in the mountains above Culcuire."

"How long has it taken you to get here?" I asked.

"Nearly two days," replied Justo. "We left Parupata yesterday at daybreak and we stayed with friends in Culcuire last night. We walked the rest of the way today."

He opened out his *bulto* and presented me with two eggs.

"*Ancha agradiciki* (Thank you very much)," I said, not really wanting to take some of their valuable food. But if I refused they would be insulted. I also knew that they were going to ask me to do something that would probably be impossible.

"I came to ask you a great favour," said Justo. Just as I thought.

"I would like to have my daughter, Nieves, baptised immediately," he said. "She hasn't been well and we think God is punishing us for not having her baptised." (She couldn't have got an illness by accident, it had to be attributed to something.)

"God doesn't do things like that," I said. "What age is Nieves?"

"She is thirteen harvests," he replied.

During all of this conversation Nieves never uttered a word and seemed to be frightened out of her wits.

"I will certainly baptise her," I said, "but because she is not a baby she will need to understand something about the sacrament of baptism first. Does she go to school?"

"At the moment there is no teacher in Parupata. Nieves minds the llamas and alpacas out in the mountain every day."

"If she could stay here for a week, Nemesia would prepare her and she could be baptised next Sunday," I suggested.

Justo talked it over with Rufina for a while and then agreed.

"She will stay," he agreed solemnly.

"But you didn't ask Nieves," I added, "maybe she doesn't want to stay."

Nemesia asked her if she would stay and be prepared for baptism.

"*Ari*," she replied.

Her parents left saying that they would return the following Sunday for the baptism. There were no emotional scenes of farewell and they left without saying a word.

Nieves had never been outside her community before. I was the first gringo she had ever seen. She had never slept in a bed in her life. Nemesia washed and combed her lovely long black hair. She also cut her nails which had already begun to curl inwards and showed her how to wash her teeth with a toothbrush. As she had never eaten sweets, Nieves' teeth were perfect apart from being dark green from chewing coca leaves. She couldn't sit in a chair and insisted on sitting on the floor as was her custom. She never saw a toilet and just peed outside the door until I asked Nemesia to show her a spot a little further away. She loved playing with my animals and seemed to have a special affinity with them.

At first she didn't eat very much. Perhaps she didn't like the food. Certainly it must have been a little strange to her. She just said she wasn't hungry. On the second day she had a severe pain in her stomach. She stayed in bed and I gave her some medicine but the pain seemed to get worse. It was then that she told Nemesia that she had *susto*. *Susto* is a very strange phenomenon, but it is very common among the children of the mountains. We would describe it as 'fright' or 'shock'. A child can get *susto* while playing out in the *chacra* or when seeing something strange for the first time, like an aeroplane. It affects them in various ways, but it usually means they can't eat or sleep and are in a state of shock all the time.

The Indians believe that one way of curing a *susto* is to have the child baptised. Now I knew why Justo and Rufina wanted Nieves baptised so urgently. With Indians, nothing is ever as simple as it looks. They never tell you the whole story. You have to know how to 'read between the lines' to know what they really want. They believe that a child with *susto* is possessed by some evil spirit. And it sometimes appears that this is the case. Many a child has seemed to go berserk as I tried to baptise it. If they are older they suddenly run away. It was a common sight during baptism to see a young boy or girl running out of the church with the parents in hot pursuit. When parents asked me what was the first requirement for baptism, I was always tempted to say,

"Capture your child!"

Sometimes they bring the child to the *curandero* or he comes to the child. He first enquires how and where the *susto* happened. If it occurred out in the *chacra* the *curandero* goes to the spot in the dead of night. He carefully looks around the area by candlelight for some living creature, like an insect. This he brings back to the hut. He places the child naked on a rug in a dark corner of a room. He then puts the insect on the child's bare stomach. He sprinkles water over the child and the evil spirit passes from the child into the insect.

Nieves hardly ate anything during the week. She wasn't in any frame of mind to be prepared for baptism. I would have liked to bring her to a doctor in Cuzco, but there was no way any doctor would do anything without the parents' permission. Justo and Rufina arrived the following Sunday and I suggested that I would take Nieves to Cuzco, but they would not hear of it. They wanted to bring her back to the mountains and cure her themselves. I wondered how she would survive the two-day journey. No doubt she would get the insect treatment. The extraordinary thing is that these strange customs sometimes seemed to work. I promised Nieves that I would baptise her one day when I visited Parupata.

☆   ☆   ☆

I was in the middle of a lesson with Elena in the Quechua language school in Cuzco when there was a knock on the door.

"There is a visitor downstairs for Padre Cristobal," said Pablo, one of the other teachers.

"I'm John Swinfield," said a gentleman with an English accent, as he introduced himself. He didn't look too well. He was accompanied by the porter from his hotel in Cuzco.

"I'm doing some television documentaries on people working against the odds in difficult situations and the bishop told me that I should get in touch with you."

"Are you with the BBC or ITV?" I asked.

He immediately began to act like a secret service agent, putting his hand over his mouth.

"It's a bit hush, hush," he whispered. "I don't want to go through all the red tape of getting permission from the government. That can take months. This chap with me speaks a little English so I don't want him to know what we are discussing. I'm only supposed to be a tourist. The British Embassy advised me against coming to Peru because of the terrorist situation. They said that if I came it would be at my own risk."

"Don't worry about the porter," I said. "I'll speak with my Irish brogue and he'd want to be a genius to understand me. You might even have a little trouble understanding me yourself!"

"It's for the 'Heartland Series' on ITV," he explained. "I'm on contract to Anglia TV. I've got one programme planned on a priest in Bolivia who is chaplain to a tin mine community, and another programme planned on a tribe in the Amazon in Brazil. I'd like to do one on the Andes. They tell me that you work in a very primitive and dangerous situation."

"Very little has changed here for centuries," I explained.

"Sounds fascinating."

"What kind of film do you want to make?" I asked.

"Just your ordinary everyday work," he replied. "What exactly do you do?"

"I live and work with the Indians," I said. "I'm a Carmelite priest and my parish covers a large area of the Andes."

"I'm an agnostic myself. I don't believe in organised religion, but I admire people like you. Could I come with you and follow you around for a while?"

"That would be no problem," I assured him, "but the first thing you must do is go back to your hotel and go to bed before the altitude sickness hits you." (By now he was as white as a sheet.) "If you are feeling up to it, we could leave for Combapata and Yauri tomorrow."

"The scenery is magnificent," observed John, as we made our way to Combapata. "The clear blue sky and the mountains and all the different shades of colour. It's a photographer's dream."

"For the tourist," I explained, "it's one of the most beautiful places in the world, except that no tourists come this way. They all go to Machu Picchu. The reality can be a little different when you live here for a while. The Indians are not really into photography. They look at the sky to see if the rains are coming or for the signs of frost as the maize begins to sprout. Those many shades of brown can often mean drought and hunger."

Ichu-roofed hut

"I suppose that lovely little house on the hillside isn't quite as pretty as it looks," he remarked, pointing to an Indian's hut.

"It certainly looks beautiful from here," I said, "but if you could see inside, you would probably find an Indian family living in squalor; a baby dying for want of a little medicine and a mother old before her time."

"It's so sad, Peru has so many riches," he said.

"It is a paradise," I said. "But the Indians are like beggars. In order to live with them and try to help them, you must become a beggar in paradise too."

"But why do you do it? What brought you here to live with the Indians?"

"That's a mystery," I replied, "sometimes even to myself. I can only put it down to faith."

As we stopped at my house in Combapata, John remarked,

"I expected you to have a humble home and I was right."

"Humble?" I responded, "this is luxury compared with where I lived when I first came. Wait until you see Yauri!"

John wasn't too impressed with Sicuani. He didn't see much prospects of good filming, especially the new Cathedral which he thought could be found anywhere in the United States.

As we reached Yauri, John began to suffer more and more from altitude sickness. At times I thought we wouldn't make it. But the worse he got, the more enthusiastic he was about the primitive situation. When we arrived I sent him off to bed and gave him some copies of the 'Letters from Peru' that I had written to students in Ireland over the years.

"This is it!" he exclaimed next morning, holding the letters in his hand. "I couldn't sleep a wink all night, and I read all your letters by flashlight. If we can reproduce some of these experiences we will have a great film."

☆   ☆   ☆

A few weeks later John and his crew arrived in Cuzco for filming. He had flown in from Bolivia, having just completed the documentary on the tin mine community. His first problem, however, was with the customs officials in Cuzco airport who, when they saw all the camera equipment and realised he had none of the appropriate documentation, saw an opportunity for a bribe.

"I was hoping to take some photos of Machu Picchu," John explained, as his cameraman unloaded about fifteen rolls of 16mm film and a couple of cameras, plus microphones, sound recorders etc.

There is no such thing as an innocent customs official, even a Peruvian one, so there was no way he was going to buy that explanation. John could never pass as an ordinary tourist. But when he slipped him two one-hundred-dollar bills the official even helped him to carry his case!

For the next ten days I became familiar with all the techniques of film making; clapperboards, booms, filters, off-camera voice sessions. Bob, the sound man, wired me up immediately so that everything I said was being recorded. We began by visiting the old Inca fortress at

Sacsayhuaman, looking down over the city. I stood on some of the massive stones and John interviewed me on the glory of the Incas.

Having experienced some of the food in Yauri John decided that they would buy all their food in the supermarket in Cuzco and take it with them. Filming could not be held up due to sick stomachs. Everything was loaded, including forty bottles of water, onto my jeep and we set off.

It was early Sunday morning when we arrived in Combapata. When John saw all the animals arriving for the market he suggested I should ride into the town on a horse in true cowboy style. This was no problem. I just stopped the jeep and asked one of the Indians to lend me his horse. Brian, the cameraman, went on ahead to begin filming. At one stage he got on the horse with me and filmed as I entered the town through the market. Even the *teniente* came out to greet me as I hitched the horse outside the church. Juan rang the church bell and the crowds arrived for Mass. No one took any notice of the camera. Many would not have been aware that they were being filmed. The Mass was for an Indian who had just died. His family put the customary table in front of the altar and covered it with a black cloth. On the table they placed a piece of dried meat, eggs, maize and some of the dead man's clothing.

"What's all that?" asked John.

"An old Inca custom," I explained, "it's so that the soul won't go hungry in the next life."

"Extraordinary!" he exclaimed, although I don't think he was convinced.

There were two people to be baptised after the Mass. One was from a very poor Indian family, the other was the daughter of a *misti* family in the town. The contrast couldn't have been greater. The little Indian child was dressed in a homespun skirt with no underclothes, the *misti* child was dressed in white. As the cold water touched the head of the Indian child she had a sudden bout of diarrhoea. I just managed to jump out of the way in time. The *misti* family drew back in disgust. I can cope with scenes like that much better than they can.

Afterwards we went to the market where Brian and John couldn't stop filming. An Indian market is a cameraman's dream.

Nothing was rehearsed beforehand. John wanted everything to be as natural as possible. When the children came to greet me in the marketplace, John saw the opportunity to pop a tricky question.

"Wouldn't you like to get married?" he asked out of the blue. "You seem to be so fond of children, wouldn't you have liked to have children of your own?"

"I have so many of other people's children," I answered, "that it is not a problem."

"But wouldn't you have liked children of your own?" John persisted. "Did you ever think of getting married?"

"I'm sure I did," I replied, "but I haven't met anyone yet who would like to marry me."

"And if you did, what would you do?"

"I don't know, that hasn't happened, and as time goes on I think the likelihood of that happening will become less and less."

Then he moved on to another controversial subject.

"Do you teach the Indians about contraception?" he asked, looking at all the children about.

"Indians are not interested in contraception," I explained. "They want all the children they can have. They know that half of them are going to die anyway. They need the children to help them in the *chacras*."

"But they are so poor."

"What we must do is help them with food and medicine to give them a better life, not prevent them from being born. Many people in Peru think that if there were no Indians there would be no problem. But Indian children are not the problem," I replied.

In the afternoon we visited the community of Huatucani and we were entertained in the home of René, the catechist in Combapata, and his wife, Maria. Maria immediately picked up some guinea pigs, killed them and prepared them for roasting on the fire of *bosta*. Important visitors had arrived and they must be given the best. John and his crew were touched by the generosity of these poor people. The poor are always the most generous.

"No one is too poor to give and no one to too rich to receive."

John couldn't be tempted to try the guinea pig but he got some of the most interesting footage for the documentary. It is difficult for anyone who is used to people keeping guinea pigs as pets to see them being roasted on the open fire.

"I don't eat the head and I don't eat the tail," I said as I started to chew. "But the rest I'll have a go at."

The road to Yauri provided many excellent shots. Just outside the town we commandeered a tricycle on which Brian rode as he filmed me driving along in the jeep. Passing Langui, he climbed on top of the jeep to get a good shot of the lake.

"Isn't that a beautiful little village on the shores of the lake?" remarked John.

"It certainly is," I said, while thinking to myself if they only knew. (I recalled the brutal murders of Tupac Amaru and his family and later Padre Ramos who almost met the same end.)

Young shepherds minding the flock and doing their homework

A little further on we came across a family minding their sheep and llamas on the barren mountainside. The grandmother looked haggard and wizened, old beyond her years. She immediately became the object of Brian's attention as she sat on the *pampa* grass chewing her coca leaves. I went to speak with her and offered her some chocolate. This produced some of the best shots of the documentary. First she had to spit out the coca leaves before trying the chocolate which she had probably never tasted before. She was completely deaf and oblivious to all around her as she ate the chocolate like a little child. Her hands were long and dirty with the nails turned in for want of cutting.

As we reached Descanso I recalled how *Sendero Luminoso* had murdered two policemen in the Plaza a short time before. Bob, who had just returned from filming in Beirut, quickly took a Rambo-type knife from where it was concealed around his ankle. He was prepared to take on *Sendero* single-handed, much to John and Brian's amusement. They could easily have picked us off from the overhanging cliffs. It was late in the evening by the time we reached Yauri. The llamas and alpacas were returning to their corrals and the orange glow of the setting sun gave them an angelic look. By now the crew was suffering from the effects of the altitude.

The next morning John was still very sick. He couldn't sleep and he couldn't eat but the filming had to go on. We decided to pay a visit to Apachaco. I could have found my way with my eyes closed. We passed the deserted chapel of Chalki. It would only come to life again for the next feast of St Isidor. I told John about the man who dug up the bones of his relatives for the Mass and how Kimichu ran off with one of the bones.

"If only we could film that," said John.

"Impossible," I said. "Some things only happen once in a lifetime."

Word soon spread around the community of Apachaco that Padre Cristobal had returned and people began to gather at the church. I called to José, the catechist, and his wife, Lourdes. She immediately began to prepare a meal for us. We filmed the concoction coming out of 'the big brown pot'. John and the crew decided to have their picnic lunch in the jeep, having been violently ill from food poisoning in Bolivia. Lourdes was very ill with pains in her head and she wanted a blessing. We made our way to the church. As John surveyed the ruins of the old town he remarked;

"It would cost millions to build a film set like this."

As Lourdes knelt down in the church to be blessed, hundreds more gathered around for a blessing.

"You are certainly working against the odds here," said John. "Don't you ever get disheartened? Do you ever feel like giving up?"

"Yes, from time to time I do get depressed," I replied, "but not because I don't think it's worthwhile, but because there is nothing I can do. I remember the father who carried his daughter down the mountain on his back and asked me to bless her leg. As he took off a dirty cloth there were holes right through the little girl's leg. The flesh had been eaten away and I could see right through to the bone. There was nothing I could do. I hadn't even a clean bandage. I knew that if the little girl was not taken to hospital for an operation she would die. But there was no hospital. There was no doctor. It was very frustrating."

"There is certainly some extraordinary power that keeps you going," said John, "I think if I was here for a while, some of your faith would rub off onto me."

"Miracles happen here all the time," I added, "I don't think you are as far away from God as you think."

"Do you remember in one of your letters you mentioned how you had to cross the river on horseback?" asked John, trying to change the subject.

"How could I forget!" I said.

"Could we get that on film?" he wondered.

"But this is the rainy season," I explained. "The river is in flood."

"Exactly!" said John, laughing.

So I borrowed a horse and we all headed for the river. John and the crew went across the bridge to film the scene from the other side.

The first place I tried, the horse just began to sink.

"I'll try further down," I shouted.

Just as I was half-way across the heavens opened and there was a thunderstorm. There was no turning back and I was drenched by the time I reached the other side.

"That was great!" exclaimed John looking out from the window of the jeep. This was to be the opening sequence of the documentary film.

On the way back to Yauri we got a beautiful shot of a rainbow over the town. This was a lucky omen in the time of the Incas. They worshipped the rainbow as a gift from the sun.

"Wonderful!" said John.

The local radio in Yauri announced that Padre Cristobal had returned and that he was making a film. The next morning thousands of Indians arrived at the parish house. It was a wonderful occasion to meet all my old friends. Melchor and the women killed some sheep and prepared a feast. We celebrated with music and dancing.

There was another shot which John was anxious to get.

"You wrote about hearing confessions under a poncho."

"That happens all the time," I said. "When they want to go to confession they just put their poncho over my head. It's their 'portable confession box'. Then they confess their sins. Sometimes they go on and on and it is very hard to breathe. There's very little ventilation in there!"

"Could we get a shot of that?" asked John.

I asked if anyone wanted to go to confession. There were many volunteers. One old woman put her poncho over my head and began to confess.

As I emerged from under the poncho I noticed that Bob had his microphone very close to us.

"Good God," I said, "you didn't get that on sound?"

"Perfectly," said John.

"But that was confession," I explained. "It's meant to be secret. You can't record confession."

"Don't worry," said John, "it was all in Quechua, no one will understand."

"That's not the point," I said. "If an Indian ever sees the film, he will understand. It just can't be used. We have to wipe it out immediately."

"No problem," said John. "Their dignity is essential, we'll drop it."

The film wouldn't have been complete without Geovanna. We filmed her in the centre of the Plaza in front of the church. The whole town came out to watch. I recalled how she was miraculously saved from the train crash in which her mother was killed and how she had become for me a symbol of all the Indian children who didn't get the chance to grow up like her.

John Swinfield produced a very moving documentary on my work among the Indians in the Andes which he called *Beggars in Paradise*. It went on to win the Premier Award of the Sandford St Martin Trust. This is the principal British and European Award for Religious Broadcasting. John's farewell remark to me before he left Peru was;

"You are my sort of priest. You have seriously eroded my agnosticism and I am less of a Doubting Thomas now than I was before. I hope you keep on writing down all your experiences among these people. It could make a superb book."

Life in Combapata moves very slowly. It follows the rhythm of life of the Indian – children are born and people die and life goes on. The tractor is now working overtime. The new threshing engine arrived and it has transformed the whole system of harvesting. No more forming a circle and letting the animals trample the corn. I built a large parish hall beside the church which is a wonderful addition to the parish. Here the catechists meet for three days each month, the children come for instruction in the faith, baptisms and marriages are celebrated and meetings are held. All the communities helped in its construction. They came in groups of thirty, men women and children all with their different tasks. This is called the system of *faena* and goes back to Inca times. "Today for you, tomorrow for me." At daybreak the leader goes to the highest hill and calls the people to work. Sometimes they sing on their way to and from work – a kind of "Hi ho, Hi ho, it's off to work we go." The early Spaniards recorded many of these *huayno* tunes which the Indians still sing on their way to work.

I also started a library where the children could come and study. Most schools in the mountains don't have any books. The teachers write everything on the board and the children just copy it down. The drawback with this system is that most of the children don't have any copybooks. One of the most curious sights in the mountains is to see the children coming to school carrying lumps of *bosta* for the fire. I recalled how, years earlier, I used to bring a sod of turf to the old national school in Rathdrum, back in Ireland.

Perhaps the most important thing I did was to provide medicines for the Indians at the parish office. I had bought large quantities of medicines in Lima and distributed them according to their needs. Soon I became more popular than the *curandero*. They all presumed that I was a doctor and would have willingly trusted me with the most complicated operation. I was working from a very valuable book called *Where There Is No Doctor*.

It always made me very sad to see the babies die shortly after being born. If only I had an incubator. So the next time I went back to Ireland I appealed for one on the radio. The tractor priest had taken up medicine! A Dublin firm responded immediately with an incubator and *Aeroflot*, the Russian airline, offered to fly it to Peru without charge. Its first occupants were little twins, no bigger than the size of my hand. The father had brought them in a blanket from the community of Jayabamba. The mother was too weak to travel. Unfortunately the twins only survived for a day. There is only so much an incubator can do without the help of the mother. Luckily many more survived later.

☆   ☆   ☆

Nemesia was pregnant again with her second child. The year before she had given birth to a beautiful boy, Juanito.

"I won't be able to go to the *chacra* with Juan until the baby is born," she announced one day. I didn't even know she was pregnant again.

"Why is that?" I asked, "you have a long time to go yet."

"It's bad luck," she explained, "a pregnant woman can't walk in the *chacra* for fear of contaminating the crops."

"That seems very strange," I said, in disbelief.

"It's an old Indian custom," she explained, "some women don't observe it any more. That's why the crops don't grow in some *chacras*. But there are many more things I can't do. It is unlucky to sit in the door of the house and I can't knit the baby's clothes before it is born."

"Is that another custom?" I asked.

"It is tempting God," she said, "maybe the baby won't live."

"You had no trouble with Juanito," I reminded her, "and I'm sure everything will be alright this time."

"If there is no thunder and lightning," she sighed. "The lightning seeks out the unborn child to kill it," she explained.

Indians have an extraordinary fear of lightning, and for a very good reason. Every time there is a thunderstorm people are killed. When I visit a community they always want me to bless the spot where the lightning struck. Once when I was caught out in a storm in the *pampa* outside Yauri, I lay flat on the ground until it was over. It didn't bother me that I got soaking wet, but I had no intention of getting struck. It's a horrible sight to see someone dying after being struck by lightning. The smell of the burning flesh is overwhelming.

"Thunder was the weather god of the Incas and next in importance to the Sun. He was responsible for sending the rain. In Quechua there is only one word for thunder and lightning," continued Nemesia.

"That's unusual," I said. "Quechua normally has words for everything. What is it?"

"*Llapa*," she said, in a whisper, almost afraid to mention the name.

"Do you know how the thunder and lightning comes?" she asked.

"It's caused by the meeting of the hot and cold air in the atmosphere," I answered.

"That's not it," she said. "There is a God in the heavens called *Llapa*, dressed in shining armour with a sling in one hand and a club in the other. His sister keeps the rain in a big jug which *Llapa* breaks with a shot from his sling when he yields to the people's plea for rain. The crack of his sling is the thunderclap, the stone is the thunderbolt and the lightning is the flash of his shiny armour. The rain is gathered from the heavenly river, the Milky Way."

Nemesia went off each midday to prepare the dinner for Juan. She usually returned at about four o'clock. One day she was a little late. She arrived back at five o'clock, very excited.

"It's another boy," she said, "and we're going to call him Cristobal."

I just looked at her in disbelief for a moment.

"Sit down, Nemesia. You don't mean to tell me that you have just given birth."

"On a blanket on the floor of my room. A woman helped me and all went well. She cut the umbilical cord and I will keep it with Juanito's for good luck."

"Congratulations," I said, a little shocked. "But you must go back and rest and look after your baby. Don't work until you are feeling better."

"I feel good," she said, "but a little sore between my legs."

The baby would be washed and wrapped tightly in a cloth with only its little face visible. Now he could be carried anywhere on his mother's back.

"I have to be careful that the baby is not exposed to the wind for the first three months," explained Nemesia, "otherwise it will die."

I had often heard the expression *"Ha dado viento"* when a baby died shortly after birth. (It had been exposed to the wind.)

Nemesia asked me if I would perform the custom of *ununchay*. It literally means 'throwing water on the child'. It is not baptism but it is a great honour to be chosen to throw the first water. Later, at about three years of age, there is the custom of cutting the hair for the first time. This is also a great honour. I still have the beautiful locks of Geovanna's hair which I cut when she was three years old.

Newborn children can never be left alone, because the evil spirit might possess the child when no one is looking. There is also the very practical custom that you must not just look at the newborn child and say it looks beautiful. You must present it with a gift. I presented Cristobal with a little baby suit which I had bought in Lima for the occasion.

☆   ☆   ☆

Juvenal, a young policeman with whom I had become friendly, came to see me one day.

"Padre, be extra careful for the next couple of weeks. There is a band of over thirty *Sendero* in the mountains above Combapata and we don't know where they are going."

This was secret information which he had received on the police radio, but it really wasn't of much help to me. What was I supposed to do? If *Sendero Luminoso* wanted to attack the church and kill me there wasn't much I could do. All it meant was that I was a little more nervous during the following weeks. It was well known that one of the terrorists' supply routes from Bolivia passed through the mountains above Combapata. They normally didn't bother us because the arms were more important for their supporters in Ayacucho and Lima. But I usually slept easier on a stormy night when I knew they wouldn't be on the move. (It reminded me of the monks in ancient Ireland who used to sleep better on stormy nights when the seas were too rough for the Viking raiders to sail.)

Then one night just before I went to sleep, all hell broke loose. The police next door had opened up with rockets and machine guns. The terrorists were attacking! Bright flashes illuminated the night sky. What should I do? There was nowhere to go. There was nowhere to hide. I just lay in bed and waited. The noise continued for what seemed like an eternity. Then there was silence. Everything stopped just as quickly as it had begun. The silence was deafening. I listened for the slightest sound and heard a dog barking in the distance. I lay awake all night waiting.

The next day I met Juvenal in the Plaza and asked him what all the shooting was about.

"*Sendero* were over on that hill," he said, pointing to the nearby mountain. "They were taunting us by displaying the 'hammer and sickle' flag on the hillside."

"Did you not consider going after them?" I asked.

"Not likely," he said, "we just opened fire from the station."

"But you wouldn't have a hope in hell of hitting them from there."

"Maybe not, but at least they know we are here. They just wanted to lure us out into the mountains to ambush us. We didn't take the bait."

I grew up thinking that martyrs were holy people who did heroic things for God and bravely went to their deaths. St Stephen was stoned to death for preaching the gospel. Most of the early saints met violent deaths in defence of their faith. As students in Gort Muire we used to read a section of the Martyrology each morning and marvel at the glorious deaths of the martyrs. In Rome I visited the sacred sites and prayed at the tombs of the martyrs. I went down into the catacombs and visited the Colosseum. I was in awe of the courage and the bravery of the early martyrs.

It wasn't until I lived in Combapata surrounded by terrorists that I realised that it wasn't really like that at all. Martyrdom is not something that you seek. Martyrs are just ordinary people doing ordinary things and because of the circumstances they get killed. I'm sure the six Jesuits in El Salvador didn't think about being martyrs as they went to bed that night before they were taken out and shot by the military. Or the cook and her daughter who slept in the presbytery that night for safety and were also shot. Or the Maryknoll sisters who were taken from their car on the way back from the airport and murdered. And above all their Archbishop, Oscar Romero, shot in the heart while celebrating Mass. He had gone to say the evening Mass in the Carmelite chapel in the Divine Providence Hospital. This was not unusual as he had gone there many times before. As he finished the homily and extended his hands in an invitation to prayer, a shot rang out. A single .22 calibre bullet was fired through the open church door from a car parked some two hundred yards away.

I often thought about that as I said the evening Mass in Combapata, looking out from the altar through the great Spanish doors onto the Plaza covered in darkness. Martyrdom is wonderful for concentrating the mind.

15
On Top of the World

As I look out my window I see my pet monkey 'Mickey' is carrying his sack up onto the roof. He likes bringing his shelter with him everywhere he goes. He usually crawls underneath it when the midday sun gets too hot for him or the cold winds blow down from the mountains. Mickey is an extraordinary animal, in fact he is almost human. He has been with me now for almost five years and when you live with an animal that long you get to know it very well. One of the lorry drivers brought him back from the jungle for me on one of his weekly trips to the market. He was only a baby monkey then and even now, although he is fully grown, he is still not much bigger than my hand.

I soon learned that no two monkeys are the same. They all have their own individual characteristics and habits. They even have their own personality. Mickey is a shy monkey. He will never look me straight in the eye. Whenever I look at him, he looks away. When I hold him and make him look at me he just closes his eyes. Sometimes I can see him out of the corner of my eye staring at me when he thinks I am not looking. Every day he is in a different mood. Some mornings he is bright and cheerful and wants to play, while at other times he is solemn and glum. At such times he just wants to be left alone. He is as free as the air and can come and go as he pleases.

I never have to feed him. He knows exactly where to find his own food. He opens the cupboard in the kitchen to get a banana or an orange, or whatever fruit he can find. He peels everything, even grapes, and quickly removes the pips. While fruit is his favourite food, he will try anything – potatoes, meat and maize. He even loves a bowl of soup, cooling it off by blowing on it. He has no manners. When he wants a drink he just turns on the tap and never bothers to turn it off.

Although I built him his own little house, he never sleeps in it. He prefers to sleep with the rabbits. He opens their hutch and climbs in on top of the furriest angora he can find. He hugs the rabbit tightly and falls asleep. The rabbits enjoy this arrangement. At first light he comes to knock on my window and continues to knock until I let him in. He takes his breakfast to the highest point of the roof to await the first rays of the morning sun. He knows the exact spot where the sun first appears.

He often puts his head around the door of my room to see what I am doing. If I am taking a snooze he comes and sleeps on my lap. He also likes to sleep underneath my jumper, peeping out from time to time to see what is happening. He hates to see me reading a book and does everything in his power to stop me. When I am not looking he steals around quietly behind my back and up on to my shoulder. Then he suddenly jumps into the centre of the book, knocking it out of my hand. He keeps up this routine until I give up and put the book down. He likes to play hide-and-seek with me too, but he always forgets that all I have to do is call his name and he comes running out of his hiding place.

His long tail serves as a fifth paw and he can do almost anything with it. He likes to swing from the roof by his tail. He always wants me to catch him by the tail and swing him like a pendulum. One day I wondered how he would like to be swung around completely. He loved it. Then I decided to catapult him up onto the straw roof by swinging him around and letting go. I wasn't sure how he would react. He jumped up on his hind paws, bared his teeth as if to laugh and came back for more.

The children love Mickey and come to see him every day. It was they who first gave him his name. They thought he looked like Mickey Mouse. He loved to play with the girls and their long black hair. He sat on their shoulders and tied their hair into knots. He didn't like boys so much and sometimes wouldn't come near them. Although he was free to wander wherever he wished, he seldom strayed very far. Then one day he went missing. We searched everywhere but he was nowhere to be found. I immediately suspected that the police next door had 'captured' him. When I asked the sergeant he assured me that the police hadn't seen him. Late that night two policemen knocked at the door. They had Mickey in a sack. One of them was bleeding profusely from the hand.

"Your monkey is very vicious," they complained, "we had terrible trouble trying to catch him. You must keep him out of the station."

"He doesn't like strangers," I explained.

"He nearly bit the hand off me," said one, holding up his bloody hand.

"I'll disinfect it and put a bandage on it," I suggested.

Meanwhile Mickey peeped out from the sack. He looked at the policemen and then at me and jumped onto my shoulders and hugged me for dear life.

This wasn't the first time that the police had seen Mickey trying to sneak in to the station, but it was the first time they managed to catch him. They had put him in the underground dungeon which they had prepared for the terrorists. (He was to be its only occupant. They never did catch any terrorists.) But Mickey was soon to get his revenge. Shortly afterwards he again entered the police station but this time unnoticed. He climbed through the window of their office and proceeded to tear up all the papers he could find. An irate sergeant came running in to tell me that my cursed monkey was destroying all their secret documents. I duly expressed my indignation while trying to suppress a smile. Maybe we are descended from monkeys after all!

☆   ☆   ☆

Bringing the lambs to church

The Indians never keep animals as pets. Even when they bring their little baby llamas and lambs to church it is usually because their mothers have died or abandoned them. Animals are kept to be eaten or for their usefulness. They very often mistreat their animals. It is a common sight to see horses hopping helplessly in the *pampa* with their front hooves tied together to stop them from wandering off. Very often the ropes have eaten into the flesh. Dogs are kicked at every available opportunity. They normally don't feed their dogs and they end up as scavengers. Sometimes the dogs wander around in packs. They all have rabies. I was shocked one day when a pig ran squealing into the office dragging its hind legs behind. A spear was protruding from its hind quarters. The *alcalde* had decided that there were too many pigs wandering around the Plaza and they must be hunted down. The children had great fun tying knives to sticks and running around 'spearing' the pigs. They could never understand why I kept animals as pets.

"When are you going to eat Mickey?" they would ask.

Soon my home in Combapata had been turned into a zoo. A friend of mine in Cuzco gave me a young falcon which I had for many years. He wasn't a very 'religious' falcon because he hated processions, especially when there was loud music! On the days of the fiesta he would fly off in the morning and wouldn't return until all was quiet in the evening. I always had to make sure he had plenty of meat, otherwise he would just help himself to one of the other birds. I also had an *ukate* which looked like an otter. The Indians called him the 'chicken eater' and for a very good reason. Whenever he got into the hen-house he would kill all around him.

I finally fulfilled my long ambition to keeping viscatchas. When the Indians heard I wanted viscatchas they brought me a constant supply. At first I kept them with the rabbits until they were accustomed to their surroundings. Then they roamed freely like all my other animals. They loved to climb to the highest point they could find and often in the early morning they would perch on the roof of the church.

I also had many species of birds which the children brought to me from all over the mountains. I had a beautiful owl which slept in the shed all day, only appearing at night as it went off to hunt its prey. I built a little pond in the *chacra* beside the church with a hole in the wall where the ducks could come and go with their ducklings as they pleased. I also kept those little kestrel-like birds called killichus which Geovanna had first pointed out to me in Yauri. An Indian brought me two baby pumas which he had found on the mountainside after a fire. They were badly scorched and although I did everything to try and save them they died after a few days. I never stopped to think of what I would do with the pumas if they had grown to maturity.

At various times I kept llamas, alpacas, deer and foxes. I had three parrots, two small green ones who were real lovebirds, and a big one who preferred my company. Funnily, I never kept guinea pigs but Nemesia had a plentiful supply on the other side of the church. She always presented me with one for my birthday. Mickey took charge of all the other animals. Whenever a rabbit got out of its hutch or the falcon attacked a duckling, he would run screeching to tell me. He pretended he wasn't afraid of anything but whenever a llama turned its long neck towards him he quickly ran and hid.

Geovanna made her First Communion in Combapata on 8 December, the feast of the Immaculate Conception. Children in Peru don't make their First Communion until they reach twelve years of age. Geovanna loved coming to the church in Combapata and had been looking forward to her First Communion for years. She loved to talk about religion and would listen to stories from the Bible all day.

"Tell me about the time that Pharaoh's daughter found baby Moses in the basket down by the river," she would say.

I had the privilege of giving Geovanna her First Holy Communion

I explained how the mother of Moses put her little newborn baby in a basket down by the bulrushes where she knew that the daughter of the Pharaoh used to bathe. When Pharaoh's daughter found the baby, she took him back to the palace and with great excitement gave him to his own mother, not realising who it was and said;

"Take this child and rear him for me."

"Wasn't Moses lucky that she found him," Geovanna said, "he could have been drowned."

"God was looking after him," I suggested, "just like He looked after you when you were thrown out of the train."

"I wasn't given back to my mother like Moses," she concluded sadly.

"God had other plans for you," I said. "Your Papa found you and brought you back to Yauri to be baptised."

"And you reared me up for God," she added.

"You were always God's child," I said, "and now God is coming to you in Holy Communion."

"What is God like?" she asked after a while.

"No one knows what God is like," I explained. "No one has ever seen Him."

"But Jesus was God," she insisted, "and everyone saw Him."

"Yes, but not everyone knew He was God," I explained, "for that you need great faith."

"The Apostles, Peter, James and John saw Him when they went up onto the mountain and a great light shone around them," she said.

"They had great faith," I replied. "If you have faith you will receive Jesus in Holy Communion."

"And will a great light shine around me?" she asked.

"I'm sure it will."

"Is that why I wear a white dress," she wondered, "like a princess?" (I had brought a beautiful white dress from Ireland for her First Holy Communion.)

"You are a princess," I said.

"You always said I was a *'chica extraordinaria'* (wonderful girl)."

"You have a great memory, Geovanna."

"Will I be white on the inside as well as the outside?" she asked.

"Of course you will," I assured her, "when you go to confession your sins will be forgiven."

"Do I have to tell all my sins?" she asked.

"All the serious sins you can remember," I explained.

"What about the ones I can't remember?" she asked.

"They will be forgiven too," I said.

"Supposing I can't remember any?"

"But you have a wonderful memory."

I thought that she might not want to go to confession to me so I suggested;

"If you wish, Geovanna, I will bring you to another priest for confession." (Choice of priests in the mountains is very limited.)

"Why should I go to another priest," she responded indignantly, "when my *padrino* is a priest?"

"You might find it easier," I suggested.

"I'll be telling my sins to God," she said. "Anyway you know all about me already, so I don't have to tell you everything!"

Just before the evening Mass I put on my Carmelite habit and she held me by the hand as we went to the church together. There is no confession box in Combapata so we just sat in front of the altar and she began to talk. She was talking to God and I just happened to be listening. She went through the story of her life, this time told from the inside, revealing her innermost thoughts and feelings. Finally I put my hand on her head and gave her absolution. Tears of joy came streaming down her face as she put her arms around me and gave me a hug.

"Gracias, Padrino," she whispered.

During Mass she received Communion for the first time. She looked angelic in her beautiful white dress. There wasn't a happier child in the world. My thoughts went back to that Christmas morning in Yauri many years before. It's not often one has the privilege of baptising a child, watching her grow up, hearing her First Confession, and giving her First Communion.

As I returned to my house one morning I came across two men trying to get into my room. They looked strange and primitive and I knew by their appearance that they weren't local. They wore bright red ponchos with their *chullos* tied around their necks and their sandals were crudely made from old tyres. Although I had never seen them before, they looked strangely familiar. (It wasn't unusual to find Indians wandering around the house. First they shout from the patio and if they get no reply they just come in as they would in their own community.) The door to my room wasn't locked but they couldn't open it. They were pulling it and pushing it but it wouldn't budge. When they heard me coming they came towards me to give me a big hug.

"*Allillanchu, Papay,*" they said, and added, "*Ave Maria Purissima.*"

Most Indians add this invocation to Our Lady to their greeting. They usually bless themselves with their thumbs on their lips as they say it. It means, "Hail to the Most Pure Heart of Mary".

"*Allillanmi,*" I replied, and added "*sin pecado concibida* (conceived without sin)." The sacred is never far away from the life of an Indian.

I had to hold my breath as I put my arms around them. There was a strong smell of a mixture of sweat, chewed coca leaves and the smoke from the *bosta* fire.

I turned the handle in the door and invited them into my room. They were surprised when they saw how the door opened. They thought it was locked. They had never seen a door handle before. They were still looking at it as they followed me in. They looked around my room in amazement, with its desk, chairs and bed. I offered them a chair but they declined. They preferred to stand. It was obvious they weren't used to chairs.

"*Papay*, my name is Julian, and this is Macario. I come from the community of Parupata and Macario is from the nearby community of Tiruma."

Ah, now I remembered. Parupata was where Nieves came from.

"We came to ask you a great favour," they continued. "At the last assembly in our community we decided to ask you to come and celebrate Mass for our fiesta."

"When is it?" I asked.

"Next week," they replied. "It will last most of the week but we would like you to come to Parupata on Monday."

"And we could come to Parupata in the evening and bring you to Tiruma," added Macario.

"Yes," I said, remembering that they wouldn't take 'No' for an answer. "Will I be able to get there in my jeep?"

For the first time a slight smile came over their faces.

"*Manan, Papay,*" they replied, "it is high up in the mountains. The road ends at Culcuire. We will meet you there with the horses."

"Will there be baptisms and marriages?" I asked.

"Very many," they replied, "as we have been waiting a long time."

☆   ☆   ☆

Nemesia volunteered to come with me as she had never been to Parupata before. We set out from Combapata shortly after four o'clock on Monday morning. Dawn was just breaking over the distant hills as we made our way up the valley by the River Salcca. This is the most beautiful part of the day as the rays of the sun slowly creep down the side of the mountain bringing everything to life in their path. Gentle wisps of smoke emerge from the *ichu* roofs of the adobe huts. Already some children were on their way to school, waving happily at the unusual sight of the padre's jeep at this early hour. The animals too were on the move, llamas and alpacas and sheep being led out to pasture by their young shepherds. As we passed Chiara I glanced over at the beautiful little chapel perched high on the side of the mountain.

"What a wonderful place to build a chapel," I remarked.

"That's Orascocha," said Nemesia, "where I was born and brought up."

"Does any of your family still live there?"

"My granny," she replied, "but you can't see her hut, it's behind the hill."

"What was life like in Orascocha when you were growing up?" I asked curiously.

"We had some good fun," she said, "especially with the boys. We all grew up together in the community. We all knew one another very well. We spent the first two years of our life tied to our mothers' backs. When we became independent of our mothers we all played together. The girls had home-made dolls, simply a piece of stick or stone wrapped in a *llicla*. We used to imitate our parents, pretending we were married. We would beat one another just as we saw our fathers beating our mothers, especially when they were drunk. We pretended to drink *chicha* out of mugs full of frothing urine. Parents didn't keep any secrets from their children. We all lived so closely together the children observed everything. We all slept together in the same bed, huddled up in llama skins to keep warm. We shared our beds with the guinea pigs and the dog and sometimes a pet lamb whose mother had died. From an early age we saw our parents having sex. It seemed the most natural thing in the world."

"Did you enjoy your childhood?"

"It was wonderful," she replied with excitement. "I spent most of my time minding the llamas and sheep out on the mountain."

"That doesn't sound very exciting to me," I said. "What did you do all day out on the mountain when you were minding the animals. What did you think about?"

"You don't have much time to think. You have to watch the sheep in case the *zorro* comes. He can kill twenty sheep at a time."

"How could the fox eat twenty sheep?" I wondered.

"He doesn't kill just to eat them, you know. Sometimes he kills just for fun."

"It must be very boring," I thought. ('Boring' is a word that doesn't exist in Quechua. Children don't know what it means to be bored.)

"But we played games all the time," she said.

"What kind of games did you play?" I asked innocently.

"*Paca paca* (hide-and-seek)," she said. "There were some great hiding places in the mountains. There was one cave where no one could ever find me."

"And if the fox came?" I asked.

"We would all begin shouting to frighten him away. We also played *Alalau – akacau* (cold – hot). We hid something and then we would shout out as the others came near the spot."

"Did the boys join in the games too?" I wondered.

"Yes, when we were young, but as we got older the girls all joined together to play their own games. The boys were always fighting and playing football. Sometimes they would taunt us by calling us names and a great battle took place."

"What names did they call you?"

"The most insulting names they could think of. They called me '*llamacunca*' (llama neck) and '*mayocunca*' (crane neck) because of my long neck. Then the boys attacked the girls and when they caught one they pulled her hair or her breasts or lifted her skirt and shouted '*kaspichaki*' (spindly legs)."

I was surprised how spontaneously Nemesia could recount such experiences. I never knew what to expect next. But she was being quite natural without any of the hang-ups about sex that we often have.

"Then the girls attacked the boys," she continued. "We would always try to catch the youngest boy and pull his *pichico* until he cried for mercy. At first he would laugh but then he shouted in pain until we let him go. Then we all went to the stream for a drink and ate our *fiambre* (lunch)."

"What does *Siquita muchay* mean?" I asked.

"It's a bad word," she said, with a smile.

☆   ☆   ☆

By now we had reached the community of Culcuire. I left the jeep beside the church and Nemesia and I proceeded to climb up the steep mountain to where our guides were waiting. They had three mule-like animals which they called 'horses'. Julian had brought his son, Santiago, with him. They quickly loaded the bags onto one of the horses. It never ceases to amaze me how expert Indians are at tying on a load. It must be all the practice. The Indians don't normally ride the horses up the mountain, they are reserved for cargo. Today the most precious cargo is the padre and Nemesia. Anyway I could never make it on foot.

Soon we are on our way and I make sure that I go first. I have learned

Overlooking the valley

from experience that horses have a nasty habit of breaking wind as they exert their energy in the climb. With the lack of oxygen at this altitude it is hard to breathe at the best of times, without having to contend with this. A blanket served as a saddle and as usual there were no stirrups so my legs just dangled down by the side almost touching the ground. I was soon to learn that my horse had other nasty habits too. As there was no bit in his mouth there was no way I could guide him. But he knew the way and I didn't.

Up and up we climbed as we went round and round on the narrow mountain path. The River Salcca soon appeared as a little stream in the valley below and Culcuire began to take on a fairy-like appearance, with its many *chacras* looking like coloured blankets left out to dry. My horse availed of every opportunity to try to scratch my legs against the sharp cactus that grew by the side of the path. He didn't like touching his back against the overhanging rock either, so he walked on the very edge of the track. One false move and we would both end up in the valley below. Also when we came to a sharp bend he appeared to go straight on, only turning at the very last moment. Looking out over his head we seemed to be floating on air before descending into the dark abyss. After a while I began to relax and admire the scenery, realising that the horse didn't want to end up in the valley below any more than I did.

Winding our way up the mountain

"How often do you make this journey?" I asked Santiago, as he trotted along in front of me.

"More often than the rocks on the mountain," he replied as he shrugged his shoulders. Santiago was just seventeen years old.

The path began to ascend through a great gorge beside a mountain stream which came gushing down in torrents. From time to time we had to cross it on narrow bridges made from the rocks. Little mountain flowers seemed to sprout from nowhere along the way.

"They are *zapatos*," remarked Santiago as he pointed to a little yellow flower growing between the rocks. "We call them *zapatos* because they look like shoes."

As I looked more closely I could see how they looked like bright yellow shoes. Further on there were lovely blue flowers which looked like lupins.

"*Tarwi*," said Santiago, as he pulled one to show me the bean-like seed which the Indians love to eat.

Suddenly he pointed up to the summit.

"Puma," he shouted with a tremor in his voice. I looked up but couldn't see a thing.

"Do we have to go that way?" I asked.

"Don't worry," he said, "they don't like Indians. Anyway I have some of their whiskers in my *chuspita* (a pouch carried around the neck) to protect me."

After about three hours we stopped for a rest. Santiago said it was for the horses but we all needed a break. I was so stiff I could hardly stand up. I couldn't sit down either as there were little cactus plants growing everywhere. I eventually found a place on a rock. The horses began to eat the *ichu* and then went to the stream for a drink. Julian and Santiago took some coca leaves from their *chuspitas*. Julian handed me a little wad mixed with ash which I began to chew. It produced a green liquid with a bitter taste, but it had a soothing effect and it helped me breathe more easily. They then took some *chuños* and roasted maize from their *bultos*. Nemesia enjoyed the *chuños* while I managed a little maize.

"Look at the fox," shouted Julian as I just got a glimpse of his bushy tail disappearing behind a rock.

"That must be the only one that escaped from the hunt last week," said Santiago.

"How do you hunt the fox?" I asked, knowing that they don't have any firearms.

"The whole community organises a foxhunt every year called a *chaqu*," he explained. "Everyone takes part. We arm ourselves with sticks and stones and tin cans and anything that will make noise. We all set out at daybreak for *Quebrada de Atocchayoc* (Valley of the Foxes), where the foxes have their dens in the caves among the rocks. When the leader blows his whistle we make a terrible din with the tin cans and when the foxes try to escape we kill them with our sticks. Before they die we cut off their bushy tails and keep them for good luck."

With that he produced the bushy tail of a fox from his *chuspita*.

"It's great for attracting the girls," he added with a smile. "I call it my *warmiquyaci* (woman catcher)."

He also showed me the whiskers of the puma which he killed last year. As long as he carries them with him he believes the puma will never attack him.

As we continued on our way we passed through narrow gorges and under overhanging cliffs. At times I had to dismount and lead the horse up the rocky face of the mountain. Eventually we reached an open space which Santiago called the *Puña Brava* (Wild Puna). This is a vast area on which thousands of llamas and alpacas graze on seemingly non-existent vegetation. These lovely animals seem to thrive in these conditions. They scrape their teeth along the ground to root up what little spiky *ichu* they can find. The intense heat of the midday sun is overpowering and I can feel the horse perspiring under my heavy weight. There is a strong breeze blowing which makes the sweat on my face feel ice cold. I keep my head down to stop my hat from blowing away.

A little further on, a large caravan of llamas came towards us, laden with sacks of corn and potatoes. Each llama is allotted its specific load, forty-four pounds (twenty kilos), no more no less. If you try to overload a llama it will just sit down and won't budge. No matter how you beat it, it will not move. They begin work at three years of age and continue until about twelve. They are never ridden. A member of the camel family, they can go long distances without water. Staging posts are scattered at intervals of nine to twelve miles across the mountain where the llamas rest for the night. Try to make them go a little further and they will sit down in protest. More stubborn than a mule, they are very proud animals, cocking their long necks in the air as they pass. Their leader has a bell around its neck while the others have coloured ribbons hanging from their ears. They don't travel quickly like a horse or a mule, but walk at a steady measured pace with half a dozen Indians bringing up the rear.

"*Allillanchu, Papay,*"call the shepherds, kneeling down for a blessing.

It is now over seven hours since we left Combapata and there is still no sign of Parupata. It must be the highest village in Peru! Why would anyone want to live in such a desolate and remote part of the world? This was where the Indians found refuge from the invading Spanish. At least here they were safe from human interference. Survival and freedom are the first laws of nature. The elements are easier to cope with. An old *mamita* stood up on a rock and waved at us from a distance. She was out on the mountain minding her llamas. I wonder what she thinks about all day. I doubt if she still plays with the boys.

As we climbed another hill I heard the faint sound of music in the distance. We must be getting near. This was the welcoming committee coming out to greet us. Around the next bend there they were, a complete orchestra. A motley group of Indians, dressed in ponchos and *chullos*, danced around like pixies as they played their merry tune with tin whistles, flutes and little mandolins as well as a big drum keeping time in the middle. As is the custom the band would accompany me everywhere I went during my visit.

There was still no sign of Parupata. But when I looked more closely there it was, blending perfectly into the surrounding rocky mountains. Tiny mud huts with roofs of *ichu*. Here and there straight columns of smoke ascended into the clear blue sky. This was the only sign of life. Higher up the peaks were covered with snow, giving the impression of a well decorated Christmas cake. It was one of the most beautiful scenes in the world but barren and desolate and uninviting. This place would rival Machu Picchu for sheer beauty, but the Incas never lived here.

Parupata is the most extraordinary community I ever visited in Peru. It is another world, another place, another time. Its natural beauty is overwhelming. It is situated just below the snow line at about 16,000 feet above sea level. Nothing grows here. Everything has to be transported at great sacrifice from the valleys below. Less than one hundred Indians live here. Their only company are the animals, llamas, alpacas, vicuñas, viscatchas, foxes and pumas.

We crossed a little stone bridge over a mountain stream and at last we were there. Everyone had come out to greet us.

"*Allillanchu, Papay,*" they shouted, "you are welcome to the community of Parupata." Each one greeted me with a hug.

The children were too shy to come near me at first. They had never seen a gringo before and this one happened to be the padre. I always had some sweets in my pocket for such occasions.

"*Miski,*" I shouted, and they all came running towards me.

"Where is Nieves?" I asked anxiously.

"She hasn't arrived yet," replied a woman who seemed to be in charge. "She lives over that mountain. She will be here soon."

They quickly placed a poncho on a rock and invited me to sit down. They brought some small potatoes and put them on the rock in front of me. Luckily they weren't *chuños*. They also presented me with a huge mug of *chicha*. I spilled a little on the ground for *Pacha Mama*, as is the custom, before I downed the rest. Riding a horse up the side of a mountain is thirsty work.

"This is just a snack for the hunger," said the woman who turned out to be the *alferado*. "The main meal is after the Mass."

The band watched my every move and continued to play. Little children played games in the Plaza. It was impossible to distinguish between the girls and the boys. They all wore the same homespun skirts with nothing underneath. Some played with home-made primitive toys. One little boy pushed around a wheel on the end of a stick while the girls had home-made dolls. The older boys played football on some nearby open ground. One little girl had diarrhoea and immediately a dog came and licked her clean. I could hardly believe my eyes and my stomach began to turn. The girl chuckled away to herself as the licking of the dog tickled her tiny legs.

I made my way with Nemesia to the tiny chapel at the edge of the village. All the life of the village was centred around their faith. The band continued to play. Nemesia would prepare the families for baptism while I looked after the marriages. The chapel was surrounded by a graveyard as is the custom. Little heaps of stones with crosses marked the graves. These stretched right up to the door of the chapel. There were no names, no dates. Everyone knew where their loved ones lay. The chapel was small and dark and just used for storing the images of the saints. Their patron saint was St Michael the Archangel.

They placed a table in front of the chapel for the Mass. Just then Nieves ran towards me and greeted me like a long lost friend.

"Allillanchu, Papay," she said, putting her arms around me. She had been cured of her *susto* and was dressed in a beautiful, colourful home-made costume. She had made it herself. On her head she wore a little bowler hat. Today was the day of her baptism and she was happy. I don't think I have ever met anyone more primitive than Nieves. She is about the same age as Geovanna, but Geovanna would be considered a jet-setter compared to her.

Nieves

The Mass was one of the most moving that I have ever celebrated as these poor Indians gathered around that tiny chapel, standing on the graves of their ancestors. This was to be a celebration for the living and the dead. I gave them general absolution before the Mass although many had confession privately under their poncho. Nobody knew the

Gathering for Mass

responses to the Mass. How could they? For most this was their first Mass. But these people have a natural sense of the sacred. They took part with awe and reverence, continuously making the sign of the cross.

"*Dios Yayac, Dios Churic, Dios Espiritu Santoc.*"

And isn't this the essence of what the Mass is all about? The passion, death and resurrection of Jesus Christ. As I looked around, the huge rock faces of the mountain peaks rose majestically to the sky like the steeples of a great cathedral. The words of the Psalm went through my head;

"The mountains of the Lord give praise to the Lord . . . and the sky . . . and the wind . . . and the snow."

I performed the marriages and baptised the children as they formed a semi-circle around the altar after Mass. All the children were wearing woolly *chullos* pulled tightly around their ears to protect them from the harsh mountain wind, only removing them as the water of baptism flowed gently over their heads. Nieves took pride of place in the centre. She didn't say anything. She was too overawed by the occasion. Afterwards the *alferado* told me this was the first time Mass had been celebrated in Parupata for twenty years.

The band accompanied me back to the hut where the meal was to be served. By now I was ready for anything. It is just as well that I am not finicky about food. The big brown pot is the best cure I know for that.

Eating from the 'big brown pot'

I have long since learned not to judge the food so much on its content as on the amount of effort that went into preparing it. By this standard I was about to take part in a feast.

More potatoes were spread out on the ground before me, together with a bowl of hot soup with a great lump of meat in the middle of it. The meat was probably alpaca but I didn't dare ask. I just took it in my fingers and began to eat. Once more I find myself thinking of Henry VIII on these occasions, but I'm sure he never ate like this. The band continued to play. A large *tomin* of *chicha* stood nearby from which mug after mug was filled and passed around. We had to shout at each other to be heard over the music. By now I just had to go to the toilet and there was no way I could go Indian style. I went outside and spotted a large rock in the distance. I began to walk towards it but the band followed me. There was no escaping them. Even when I eventually disappeared behind the rock, the band played on. I suppose that's what they call 'chamber music'! Not even Henry VIII was treated like this!

Late in the afternoon a great cry went up.

"The horses are coming, the horses are coming!"

Looking into the distance I could just make out three specks coming over the horizon. It was the horses with their guides coming to bring Nemesia and me to the community of Tiruma. It took them almost another hour to reach us. One of the 'horses', which was really a mule, was very lively, prancing and jumping around. My two guides were Celso and Toribio. Celso suggested that as I was the heaviest I should take the lively horse, who soon stopped his antics with me on his back.

"*Vamonos, Papay*," shouted Toribio as we set off. The whole community of Parupata came to wave goodbye and the band continued to play.

As we began to climb the steep mountain a fierce wind began to blow. My hands were beginning to go numb as I tried to put on my woolly gloves. There were viscatchas everywhere, darting here and there between the rocks. A little further on we reached the snow. It was now bitterly cold. We passed through a series of gorges and steep hills. As we approached a particularly steep part of the mountain I shouted to Celso;

"Do you think the horse can make it?"

"Just keep going," he shouted, "no problem."

When I reached the top there was a sheer drop on the other side. I was terrified. I thought the horse was going to go head first over the top, but he just sat down on his hind legs and slid to the bottom. The next time I won't ask any questions, I thought. I'll dismount and walk. The only trouble was that I felt so stiff, I doubted if I could walk very far. As I began to dismount, the horse reared up and I landed unceremoniously on my back on the ground. Celso and Toribio were doubled up with laughter. Luckily I was not hurt as I began to walk slowly along the rocky mountain track.

Darkness had fallen by the time we reached Tiruma. Celso showed me to the *alferado*'s hut. People began to embrace me like a long lost friend. There was a strong smell of drink. They had started the festivities early and by now they were all very drunk on pure alcohol. I have become an expert over the years at knowing how the Indians get drunk in Peru. It was either *chicha*, beer or alcohol. Each had its own degree of stupor. Alcohol is the worst. Everyone just looked at me with a blank stare as they put their arms around me to give me a big hug. The smell of their breath was terrible. I could see there was no hope of getting anything to eat as they wandered around in the dark.

"*Papay*, won't you have a drink with us to celebrate the feast?" said the one of the men who was supposed to be the *alferado*.

"Just a little *chicha*" I said, "for the thirst. I am so tired I just want to go to sleep."

"It's early yet, *Papay*," he said, "we have to celebrate a little more."

"I'm too tired," I said, "where can I sleep?"

"We all sleep here," he said, showing me into a smoke-filled hut with guinea pigs running around the floor. There was a fire of *bosta* smouldering in the corner. As I looked around I counted three couples plus three children in the family. How could we possibly sleep in such a small space and they all drunk?

"Is there nowhere else I could sleep?" I asked in desperation.

"You could sleep here," he said, as he opened the little door of the adjacent hut where all the rubbish was kept.

I crawled through the tiny door, opened out my sleeping bag and got into it without taking any clothes off. I couldn't wait to lie down but I was too exhausted to sleep. I just lay there tossing and turning for what seemed like an eternity. Eventually I put on my flashlight and looked at my watch. It was ten minutes to eleven. I decided to look around the hut with my torch. There were skins and rugs piled high in one corner. Old clothes hung on pegs made from llama bones on the wall, together with laths and wool used for weaving the ponchos. As I looked up at the roof I suddenly saw two huge eyes staring down at me. I quickly switched off the light. I wondered who could be looking at me. As I turned on the light again I saw it was a sheep's head. All around was the meat from the rest of the sheep. This will be heavily salted and left in the sun to dry to become *charqui*. Like the *chuños* this is a method of preserving meat so that it will last for ever. There were all kinds of ropes, musical instruments and a variety of old pots. My contemplation was disturbed by an army of fleas which had just entered my sleeping bag. I thought the morning would never come.

A little glimmer of light began to peep through the cracks in the door. It was the dawn. I could hear the sound of falling rain in the patio outside. Suddenly it stopped. Then it began again. "That's not rain," I thought, "it's the family urinating from the door of their hut." I could hear the constant loud coughing of the children. The parents too were coughing as they moved around doing their morning chores. Someone was sweeping the patio outside my door. I could see the dust on the beams of light entering my hut. I too began to cough. I had to go to the

Handing out *miskis*

toilet and I couldn't wait any longer. I crawled out the door and went around the back to look for a rock.

Everywhere was covered with a thick white frost. It had all the appearance of a blanket of snow. As I passed behind the hut an old woman was washing her hair in a bucket of urine. Now I knew it was true. I had seen it with my own eyes. Hundreds of llamas and alpacas waited anxiously in their stone corrals. A great cloud of steam rose high into the morning air. Soon they will join with all the others from the nearby huts and make their way out into the surrounding hills. When evening comes they will all return together, only separating at the last moment to enter their respective corrals.

My hands and face are numb with the cold. The little mountain stream is a long way off and is almost frozen over. No wonder the Indians in the mountains don't wash. As I return to the hut one of the Indian women is sitting in the patio picking the fleas from her daughter's hair. The girl has her head across her mother's lap as her mother searches through her tangled black hair. Now and then she squeezes the fleas between her thumbs, before eating them so as not to lose any of her daughter's blood. My breakfast consists of a *mate* made by pouring hot water on some mountain herbs and a few pieces of rock-hard wheaten bread.

The sound of the chapel bell re-echoed around the mountains and soon families began to arrive from all directions for the Mass. The fiesta

313

was in honour of St John the Baptist, the patron saint of Tiruma. They took a giant statue of him from a box and placed it on the altar. The Mass was celebrated outside. Nemesia helped me with the many marriages and baptisms afterwards. Even the wildest looking Indians with their long black hair and stony sculptured features attend the Mass with awe and reverence. Afterwards they come and humbly kneel before me and ask for a blessing. Then they kiss my hand, embrace me and thank me for coming.

I declined the offer of the horse for descending the mountain, deciding it would be safer to walk. After many hours we finally reached Culcuire and the jeep. It won't be long now until I am home in Combapata and back to civilisation. As I came in the patio gate Mickey jumped for joy. He had been busy picking the fleas from the backs of the angora rabbits. I just wanted to have a shower and get into my nice warm bed.

So my time has come to leave the mountains of Peru. I suppose it was inevitable that it would happen one day but I never wanted to think about it. It was a decision that was very difficult to make and will be much more difficult to live with. But I must face reality. The prevailing medical opinion is that it is not advisable for us gringos to live at high altitudes after we reach sixty years of age. After all, that is much older than most Indians ever reach. I have long since passed that milestone. I know that no-one is indispensable and that life will just go on as before. Even if I were to live here for a hundred years not much would change. My most important contribution has been simply to live with these poor Indian people. I haven't got the heart to tell them that I am leaving. Anyway they wouldn't understand. They would always imagine that I would be back one day, and that maybe I would bring another tractor.

The evening before I left I played volleyball in the patio with the children from the town. These games were always taken very seriously and each side played to win. We laughed and we joked as the sweat poured down our faces in the evening sun. Mickey tried to distract us as he did handstands on the nearby straw roof.

When the game was over and it was time to leave, Zorenayhua, a young teenage girl, put her arms around me and gave me a hug.

"*Paqarin kama, Papay* (See you tomorrow, Father)." she said as she ran out the door. I could feel the beads of sweat form into a trickle as they ran down my face.

Early next morning Juan drove me to Cuzco to catch the plane to Lima. All along the way the sheep and the llamas were being led out to pasture. Children hurried barefoot on their way to school. Whiffs of smoke rose from the mud huts on the mountainsides. The little chapel high up on the hill outside Quiquijana still stood like a sentry guarding the valley below.

It was the beginning of another day in the mountains. These were the sights that I had seen a thousand times before but today they seemed to take on a different meaning. It was just like seeing them all for the first time. Juan said very little. It was as if he knew that I wanted to be left alone.

When we got to the airport Juan put his arms around me without saying a word. Indians are not used to saying goodbye.

"Keep ploughing the *chacras* with the tractor," I said, "and be careful that you don't drive into the river." He smiled.

As he got back into the jeep for the lonely journey back to Combapata I shouted;

"Look after Mickey . . . and don't eat him!"

I remembered to get a seat by the window on the right-hand side this time. As I gazed out on the snow-capped peaks it still seemed impossible that Pizarro and his one hundred and eighty men could have made their way across these mountains. But he did. And the entire history of South America was changed forever.

"What did you think of Machu Picchu?" asked the man sitting beside me.

"Wonderful," I said and closed my eyes. I just wanted to be left alone with my thoughts.

Epilogue

Silence has descended on my Wicklow home and I am alone in the peace and quiet of my room. Through the window the clear night sky reflects a million stars and the only sound that breaks the stillness is the barking of a dog in the distance. My mind begins to wander . . .

I remember the first night I arrived in Yauri, tired and suffering from altitude sickness and wondering what in the name of God had brought me to such a dreadful place. And when I first said Mass and looked down from the altar and saw the old Indian women sitting on the floor looking up at me stony faced, expressionless, chewing their coca leaves, I was puzzled. What goes on inside their heads? What are they really thinking? Why did I come here? What is the meaning of it all? Now as I lie here I am a little nearer to answering these questions.

I travelled the length and breadth of the immense territory which is the prelature of Sicuani, on mountain tracks that all but disappear in the rainy season. I endured the freezing cold of winter and the hot Andean summer sun. At times I was violently sick and I suffered constantly from bouts of diarrhoea. Like a baby I was reduced on numerous occasions to wearing a nappy. Frequently I slept on the clay ground in Indian huts and ate from 'the big brown pot'.

At first it was all just an interesting experience, an adventure, but soon it took on a different meaning. The young barefoot mother, dressed in her multicoloured costume, trotting along with her baby on her back looked so strange and beautiful at first. Now I know that for every baby I saw, another had died. Some die at childbirth, others die later of disease or lack of nourishment. Many could so easily have been saved. When I picture Geovanna with her lovely eyes and long black hair I think of all the 'other Geovannas' who have not survived. In the Andes it is still the survival of the fittest. Three-quarters of those who do survive don't know how to read or write. That little thatched mud hut perched high on the mountainside seems so quaint and picturesque, yet I know that if I crawled inside I would find a family in abject poverty, struggling to survive. The mountains look so majestic and breathtaking with their

316

snow-covered peaks. Such are the scenes of picture postcards, but the reality is so different. It is not easy to live on a cold and barren mountain.

But above all I have come to know the Indian people, a beautiful and forgotten people and my life will never be the same again. The longer I lived among these Inca Indians, the more I realised how they have been exploited and suppressed. In Inca times they lived in relative peace and tranquillity. They worshipped the Sun and worked the earth. They have always had a wonderful spiritual relationship with nature and especially the earth. They have sprung from the earth and they will be laid to rest in it. To them it is sacred – *Pacha Mama*, the fountain of all life. The earth gives them everything. It is not just a means of nourishment and survival, it expresses the harmony which exists between God, their fellow man and nature. The earth is where we all share our common humanity.

So it was that these people were terribly wounded when the white man came to take their earth from them, to exploit it, to make it more productive, to level it down and at times to destroy it, without respecting it. The conquistadors took tracts of the best land and formed them into great haciendas where the Indians were treated as little more than slaves. They were forced to work for a symbolic wage and a few miserable gifts, such as a small plot of land, or grazing for their few animals. The conquerors robbed the earth of its treasures, gold and other precious metals and used the Indians as cheap labour because they were the only ones who could work at such high altitudes. This exploitation and suppression continues to the present day.

The Bishop of Puno, Monsignor Metzinger, wrote recently;

> How sad to think that these people who once knew the glory of a grand empire have been changed after the conquest into a famished people – beggars, slaves, victims of disease. An exploited people who live at the margins of the national population. Our Indians are not poor, they are miserable. Decent people would be ashamed to keep their animals in the huts they live in. They walk with bare feet in the extreme cold of the high mountains. They still work the earth with the primitive tools that they used in the time of the Incas.
>
> They are criticised for using ancient pagan customs mixed with Christian rites and gestures. We should be more surprised that the Faith has survived among these poor people who only see a priest

every ten or twenty years, or worse still, have been exploited in the name of religion. This is the result of four centuries of civilisation which we call 'Christian'.

The Christian faith arrived with the conquistadors. It was born and took root in the midst of hatred and bloodshed, destruction and robbery. In such circumstances it would have been difficult to preach a gospel of love. So a Christianity of authority, law and commandments took its place. The Church is an Institution, a beautiful construction built on a rock that was chosen by Christ. So all the pagan temples had to be razed to the ground and Christian churches built on their ruins. Places of worship were adorned with gold and silver altars and beautiful ornate pulpits from which it was so hypocritical to preach the gospel of the poor.

The Church was preoccupied with law and order and the trimmings of the faith. To enter this Church one must be baptised. So the Indians were baptised under the cold eye of the Inquisition. From then on they were Christians. They had no option but to accept the religion of the foreigner. As he bowed his head under the Spanish yoke and pledged submission, the Indian thought within himself;

"The white man can conquer us but he will never know what we think!"

The Indian soul has been trampled on in so many ways, from not recognising it, to brutally suppressing it. Now we must start again at the beginning and sow the real seed of the gospel in the heart of the Indian, taking into account the seeds of the Word which lie in their native religion, recognising all the good that is in the hearts and minds of every Andean. The Indian of the Andes must be free. Every race has a right to be different. All peoples need to better themselves and become more civilised, ourselves included. But we must do it according to our own lights, experiences and observations.

The Gospel must be preached out of love. The Indians have to be given back their dignity. They must be freed of their complex of being conquered and colonised, of being poor and good for nothing, of being backward and marginalised and of being discriminated against. They must be helped to stand on their own two feet, to reject all forms of exploitation, domination and dependency. They must restore security and confidence in themselves.

St Francis of Assisi was coming home one evening with some of his brethren. They arrived at the top of a mountain overlooking a tiny village. It was bitterly cold and it was beginning to snow. The brothers began to gather firewood to light a fire and prepare some food. Francis gazed down on the village as the lights began to go out for the night.

"Look at those poor people," he said, "they have neither food nor heat. Tonight they go to bed hungry."

"But what can we do to help them?" asked one of his companions, "we have no food to give them."

"No, but we can share with them the cold and the hunger," said Francis, "let's not prepare a fire tonight."

This I have tried to do in my own simple way. I came to Peru as a pilgrim with no preconceived plan and carrying no mental baggage. One of the things that I have learned during my time there is that the Indians are just as good as I am. Actually they are much better in so many ways, especially at living at high altitudes. Thank God I didn't come to change them! I just wanted to live in solidarity with them, to be present for them, to suffer with them, to feel the cold with them, to go hungry with them and to be humiliated with them. I have no monopoly on wisdom. They must be allowed to develop in their own way and at their own pace. I have learned that I can never become an Indian, even though I wear a poncho, and the Indians can never become like me. Of course I want to help them but with a mutual unconditional exchange, respectful, equal to equal. I bring my little bit of light and they bring theirs, and hopefully all our lives become brighter and more meaningful and a little happier.

So living and working with the poor Indians can never be just an interesting experience. You must identify with them, share their lives, be present among them as one who cares. You can never be just an observer on the outside looking in. You must go all the way. It means enduring hardships, the altitude, the cold, being without water and electricity, cooking your own food, eating unpalatable food in the communities. It means loneliness and lack of communication with the outside world. But there is another side to it that makes it all worthwhile. It means coming close to people, getting to know them, forming relationships and becoming friends. Thomas Merton put it so well when he said;

> Do not depend on the hope of results. When you are doing the
> sort of work that you have taken on, you may have to face the fact

that your work will be apparently worthless, and achieve no results at all, if not results opposite to what you expect. As you get used to this idea you start more and more to concentrate not on the results but on the value, the rightness, the truth of the work itself. In the end it is the reality of personal relationships that saves everything.

Mother Teresa was once asked during an interview on television;

"But there is such immense poverty in India and all you are dealing with is a drop in the ocean?"

"I don't know anything about the ocean," she replied humbly, "I only see the drop that is in front of me."

As his filming expedition was coming to an end, John Swinfield asked me a very pointed question.

"Do you think you have been successful in your work here among the Indians?"

"God doesn't ask us to be successful," I replied, "He only asks us to be faithful."

I am consoled by an incident that is recorded among the papers of the viceroy, Francisco de Toledo, shortly after he massacred the last Inca, Tupac Amaru, at the end of the sixteenth century. He asked a Dominican, Reginald de Lizzaraja, why members of a hostile tribe of the Chiriguanes in the Peruvian Andes were accustomed to making the sign of the cross. The Dominican explained that this tribe had been taught by a Carmelite missionary who had lived with them for a time and built churches in honour of Our Lady of Mount Carmel. Maybe my work among the people of Yauri and Combapata will have some impact also.

When I had told Mercedes that I was leaving Yauri she just looked at me in silence for a moment and said;

"We will never forget what you have done for us. And when there is trouble again in Yauri, we will wish that you were back here once more among us."

———— ☆ ————